The New Engineer's Guide
to Career Growth
and Professional Awareness

The New Engineer's Guide to Career Growth and Professional Awareness

Edited by
Irving J. Gabelman

IEEE PRESS

IEEE United States Activities Board, *Sponsor*

The Institute of Electrical and Electronics Engineers, Inc., New York

This book may be purchased at a discount from the publisher when
ordered in bulk quantities. For more information contact:

IEEE Press Marketing
Attn: Special Sales
445 Hoes Lane, P.O. Box 1331
Piscataway NJ 08855-1331
Fax: (908) 981-9334

Printed in the United States of America

10 9 8 7 6 5 4 3 2 1

ISBN 0-7803-1057-8
IEEE Order Number: PP4119

Library of Congress Cataloging-in-Publication Data
The new engineer's guide to career growth and professional awareness /
edited by Irving J. Gabelman.
    p.   cm.
    Includes bibliographical references and index.
    ISBN 0–7803–1057–8 (paper)
    1. Engineering–Vocational guidance.   2. Career development.
I. Gabelman, Irving J.
TA157.N3765   1996
620'.0023–dc20   96-6440
                                                 CIP

Contents

Chapter 4   The Entrepreneur   55
Orin Laney

Chapter 7   Intellectual Property   123
Howard Rose

Chapter 8   Legal Aspects of Employment   148
Larry P. Malfitano

Foreword

How do you talk about a book that is "must reading" for all students of engineering, new engineers, and experienced engineers? The authors who have worked with Irv Gabelman to write this excellent book are outstanding. They bring an incredible body of knowledge and experience to this task. Irv and his team can be very proud of what they have accomplished.

During the early 1970s, the IEEE, along with most of the other engineering societies, realized that it was absolutely necessary to become involved in nontechnical areas. This was a period of engineering downsizing with little regard for the good of the nation or the individual. It was clear that we as professionals must become involved in the political arena.

To that end, IEEE developed a Washington presence and worked together to improve such things as pensions, patent rights, prevailing wages on service contracts, and other matters related to the economic well-being of engineers' careers. IEEE, concerned with educating their members, expanded the education process to include student members by creating the Student Professional Awareness Conference program. The basic concept is to bring several of the best and most knowledgeable speakers in the IEEE to the campus to speak to students on topics related to professional activities and career enhancement. This highly successful program has now reached thousands of students.

This book provides needed information for all students planning engineering careers and could support dedicated classes for undergraduate as well as graduate programs at every university. Students who are fortunate enough to have such a course would find that they have learned many things that will help enhance their careers as well as provide many of the tools necessary for a long, productive, and exciting engineering career.

This is one of the most exciting periods in the history of engineering. In fact, we are just now entering the Golden Age of Engineering! I can say that because we finally have computers powerful enough to realize what we only dreamed about in the past. Unfortunately, this tremendous time technically also is accompanied by one of the worst periods for employment. Thus, the importance of this text and all that it offers!

Charles K. Alexander
Dean of Engineering,
California State University, Northridge;
President-Elect, IEEE

Preface

Generally, engineers tend to immerse themselves in their disciplines, intent on solving the ever-emerging problems created by the requirements of society and advancing technology. They are politically naive and indeed apathetic about participation in government and community activities that affect them socially and economically. This attitude is due in part to the training that they receive at colleges of engineering. These colleges, with an occasional exception, have curricula which are almost totally discipline-oriented with little or no attention given to career and professional issues.

McNeill[1] has stated that "We should examine the training tomorrow's engineers are receiving in our colleges and universities. The focus must remain on science and technology. But engineering education must expand to include more courses in history and political science, so that young engineers learn how to make effective contributions once their careers begin." One might add that courses in career planning, professional awareness, and the legal aspects of their professional lives are also necessary.

The Institute of Electrical and Electronics Engineers (IEEE), recognizing the need for active participation by its membership and by the engineering community in career and professional activities, established the United States Activities Board (USAB) in 1972.

One of the USAB programs, the Student Professional Awareness Conferences (SPAC), brings speakers to engineering college campuses to address undergraduates on career related issues. While SPAC are needed, a more effective method of educating engineering students would be to include a course covering pertinent subjects in the engineering curriculum. A one-semester course in which a relatively brief introduction to the various career influencing factors is given would be a desireable and valuable addition.

IEEE Bylaw 312 states that, "The United States Activities Board shall recommend policies and implement programs specifically intended to serve the members in the United States in appropriate non-technical professional areas of economic, ethical, legislative, and social concern." The volunteer IEEE members of the many USAB committees strive to achieve that objective. This book reflects much of their work, and several of the contributing authors are USAB committee members.

Part I: Jobs and Careers   The employment of young engineers and the factors which will influence their choice of career is reviewed. Almost without exception, newly graduated engineers will begin their careers as employees of an engineering company or the government. A description is given of the job market and the strategies for obtaining a position are discussed. Most engineers will continue working for companies or the government for the remainder of their careers while some, after a learning period, will strike out on their own. Entrepreneurship and consulting are two possible avenues open to them. A look at pensions is given so that early on, whatever their career status might be, they can begin the planning for their retirement years.

Part II: Law   This part addresses the legal aspects of employment, intellectual properties, and licensing and registration. The legal aspects of an employment contract for an engineer pertaining to their pre-employment and post-employment rights do not differ significantly from those of other professionals. These aspects and rights are presented and discussed. The chapter on intellectual properties is a discourse on patents, trademarks, service marks, and copyrights. It answers some of the most commonly asked questions in this area of the law. The services which engineers provide impact directly on the public. Engineering should only be practiced by individuals who have demonstrated their competence to the state boards of registration. Licensing and registration is the subject of the last chapter of Part II.

Part III: Professionalism   In this part, ethical conduct by engineers is described. It relates the responsibilities of engineers to employers, society, the engineering community, and clients. It looks at the problems that arise when these responsibilities give rise to a conflict of interests. The final chapter shows the several ways in which the various engineering societies serve the engineering community and the public.

Part IV: Government   This part describes the organization and functioning of the federal, state, and local governments. The preoccupation of engineers with their professional disciplines and their general apathy toward participation in government activities is noted. It advocates action by the engineering community which will help achieve one of the objectives[2] of the IEEE Professional Activities Council for Engineers (PACE) by "engaging in government action at the local, state, and national level, by making the technological and problem solving experience of engineers available to the legislative process, and by influencing legislation that affects the professional careers of engineers."

ENDNOTES

1. McNeill, "Engineers Must Become as Effective in Politics as They Are in Science," *Plant Engineering* (September 1992).
2. PACE Leader's Handbook, IEEE United States Activities Board, Revised August 1994, p. 10.

Irving J. Gabelman

List of Contributors

(Listed in alphabetical order)

Richard Backe
Program Director, Unisys Corporation, Lanham, MD;
Chairman IEEE-USA Employment Assistance Committee;
Editor-in-Chief, *IEEE Employment Guides*

Ruth Barwick
Executive Assistant to the President,
Utica College of Syracuse University, Utica, NY

Chris J. Brantley
Senior Administrator, Technology Policy Council,
IEEE-USA Washington, DC;
Former Executive Assistant to the Director,
American Association of Engineering Societies

Irving J. Gabelman (Editor)
USAF (Ret.), Chief Scientist,
Rome Laboratory, Rome, NY;
Member, IEEE-USA State Government Activities Committee

John J. Guerrara
Professor of Electrical Engineering,
California State University, Northridge, CA;
Past President, IEEE

Deborah G. Johnson
Professor of Philosophy,
Rensselaer Polytechnic Institute, Troy, NY;
Author, *Computer Ethics* (Prentice Hall, 1994);
Editor, *Ethical Issues in Engineering* (Prentice Hall, 1991)

Orin Laney
President,
Avocado Computer Co., Silver Springs, MD;
Past Chairman, IEEE-USA Intellectual Property Committee

Larry P. Malfitano
Attorney and Partner,
Bond, Schoeneck & King, Syracuse, NY;
Member, New York State Bar Association's Labor and Employment Section

George F. McClure
Technical Director (Ret.),
Martin Marietta Electronic Systems, Orlando, FL;
Past Chairman, IEEE-USA Pensions Committee

Robert W. McClure
Vice President of Engineering,
CONDUX, Inc.;
Chairman, IEEE-USA Licensure and Registration Committee, Wilmington, DE

Charles C. Olsefsky
Professor of Engineering,
California State University at Northridge;
Past Chairman, IEEE-USA Committee on Age Discrimination;
Past Chairman, IEEE-USA Committee on Legal Aspects of Engineering

Marlin P. Ristenbatt
Research Engineer,
Department of Electrical Engineering,
University of Michigan, Ann Arbor, MI;
Member, IEEE-USA Career Activities Committee

Howard L. Rose
Patent Attorney,
Bethesda, MD,
Member, IEEE-USA Committee on Intellectual Property;
Past Chairman, IEEE-USA Task Force on Patents

Richard A. Schwarz
Manager Metering Services,
PP&L, Hazleton, PA;
Vice Chairman, IEEE-USA Licensure and Registration Committee

Richard G. Weingardt
President,
Richard Weingardt Consultants, Inc., Denver, CO;
President, American Consulting Engineer's Council

PART 1   JOBS AND CAREERS

1

Engineering Careers in the United States in the 1990s

Marlin Ristenbatt

1.0 INTRODUCTION

As readers of this chapter, you have taken the initial steps along your career paths. You have chosen engineering from among a very large number of other possibilities. In the future you will encounter other branches in this career path and will need to decide which direction you should take. The first parts of this chapter describe the scope and types of engineering in the United States, the employers of engineers, and their policies. This description of the engineering environment is essential to making intelligent employer choices and career decisions down the road. The latter part of the chapter presents some of the alternatives.

The entering engineer will find that most of the public is unaware of how engineers function. That is because they experience an engineers work only through the products and services they purchase, rather than by direct interaction as with accountants, lawyers, and physicians.

2.0 OVERVIEW OF AN ENGINEERING CAREER

An engineer's career begins and develops in an organization. Unlike an accountant, lawyer, or physician, the engineer does not begin by setting up a "practice." For engineers, working alone as a consultant usually is possible only after a successful career in some organization.

Dalton[1] notes that the first stage of an engineer's career is that of an apprentice, or "contributing dependently," characterized by helping, learning, and following directions. The work is supervised and judged by others who are in responsible charge. One is expected to demonstrate competence on a portion of a larger project and on detailed nonroutine tasks. One should show creativity and initiative and be able to perform well under time and budget pressures.

A second stage, called "contributing independently," occurs when the engineer has evidenced enough skill and judgement to warrant self-management. The independent contributor's area of responsibility necessarily involves some specialization. Networking with peers, both inside and outside the organization, is especially helpful in this stage. A significant fraction of U.S. engineers conclude their careers at the independent contributor stage. They enjoy the technical challenge of their specialized area.

After gaining a broader knowledge of the technical fields, an engineer may enter the third career stage, "contributing with and leading others." An engineer at this stage may be in a recognized management position or from any position may be using experience, knowledge, and gained confidence to exercise leadership by originating ideas, mentoring others, and consulting. The engineer may be a co-worker on a project whose technical expertise is recognized by peers.

A fourth and final career stage has been labeled "leading through vision." Engineers at this stage are top management or senior technical staff. They provide technical direction to the organization and plan the allocation of financial and technical resources.

3.0 CATEGORIES OF ENGINEERING ACTIVITY

There are four categories of engineering activity: basic research, applied research, prototype development, and production.[2]

3.1 Basic Research

Basic research attempts to advance the frontiers of science by discovering new scientific facts and theory. In the United States the federal government finances most of the basic research, with some investment by large corporations. The research is mostly carried out in universities and in nonprofit institutions under contract to the government. Basic research may be led by scientists with engineers supplying technology or instrumentation support. In some areas such as solid-state electronics and computer science, engineers with advanced degrees may be the project leaders.

3.2 Applied Research

Applied research uses the available scientific and technology database to develop a new or improved technique or product. Here again most of the financial support comes from the federal government via contracts awarded to industry by the various government laboratories. Industry also does a substantial amount of applied research in an effort to lead the market in producing improved products.

3.3 Prototype Development

The result of applied product research is usually a breadboard assembly which demonstrates feasibility. Prototype development takes the next step and constructs a working model of the product. Financial support and areas of activity parallel those in applied research. If the end result is a consumer product, prototype development will occur in private for-profit companies. If the end result is used by the Department of Defense or other government agency, the prototype will be developed under contract to industry, a university, a nonprofit institution, or a government laboratory.

3.4 Production

All engineering prior to production is performed in a laboratory environment. The mass production of a product modeled in prototype involves design engineers and engineers skilled in the assembly line manufacturing techniques. Here, large and small commercial companies are the major participants, with government in a secondary minor role. For consumer products, financing for this category comes from stockholders of privately or publicly held corporations. The supplying of a service, such as power or telecommunications, may be considered in this category. The organizations involved are public, private, or government. Engineers are employed at all levels, from design and installation to the executive suite.

4.0 U.S. COMPETITIVENESS

The 1990s will be a time of change for the engineering community, as it is for all other economic sectors of the United States and for other industrialized nations. Two large drivers for change in the United States are the downsizing of the defense budget and the global competition in all product categories. In the consumer product area, the United States competes favorably in basic research and prototype development. It is especially good at basic research, as shown by the record of Nobel prizes, and at prototype development. U.S. companies have not invested in applied research to the extent that its competitors have. Pressured by the investor community, U.S. companies have looked for short-term results, while foreign competitors emphasize the long term.

The greatest challenge for the United States is in the production of consumer products, where the United States is losing out to the competition. And yet here is where the real payoff lies. This is where the United States needs to focus attention if it hopes to improve its competitive strength.

5.0 EMPLOYMENT SECTORS

5.1 Industry-Commercial

The largest employer of U.S. engineers are those companies engaged in mass production. This sector is financed by investor-owned companies with income provided by the products and services offered. It is one of the major drivers of the U.S. economy, and engineers are essential, critical employees of these companies. This sector appears healthy for the 1990s, but is under severe global competition.

Large companies often have good training and apprenticing programs, which attracts new graduates. Until recently, some large companies could offer the prospect of lifetime employment, but this can no longer be assured. Job security is still fairly good so long as one remains a strong contributor. Engineers are expected to work hard and be effective producers. In past decades the growth in the U.S. economy has been borne mainly by the smaller companies. There is a stronger work ethic and less bureaucracy in smaller organizations.

5.2 Industry-DOD/Aerospace

The second largest employer of engineers in the United States are those commercial and nonprofit organizations who produce military or aerospace products, or do applied research that support such products. The work is funded by the federal taxpayer. This sector includes support of challenging and interesting technical programs which attract engineering graduates. Edge-of-technology efforts such as the moon landing and the space station are funded with tax dollars. The industry-conducted projects are administered by DOD or NASA employees. Industry engineers working on these programs earn relatively high salaries because of the sometimes unstable employment conditions that go with the winning or losing of military or space contracts by their employer. The engineering jobs include those that are technically exciting along with a large number of mundane jobs that come with the government regulations and associated paperwork. This sector is not expected to grow in the 1990s, and may diminish, due to the ending of the Cold War.

5.3 Public Sector

The employer is a government agency (federal, state, or municipal) or a university. The government jobs are subject to the civil service regulations. Most engineering jobs are with the federal government, mainly in the Department of Defense. These jobs are in all aspects of engineering, with the least percentage in the production engineering area. In the past, the salaries, particularly for the higher civil service grades, were less than those paid to engineers in comparable positions in industry. Recently, the salary structure in the federal sector has been raised so that they are roughly comparable. Government positions are more secure than other employment sectors. When there are changes in workload, personnel reductions are usually accomplished by attrition, that is, personnel retirements and voluntary resignations. Retirement plans and health benefits are as good as the best found in industry. The government jobs offer engineers the opportunity to administer technical projects, and emphasize planning and control. Some applied research and prototype development are carried out in government laboratories, but most technical developments are accomplished under contracts to industry or nonprofit laboratories.

University tenure-track jobs are subject to the special conditions associated with tenure. Nontenure-track engineering jobs at universities are placed in the nonprofit laboratory category. Employment security for tenure-track jobs is the highest, at least after tenure is granted. Non-teaching engineering activity is financed by grants and by government contracts. Basic and applied research are the principle areas of work. Here, as in the government sector, health and retirement benefits are excellent.

5.4 Public Utilities

Public utilities (power and telecommunications) are regulated by state utility commissions and depend on income from ratepayers. The utility is usually a private industry, but their finances are under the control of the commission. Until recently the job security was comparable to that in the public sector because of the stability of the ratepayer base and demand, but recent efforts to deregulate the utility business has brought stiff competition to this sector.

5.5 Nonprofit Organizations

These organizations either are in practice subsidized by the government or are financed by grants and by the income from their government and industry contracts. The MITRE Corporation in Bedford, Massachusetts, and Batelle Institute in Columbus, Ohio, are typical nonprofits. In general the engineers both propose and carry out technical work, either in response to some request for proposal (RFP) or an unsolicited proposal. The projects are technically challenging and interesting.

5.6 Private Practice

After practicing engineering for a number of years, engineers may acquire sufficient experience in some area of engineering so that they can offer their expert services much in the manner of doctors or lawyers. Their clients may be nonengineers or engineering companies that require their particular expertise.

6.0 ORGANIZATIONAL POLICIES

6.1 Employee Relations

Since the onset of global competition in the 1960s, U.S. organizations have been trying to boost their productivity. There is increasing use of customer-focused business models, employee diversity, and flattening of organizations. A critical factor in productivity is the treatment of employees. Longrigg[3] discusses this issue:

> Organization managers should do all they can to improve morale for these professionals (and all employees) by moderating the tendency towards greed and self-aggrandizement that seems exaggerated in our Western Civilization organizations.
>
> Management and all employees must become aware of, and suitably nurture, leaders as opposed to managers. A leader may be described as a person that other people want to follow; a manager may be followed only because it is necessary to get the paycheck, and may be due solely to a hierarchical position. Our industries need to increase the fraction of leaders relative to managers. In addition, for long range purposes, we must develop some form of consent mechanism so that leaders have the consent of the led, if we are to secure our future in the global economy.
>
> The United States has a much larger fraction (12%) of employees engaged in supervisory roles, than does Europe (4%) or Japan (3%), as opposed to roles that directly contribute to the product. It has become painfully clear in the last few years that the companies with the resulting large bureaucracies are in the most trouble. Companies in our capitalistic system must improve their treatment of people. Workers in the West are too often treated like an expense to be managed and curtailed rather than a resource to be nurtured and developed. Japan, which practices a vigorous form of capitalism, attempts to provide employment stability (at least to age 55) in many employment sectors, for the core employees. Satisfied workers are perhaps a necessary condition for high productivity organizations.

6.2 Desirable Practices

Engineers assessing future employers should be aware of and should evaluate their organizational practices. An engineer contemplating joining a company should look for the following recommended practices:

6.2.1 Business Continuity
The company policy should emphasize staying in business and continuing to provide a product or service. As Deming noted,[4] it is important for organizations to create constancy of purpose for improvement of product and service. While making an appropriate amount of money is certainly a necessary condition for any private organization, all the stakeholders with the possible exception of some investors, have the vested interest of having the company stay in business and provide jobs through innovation, research, and constant improvement.

Of all the employees, engineers especially have their interest and career satisfaction invested in the planning for and development of increasingly better products. Companies that overemphasize the money-making goal almost always focus on short-range performance and tolerate exaggerated money rewards to managers or stockholders. This attitude jeopardizes long-term stability and growth. The more successful companies are those that measure success by doing the greatest good for the greatest number of people. Just as the investment community is now awakening to the "don't harm the environment" dimension in their investment decisions, it may in the future take into account a "balanced scoreboard" that has recently been advanced,[5] when weighing investment decisions. Society is now beginning to hear about "socially responsible investments," where social factors in addition to the monetary return are being considered. The long-range economic strength and the stability of the U.S. economy would be improved if investors were encouraged to expect reasonable rather than unusual returns on their investments.

Corporate activity in the 1980s emphasized the leveraged buyout and an epidemic of financial manipulation. Here's how Ron Tucker, a financial analyst described the result[6]:

> Instead of replacing an outdated plant and its equipment, upgrading the skills of their labor force, or investing in research and development—all necessary for long-term competitiveness—these corporations have been forced to distribute hundreds of billions of dollars in accumulated earnings to greedy investors. Besides the obvious damage to the American manufacturing base, this policy change has resulted in a significant drop in expected government revenues, due to massive layoffs and a rise in government entitlements.

6.2.2 Leaders
The organization should encourage employees who show leadership qualities and should give these individuals appropriate responsibility.

The requirements for being a leader, according to Hanson and Miller, management consultants are[7]

- Be willing to become personally involved with subordinates and peers
- Exert leadership by motivating and inspiring others, but also get things done; require people to be accountable for agreed-upon action
- Be proactive; exercise initiative

- Be prepared to handle complexity; don't overly focus on singular goals but be goal-oriented
- Do person-to-person inquiring and probing for information
- Monitor the work; establish controls and constraints
- Be consumed with effectiveness and making a significant difference; doing right things rather than becoming more efficient; in other words, doing things right
- Be conceptual and grasp and assimilate abstractions like missions and visions.

6.2.3 Management Hierarchy   The best technical organizations have a minimum hierarchy. While bloated hierarchies do provide some middle management jobs for engineers, the penalty in lost efficiency and reduced enthusiasm of employees far exceeds such benefits. Morale, productivity, and long-term success are highest with the minimum hierarchy. Excess layers of management discourages lower levels of employees from taking responsibility and encourages some employees to pursue promotion for prestige instead of working to contribute to the quality of the products or services.

Many U.S. organizations are making strong attempts to improve their practices with regard to technical employees, and one should look for organizations that are doing this. Assigning responsibility to the lowest viable level allows more employees to manage themselves. This strategy has the best long-range potential for both the employee and the organization.

6.2.4 Compensation   Executives should be compensated at a reasonable rate compared to others in the organization. Paul Longrigg states[8] similarly we see many CEOs who take obscene emoluments from their often-failing operations and then depart the scene on golden parachutes, leaving an horrendous mess behind. In Japan CEOs salaries are only 7 to 10 times larger than that of the lowest-paid worker. In the United States and elsewhere, this figure is often 85 to 1 or larger.

6.3 Recommended Practices for the Engineer

While the entering engineers have little influence over organizational practices beyond choosing whether or not to join it, they do have control over their own behavior. The following advice for the entering engineer is quoted from Werne and Lafranchi.[9]

Be Technically Skilled: Being skilled means committing yourself to career-long learning in a manner which keeps your skills current so that you may meet the needs of your organization in this increasingly competitive world. It also prepares you for new assignments and perhaps even going to a new employer.

Find a Mentor: The message here is simple—learn from experienced, senior co-workers; they typically have a wealth of knowledge and experience and love to share it.

Be Selfless: Furthering your career advancement through appropriate preparation and experience is expected, but to do it at the expense of others or your organization is usually detrimental. Teamwork and cooperation are essential in today's competitive work environment.

Try to Do the Best in Everything You Do: Ultimately your career success will hinge on the quality and quantity of your work. Recognition and opportunities for advancement come as a result of doing your job, all aspects of your job, and doing them well.

Be Willing to Help: Teamwork is an essential element in the successful accomplishment of engineering projects. Willingness to help your co-workers and therefore your team will further enhance the possibilities of team success.

Speak Up on Issues in a Constructive Versus Destructive Way: Coming up with the best answer to a problem usually becomes a competition among ideas and proposals. . . . Those who constantly complain about the organization and make no constructive suggestions about how to improve things may become labelled as "malcontents." Such labelling can have long-term negative impact on an individual's career.

Be Active in Your Professional Society: Technical skill, mentors, professional networks and recognition of your work, can all be obtained or enhanced through your professional society.

Other articulations of what works appear in Rosen[10] and Hutcheson.[11] The observations of King,[12] although communicated in 1944, contain practical on-the-job advice that is valid today.

Research has shown that having a challenging first assignment is highly correlated with career success. Of course, challenging assignments are critical throughout the career, but especially so at the outset. However, an engineer must learn to cope with boredom when engaged in less interesting aspects of the job. No matter what stage an engineer is in and whether on a technical or a management path, he or she must constantly keep learning to survive.

7.0 DECISIONS

This final section discusses path choices available to engineers during their careers. Some of this section paraphrases a talk by Merrill Buckley.[13] All choices are purely a personal matter for each engineer, being dependent on the engineer's interest, aptitude, and ambition. No matter which choice is selected, the engineer will have the satisfaction of knowing that he or she will be making a contribution to society.

7.1 Job or Graduate School

The first decision that the newly graduated engineer will make is whether to seek a job or continue in graduate school. This decision should consider (1) interests, aptitude, and past scholastic record; (2) the current and predicted job market; and (3) future objectives.

7.2 Career Areas

7.2.1 Engineering   This is the area that will appeal to most engineers. It involves the application of the engineering principles they have learned in their academic years to the production of improved products for society. They are interested in problem solving and demonstrate their abilities by writing books and journal articles and by their contributions to engineering projects. They seek the recognition of their accomplishments by their peers.

7.2.2 Teaching   A possible career choice for the engineer is to become an academic and thus help teach and guide the next generation of engineers. Graduate study and an advanced degree are always required for entry into this field, and a Ph.D. is almost mandatory for an academic career. An academic can be involved in teaching and in basic or applied research conducted under grants or contracts.

7.2.3 Marketing   While engineers are logical in their thought processes, some will prefer using this personality trait to expound on the benefits that accrue to using their company's product rather than being involved in the problem-solving environment that develops them. These engineers are people oriented, and marketing or sales should be their forte.

7.2.4 Management   Since, in most companies, managers have responsibility for the financial and many of the technical aspects of the project, depending on project size, it is no surprise that management positions carry higher salaries, greater control over decisions, and more prestige. Companies may have a dual ladder structure where technical personnel salaries parallel management. There are negatives to being a manager, such as less technical development; more competitive stress, since the number of people seeking promotion exceeds the number of positions available; and greater strain on family life because of longer work-hours. Achieving success as a manager requires that one be capable of leading. Thus, a management position should only be considered when one is confident enough and experienced enough to exert leadership and when one desires the recognition that goes with executive positions.

7.3 Specialist or Generalist

Another decision for engineers to make is choosing whether to specialize or to broaden one's scope of knowledge and become a generalist.

There are many engineering specialties, particularly in electrical engineering. The IEEE has 37 societies, each devoted exclusively to an engineering discipline. The engineering state of the art in most of these is changing rapidly, particularly in the computer, communications, and solid-state areas. In a general sense one might characterize the advance by saying the technology base in most special fields has a half life of 5 years. Since the average engineering lifetime is about 40 years, it is easily seen that an engineer, to remain competent, is in a continual learning cycle. It becomes obviously evident that being a competent technical specialist is a full-time job.

The design and implementation of a system requires interfacing and integrating the services and products of several special technology areas. This is the purview of the generalist. The generalist must have a broad knowledge of the various technologies employed in the system and an ability to interact with specialists so as to do the necessary systems analysis and guide the system implementation.

7.4 Public Sector, or Industry

The characteristics of these employment sectors have been described in Section 5.0. The public sector offers maximum security and stability. In large companies, it is difficult to obtain the "big picture." Engineers work on some segment of a large project, and unless they are in higher-level management or on a planning staff, they rarely get to participate in the systems integration. They are also less likely to initiate new projects or promote innovative concepts. On the positive side, engineers will have relative freedom in establishing design criteria for an assigned area of work and will enjoy working closely with a team of peers.

The small company allows participation in the company projects from cradle to grave and more opportunity for introducing innovative design. There is less bureaucracy and a more informal working environment.

In the past, companies large and small favored conservative dress styles. Many companies, for example, IBM and AT&T, still do. There is a growing trend, particularly in Silicon Valley on the West Coast toward adopting casual attire in the workplace. While admittedly a minor career consideration, it may be a personal factor.

8.0 CONCLUDING REMARKS

Engineering careers are diverse and idiosyncratic. They are affected by organizational types and practices and by individual interests, attitudes, and personality traits. Career planning is an individualized process that depends a great deal on needs, aspirations, and expectations and on a self-analysis of capabilities and skills. An engineer should attempt to match personal characteristics with those required by the job. Describing the techniques that can be used to perform this essential self-assessment is beyond the scope of this chapter. An excellent treatment of this aspect and others of professional career planning is given in Raelin.[14]

ENDNOTES

1. Gene Dalton, "A Tested Method for Recognizing and Rewarding Technical Leadership and Contribution, p. 45 of *8th Biennial Careers Conference Record,* April 14, 1994, Fort Worth, Texas, IEEE Cat. No. UH0195-8, is the most recent of a large series of articles about career stages that began in 1977: "The Four Stages of Professional Careers—A New Look at Performance by Professionals," in *Organizational Dynamics* (New York: AMACOM, a division of American Management Association, 1977).

2. This section is based on a talk by Edward J. "Jack" Doyle, presented to the Professional Activities Committees for Engineers (PACE) meeting in 1992.

3. Paul Longrigg, "On Some Aspects of a Multi-National Career in Electrical Engineering over Four Decades," p. 160 in *IEEE-USA's Seventh Biennial Careers Conference Record,* October 10, 1991, Denver, Colorado, IEEE Cat. No. UH0190-9.

4. M. Maccoby, "Deming Critiques American Management," *Research/Technology Management* (May–June 1990).

5. Robert S. Kaplan and David P. Norton, "The Balanced Scoreboard—Measures That Drive Performance," *Harvard Business Review* (January–February 1992).

6. Ron Tucker "Other Voices," Ann Arbor News, Ann Arbor MI, 6/28/92.

7. Marlys Hanson and Arthur Miller, Jr., "When You Choose Leaders—Beware of the Smile Factor," p. 82 in *1991 IEEE-USA Career Conference Record*. Washington, DC.

8. Paul Longrigg, "On Some Aspects of a Multi-National Career in Electrical Engineering over Four Decades."

9. Roger Werne and Edward A. Lafranchi, "Career Advice for the Young Engineer," p. 171 in *1991 IEEE-USA Career Conference Record*.

10. Elizabeth A. Rosen, "Working Towards Career Satisfaction: Cases from an R & D Environment," p. 166 in *1991 IEEE-USA Career Conference Record*.

11. Peggy C. Hutcheson, "Are Engineering Careers the Fast Track to Nowhere?" p. 74 in *1991 IEEE-USA Careers Conference Record*.

12. W. J. King, *The Unwritten Laws of Engineering* (New York, NY: American Society of Mechanical Engineers, 1944).

13. Merrill Buckley, presentation at an IEEE-USA Student Professional Awareness Conference, Philadelphia.

14. Joseph A. Raelin, *The Salaried Professional, How to Make the Most of Your Career* (New York: Prager, 1984).

2

The Job Market

Richard Backe

1.0 INTRODUCTION

For the past century, most engineers (more than 95 percent) have worked directly for an employer in industry, the government, or academia. Unlike our self-employed colleagues in medicine or law, the engineer will have to find an employer to work for and must do so in an increasingly competitive job market.

Although self-employment is a growing option for many entrepreneurial engineers, most professionals in engineering will face the prospect of finding an employer at least 5 to 10 times in their 40 years or more of technical practice. Whether the reader is a recent graduate or a seasoned professional, this chapter will help in finding and in choosing the next career job.

This chapter is certainly seeded with personal biases developed in the 40-year career of the author which involved interviewing and hiring hundreds of engineers. However, the advice is also based on formal surveys and follow-up research with several hundred engineering and personnel managers. As such, it reflects the conventional wisdom of many individuals.

All rules, however, have exceptions and that is true of the guidelines here. Moreover, there is room in engineering for mavericks, both as employees and employers. If the job seeker wants to find a position in a nontraditional setting, he or she should tailor the search by taking exception to some of the rules. After all, the idea is not to get just any job but one that can be looked forward to with enthusiasm each day.

What is described is the engineering employment world as it really is, not as the reader or author might like it to be. To portray a different picture would not serve anyone very well in their search. In a more ideal future, conditions might be more employee-friendly concerning employment-at-will contracts, patent agreements, work hours and job sharing, and so on. The reader might even be among those who change some current industry practices, but the best time to do that is not during the employment search process.

1.1 Preparation

It is quite amazing that some engineers believe that their first (or next) job will fall into their laps effortlessly. There may have been some basis for this in the halcyon days of technology-driven eras when the United States had a virtual monopoly on engineering development, and budgets were subordinate to the quest for supremacy in defense and space programs. Now, however, a shrinking economy, both public and private, the demands of our social programs, a worldwide move toward a more peaceful climate, and the competition from other countries in both low- and high-tech labor markets have all changed employment ground rules.

The first thing to recognize in the job search process is that this very task is a full-time job in itself. As such, it demands the same discipline, inquisitiveness, data gathering, judgment, structured action, follow-up, and ethics that characterize other professional activities. The engineer is likely to work about 85,000 hours in a lifelong career and earn between $2 and $3 million (in 1994 dollars) over that period. For a contract of several million dollars, an engineering company will spend at least 1 percent of the contract value in developing a technical proposal. The individual professional should be prepared to spend 100 hours or so before each career move to meet that 1 percent criterion. A lesser effort might result in a less than optimum job search, or it might not succeed at all.

2.0 THE NEXT JOB

2.1 Job Location

Engineers find employment in a variety of work situations. A recent survey of electrical engineers shows them distributed as shown in Table 2.1.

Some changes in these distributions will occur throughout the 1990s and into the next millennium. The distribution by sector is unlikely to change much; the majority of engineers will still find employment in the private sector, and perhaps somewhat fewer will find federal government jobs. In terms of industry type, barring another shift in world stability, there will be a decrease in the number of engineers employed in defense-related jobs, but current developments suggest continuing increases in employment in both the computer and communications industries.

The referenced IEEE survey shows an unusually high percentage of engineers (18 percent) in management functions. The survey population

Table 2.1   Employment of Electrical Engineers in 1993 by Field, Type Employer, and Function

TECHNICAL FIELD	PCT	EMPLOYER TYPE	PCT	JOB FUNCTION	PCT
Computers–software, hardware	25%	Private industry–non-defense	47%	Design and development	25%
Power and other energy	14%	Private industry–defense	17%	Technical Management	18%
Circuits and devices–systems, electron dev., hybrids	12%	Utilities	12%	Programming S.W. Engineer	11%
Communications–broadcast, consum. electronics	12%	Federal government–defense	7%	Systems engineer	8%
Systems and control–control syst, medical, robotics	8%	Federal government–non-defense	3%	Consulting	6%
Signals and applications–electronic, acoustics, geoscience	7%	Education	8%	Education and training	6%
Industrial application and instrumentation/measurement, insulation	7%	Non-profit institutions	3%	Basic research	5%
EM and radiation antennas, u-wave, EM comp.	5%	State/Local government	1%	Engineer support	5%
Management and education–reliability, communication	6%	Other	2%	General management	4%
Other	4%			Sales, construction, quality, maintenance, other	12%

was a fairly select group. More extensive Department of Labor surveys of engineers in all technical disciplines have consistently shown a smaller number (11 percent) in supervisory roles. The number of engineers in purely management roles is expected to decrease further as U.S. companies are budget-driven to flatten their organizational structures and as self-directed work teams become the norm in more and more industries.

Thus, the "average" electrical engineer will be looking for a nonsupervisory job in the private nondefense sector, probably in a computer or communications company and most likely doing design or development work. However, the thrust of this chapter is to allow individuals in all disciplines to tailor their job search to their preferences. It is useful to know where the majority of jobs are by type and geography, particularly if you are unemployed and wish to enlarge the target field.

You should also not overlook the fact that there are thousands of jobs, many not advertised, in less well-known and popular areas. So if you are really interested in doing research for a nonprofit company on biomedical equipment, you should not be deterred by the demographics in that field compared to others; the numbers don't tell the whole story.

2.2 Important Factors

No one can tell you what to look for in your next job. If you are out of work or are just entering the engineering work force, and if the economy is generally poor or is depressed in your major interest area, some compromises may have to be made. Even then, it should be possible to aim close to the ideal. Perhaps there are no jobs at the time developing on-board flight computers for NASA, but there might be close analogs in the automotive or transportation industry. While waiting for the perfect choice, the engineer should use technical publications and professional society meetings to maintain current skills in the space industry; a lot can change in a few years.

The job-seeking professional should not focus only on those jobs that promise a high salary, benefits, and little else. Analyses of many opinion surveys over the past several decades reveal that engineers show a remarkable consistency in the factors they consider important in selecting their next job, and compensation is not the first. Their work content and environmental conditions consistently outrank compensation. (See Table 2.2.)

Table 2.2   Factors of Importance, Percentage Rating Most Important

---

Challenging work assignments 50%

Opportunity to advance 32%

Geographic location 26%

Higher salary 26%

Professional development 19%

Job security 19%

2.3 Job Openings

When engineering employers were surveyed on the subject of how they obtained most of their engineering staff, they cited the following means, listed in order of preference and effectiveness:

- Employee referrals
- Walk-ins
- Advertising
- Job fair/Open house
- Corporate transfers
- Employment agencies, executive search firms

2.3.1 Employee Referrals   This mode is the most preferred, particularly if the employer has only a few openings. More significantly, such personal networking may lead to job interviews even if the company has no employment requisition open at the time matching the skills of the applicant.

Employee referrals generally result in candidates well matched by talent and temperament to jobs in a particular company or department. The referring employee has something at stake both with his or her friend and with the employing manager. He probably has a good knowledge of the job requirements, the general work ambiance, and his friend's qualifications and personality. For all these reasons, he is likely to make a careful recommendation.

Another positive factor to the employer is that such hires generally cost the employer less than $1000 in finder's fees and related costs. From the job candidate's point of view, a personal referral affords a better than 1 in 50 chance of being hired and for a job with a built in mentor via the referring colleague.

2.3.2 *Walk-ins*   Cold calls intrigue many employers. The technique used to make such contacts may show that the prospect has a lot of initiative and may demonstrate a level of interest and persistence that will be an asset on the job. There are lots of ways to make cold calls: you could show up at the personnel office to drop off a resume and ask for an informal interview, or get the name of one or more engineering managers and call them at 5 P.M. (they probably work late, but their calls are not screened after hours), or follow-up on a contact made at a social or professional society meeting by asking for a brief visit to get some job-hunting advice.

For the serious job seeker, a cold call provides good practice in handling oneself in an interview; it risks little, and it may produce a long-shot winner. From the employer's vantage point, it could constitute a minor schedule interference, but it could also offer the opportunity to meet a qualified candidate in an unusually candid setting and to make a zero-cost hire. It is worth the effort.

2.3.3 *Advertising*

Print Media   Responses to advertisements probably net the largest number of candidates and are second only to personal referrals in employer preference. If a large number of engineers are needed in a short period of time, advertising is an indispensable tool. An employer will typically place ads in several major daily newspapers (e.g., *The New York Times, Washington Post, The Wall Street Journal*) which yield a quick response.

If the employment needs are likely to be sustained, the employer will also place ads in monthly periodicals of the trade press (e.g., *The Mechanical Engineer, IEEE Spectrum, Electronic Design*). These ads require at least 30 days' lead time and responses come in over a longer period of time. Such long lead opportunities are frequently described in generic terms and may not represent currently available openings; they are intended to fill anticipated attrition-based vacancies or new business requisitions.

The cost of placing a display ad will run from $5000 to over $25,000, depending on the circulation of the publication. Employers report that the average cost per engineer hired by this means is about $5000 just for the cost of advertising. If the ad is fairly specific with respect to requirements, many potential respondents will be able to do an honest job of screening their qualifications against those of the job. Nevertheless, the odds of hiring any single respondent are about 1 in 90.

Electronic Media   Not all ads are placed via the print media. Although there is no reliable data about the success rate of ads placed in less

conventional media, the reader is encouraged to investigate all such opportunities. Employers will occasionally use ride-time radio to advertise their
openings. Costs for radio ads are relatively low. Although the contact rate
may not equal that of a daily paper ad in the same city, the impact is high.
Paid-over-the-air TV is used less frequently. In many cities, cable TV is
used by a fee-paid agency or is placed free by the local government on an
open channel. All such broadcast ads are for real and immediate openings
so they are worthy of attention. There is an increasing use of on-line and
off-line electronic data bases to list job openings or to store resumes for
employers to scan. The on-line service of Prodigy is one of the better known
commercial services. Information is available in any computer store. The
U.S. Department of Labor lists job openings on an open line. Call their local
office for information. Many of the professional societies sponsor electronic
data bases that are worth investigation.

2.3.4 *Job Fair / Open House*   Employers seeking to hire a large number
of employees, particularly at the beginning of a major contract or at the
opening of a new facility, may run an open house or employer-run job fair.
These gatherings are typically staffed with the company's engineering
managers.

Whenever the company has immediate vacancies to fill, job fairs
represent an easy way for the employment seeker to make a first contact
with a prospective employer. A senior engineer interviewed at such events
is very likely to be asked to return for a follow-up interview.

Employers are less enthusiastic about the effectiveness of agency-
run job fairs. The cost for the employers to participate is somewhat
higher than that of a display ad in a major daily. However, the number
of qualified candidates obtained for interviews is likely to be low,
particularly in view of the time involved in preparing for and staffing the
interview rooms. If the job fair is run well, the recruiting agency will
have contacted potential applicants several times and will have matched
them to the participating companies' job openings. Those companies will
have been given summary resumes in advance, and specific interview
times arranged and confirmed.

Unfortunately, some agencies do a poor job of screening, matching,
and scheduling, and candidate no-shows are frequent. These fairs seem to
be most effective when focused exclusively on a specific theme such as
attracting minority engineers, or those interested in overseas assignments,
and so on.

2.3.5 Corporate Transfers   A typical company will probably state as a matter of policy that they prefer to fill openings by internal transfers and promotions from within. However, few new jobs are filled by this means, in contrast to the number filled by outside hiring. One reason is that there are frequently not enough personnel resources in the company to match new openings to existing staff. There are also other factors inhibiting intracorporation transfers:

1. Few companies have an effective reward system to motivate managers to transfer any of their staff, much less their best engineers, to another job.

2. Not many companies have well-maintained, on-line personnel skills data bases, monitored by senior management, to ensure timely transfers occur.

3. Intracorporation employee relocations can cost over $40,000 in contrast to $10,000 for a new-hire relocation (or to no cost for hiring a locally available engineer).

All this means that job seekers should plan to work just as hard for their next job within their present company as they will for one outside the company. Their networking opportunities should certainly be much better among current company contacts.

2.3.6 Employment Agencies   Employment agencies are generally the last recruiting resort of an engineering employer, because costs are high and the process is not efficient. Although the company will pay only upon candidate placement, the fee is typically 10 to 20 percent of the offered salary. This cost, $5000 to $15,000 in today's market, is usually higher than the cost per hire by any other means.

- Recent graduates should not count on agencies to help them; few companies will pay an agency fee for those just entering the field, relying instead on their own college recruiting programs for such help.

- An engineer should never pay a fee nor sign an exclusive contract with an employment agency. In the engineering industry, employers pay all placement fees.

- Engineers should not depend on agencies to protect their identity in a supposedly confidential search. Those engineers who are still employed might be in jeopardy if their resumes ended up with their current employer.

With these factors in mind, the job-seeking engineer may still choose to send a resume to several agencies, but should not depend on them for anything other than a mass mailing service. The odds of an employer filling a job by this means are less than one in a hundred.

2.3.7 Executive Search Firms   Executive search firms are retained by companies to do a dedicated search for very special needs, typically in the management area. Most such firms will not accept unsolicited resumes. They will find appropriate candidates by networking among their contacts in the field.

2.4 Focusing the Job Search

Armed with the knowledge about how employers typically fill their jobs, the job seeker can decide on the best strategy to use in the search. There are three courses of action: (1) investigating the jobs that are formally advertised in the various media, (2) looking for the hidden jobs, (3) networking.

2.4.1 Advertised Jobs   The first or more conventional method means studying all of the advertising media to learn about currently advertised jobs and about job fairs. A few sources for these are

- Personal subscriptions, at least for the length of the job search, to the prime national daily newspapers (e.g., *The New York Times, Los Angeles Times, The Wall Street Journal, Washington Post*) as well as the local papers in areas of particular interest. The Sunday editions contain the majority of the employment ads either in the classified sections and/or in special business sections.
- Special "newspapers" that focus only on job searches. *The Wall Street Journal* publishes an "Employment Weekly," and there are several Washington, DC–based newspapers that list government jobs (e.g., *Federal Employment Newsletter*).
- The public libraries for copies of other daily newspapers, in hard copy or microfiche
- The trade press, both weekly newspapers and monthly magazines, such as *Design News, Research and Development,* the *EE Times,* and so on. There are literally dozens of these in every area of engineering,

and many are available as a free subscription for those already working in the field. Copies are also available in the libraries of engineering schools, employers, major city libraries, and government laboratories

- Professional society journals such as IEEE's *Spectrum,* NSPE's *Professional Engineer*, ASME'S *Mechanical Engineer,* AIP's *Physics Today,* and the like and their technical and regional chapter newsletters or magazines

- Computer network services which frequently carry job listings and also carry some editions of daily newspapers. Those who do not have a personal computer with a suitable modem or who are not connected to a network should try the public library, outplacement office of their alma mater or local engineering schools, the local office of professional societies, or state employment agencies.

2.4.2   The Hidden Job Market   As mentioned earlier, not all jobs are advertised. Some jobs may be potentially available even though a company has not opened a formal job requisition. A really proactive job seeker can find these hidden jobs.

The task may take a good bit of the 100-hour estimate mentioned earlier, but it is no more difficult than the research required in any engineering task. It involves identifying:

- The employers who are involved in the type work and in the location(s) that is preferred

- Those individuals within those companies with whom to investigate job opportunities

The engineer who has been in the field for a while will know many of the companies that are likely candidates. In addition, several technical publications compile annual lists of the "top" engineering employers. Certainly starting with a Fortune 500 or equivalent list will include a large number of potential employers.

The list in Table 2.3 does not include all major employers and/or may not include employers in your preferred field of work or in the geographic region in which you want to work. You can develop your own list using a number of sources, such as the following:

Table 2.3   The 25 "Most Admired" Engineering Companies

3M	Honeywell	Rolm
Advanced Microdevices	Hughes	Sun Microsystems
Apple Computer	IBM	Tektronix
AT&T/Bell Labs	Intel Corporation	Texas Instruments
Control Data	Kodak	TRW
Digital Equipment	Microsoft	Unisys
General Electric	Motorola	Xerox
Harris	RCA	
Hewlett-Packard	Rockwell	

- IEEE's *Employment Guide for Engineers and Scientists,* Volume 2, is a directory of more than 1000 engineering employers conveniently listed by location.
- *Peterson's Guide to Engineering, Science, and Computer Jobs* is particularly valuable for recent graduates.
- State and local economic development commissions' directories of high-tech employers; Maryland, for example, has published a *Directory of Maryland Manufacturers* listing over 3000 employers, their addresses, product lines, and key officials as well as a separate but similar directory listing only high-tech companies.
- State and local chambers of commerce are also good sources of directories of employers, and these associations may provide the opportunity for local networking.
- Engineering trade associations often publish directories of their member companies; for example, the Electronic Industries Association (EIA) publishes a directory of its more than 300 member companies with the addresses and key officials of principal locations. The National Securities Industries Association does the same. To find the appropriate association, contact the Association of Association Directors in Washington, DC, or go to the library to get a copy of the National Academy of Science's *Scientific, Technical, and Related Societies of the United States* or AAES's *Directory of Engineering Societies.*
- Trade publications, both regional and national, frequently publish annual directories of employers in their disciplines or geographic area. As one example, *Design News* publishes an annual directory with over 1000 pages listing 6500 manufacturers of various products, their addresses, and telephone and fax numbers. For a small fee, some publications will make available a mailing list of their advertisers for your direct mail campaign.

- The well-known business magazines all publish annual directories or lists of the largest employers. Look at those published by Fortune, Barron's, Inc., Business Week, and others.
- State employment offices have listings of local employers who have frequent job offers; in larger states and cities, there will be a special employment office to assist professionals such as engineers in making contacts. Under federal law, government contractors must list all their openings with such agencies. Not to be overlooked are local offices of the U.S. Department of Labor for useful publications.
- Financial publications will be valuable sources not only of contact addresses but of data to help gauge the health of prospective employers. The Securities and Exchange Commission publishes lists of all publicly traded companies which can be used to secure annual financial reports. Indices such as Standard & Poor's should not be overlooked.
- The telephone Yellow Pages may be a gold mine, not only of the local companies but also of useful government agencies in the area. In this latter connection, the reader should be aware that most major federal agencies publish periodic lists or maintain current data bases of all their contracts and contractors, and these are available at low or no charge under the Freedom of Information Act.

2.4.3 Networking   Engineers, and most other professionals, are dependent throughout their careers on a network of colleagues for technical and business advice as well as career support. This network is an important tool in the job search process and should be explored as aggressively as any reference library or data base.

The process of network development begins in school. Individuals generally maintain contact with their closest friends, even as they disperse through different parts of the country and industry. Moreover, most universities maintain an active alumni association, placement facilities, and directories of graduates with employer names and contact information. Many of these are going on-line, accessible to anyone with a personal computer and an access code.

Every engineering student should join the chapter of his or her professional society while in college. Most of the engineering societies (ASME, AIDE, IEEE, etc.) have active student member programs, offered at affordable rates. The benefits in terms of activities are alone worth the price, but the biggest benefit is the beginning of a lifelong habit of professional interaction.

After graduation, the engineer should maintain this relationship with peers, not just through society membership but by active participation in local meetings. This should not be limited just to the particular specialty of the engineer. The radar specialist who attends meetings of the computer society or medical applications group will not only increase in technical knowledge but will also meet individuals in different associated fields and companies.

When it's time to look for another job, these contacts may be the best source of referral. Sometimes engineers who are unemployed, or substantially underemployed, are wary of using their associates in this way. This concern is not well founded. Most individuals are flattered to be asked to help.

Benjamin Franklin said that the best way to gain a mentor or sponsor was to ask for a favor, but only a little favor. Upon arrival in Philadelphia, Franklin borrowed a book from an established businessman, became his protege, and launched a distinguished career, starting as a printer.

When looking for a job, the engineer may find it useful to avoid directly asking personal contacts for a job. Instead, the initial call is more relaxed if the contact is asked about job opportunities in the company or nearby area. This takes the pressure off the respondent, who may not want to directly evaluate the caller as an employee or do so at that time. This opening lends a certain dignity to the discussion and frequently leads to productive referrals and excellent references.

Not to be overlooked are the staff personnel and volunteer officers of the job seeker's alumni office, local and regional engineering society and former bosses, fellow workers, and even neighbors.

3.0 THE RESUME

The resume is a tool that should be designed by a professional for one exclusive purpose: to get an invitation to an employment interview for a specific job. The resume may be mailed to an agency, sent directly to a company's employment office, dropped off during a cold call, or circulated via a personal network of professional colleagues. It is a marketing tool, one that must be designed to sell the professional abilities of an engineer as a prospective employee.

3.1 Resume Facts

Many engineers are not inclined toward selling. Their naturally conservative nature and methodical writing style result in a resume that does not make their special skills leap off the page like a three-dimensional holo-gram. For those individuals, a few important resume facts need to be disclosed.

FACT—The typical reviewer of resumes spends only 10 to 20 seconds in the first review of a stack of as many as 25 to 100 that are being scanned at any one time.

FACT—The first review of a resume is likely to be used to deselect candidates for a job, based on information that is missing or on information that is provided but that is a negative discriminator.

FACT—Resumes are viewed as a request for an interview for a specific job. If the resume is not tailored to that particular job, or if it contains a lot of irrelevant material, it is not likely to survive the first deselection review.

FACT—No resume reviewer expects to see a resume more than two pages, no matter how experienced the applicant, and the primary selling features must be on the first page.

A common mistake made by engineers is to confuse a resume with an employment application, a curricula vitae, a technical biography, or a chronological employment history. It is none of these, although all may be used as a source of data for the resume.

3.2 Resume Contents

The resume needs to convey three major kinds of information, namely,

- The identity and contact information for the individual engineer or scientist
- The engineer's education and related credentials
- The professional experience and accomplishments

Other information may be useful, useless, or damaging to the prospect's chances of securing an interview, but the three features just outlined are essential.

3.2.1 Identification   The full name of the candidate is normally the first item on the resume, without gender prefixes (e.g., Mr., Mrs., Ms.), but it is acceptable to include the honorific title Dr. Note, however, there could be a good reason to omit the latter; if the job in which the applicant is interested does not require a Ph.D., inclusion of this reference might dissuade further review by a manager who is disinclined to hire an overqualified applicant. For many jobs, state registration is mandatory or useful, and it is never harmful to use the earned suffix, P.E.

Inclusion of one's home address and telephone number is conventional, in addition to other contact addresses if the candidate is at school or a temporary work site. One should not use a current employer's phone number or address without permission. It is useful to note the hours available for contact, or the availability of an answering machine, as well as to furnish any available telefax and Internet contact numbers to accommodate companies interested in a quick response.

3.2.2 Education

A simple statement of degree(s) earned and the granting college or university is sufficient. Very recent graduates, as well as very mature engineers, might want to leave out the year the degree was obtained, lest they be deemed too young for some jobs or too old for others. Age discrimination is patently unfair and illegal, but there is no reason to provide negative discriminators.

An engineer who has graduated with honors (magna cum laude) or with an excellent grade point average (3.6 to 4.0) might want to list it. This applies particularly to the recent graduate who does not have any substantial experience. Scholarships, fellowships, and other credentials should also be noted.

The "engineer" without a degree should not cite a half page of courses as a substitute. It merely makes the absence of the degree stand out. A person qualified by experience and nondegree technical education should cite this succinctly (e.g., armed forces technical certificate plus B.A. in economics) and trust the reviewer will move on.

3.2.3 Experience

This is the key element of any resume and the data block that all reviewers go to at once. The engineer's experience can be presented in one of three ways.

In the chronological presentation, the engineer lists all the professional jobs held in reverse chronological order, typically giving the employment times and the employers' names and locations. This is followed by a statement of the work done, using brief phrases and only those abbreviations and acronyms that an engineering reviewer should be expected to recognize.

Reviewers are trained to look for gaps in such chronologies. These should be covered by short, and perhaps euphemistic, phrases: educational leave of absence, self-employed, career advancement.

Note: Purely chronological resumes are the most traditional. They are the easiest to update and use for broadcast distribution for a variety of jobs, but they are the least effective when a particular type job is targeted.

In the skills-ordered resume, the engineer will present his or her unique special talents in one or more phases of engineering. This presentation lends itself to tailoring for particular jobs. Several sentences describing current computer-aided design skills in photolithography would certainly interest an employer seeking an integrated circuit designer.

Such a skills listing can be followed by a brief chronological listing of jobs, employers, and duties to give a more complete sense of professional experience and diversity.

The accomplishments resume is a variant of the skills resume but one in which the engineer not only lists achievements but also points out that which was unusual and eye-catching. The idea is to make this resume stand out among others citing similar skills.

A statement that one has considerable mechanical engineering experience in telerobotics is considerably enhanced by

> performed all mechanical design work, from initial concepts through manufacturing reviews, testing and integration on remote manipulator arm for space shuttle retrieval of the Hubble Space Telescope. Mission satisfied all goals during five-day mission in 1993, and work was completed slightly under budget (about 3.5 percent less) and two weeks ahead of a critical launch window.

The objective should be to tailor the resume to a specific job, not just to any job. Part of the job seeker's initial research should have disclosed specific opportunities or at least the most likely opportunities in a target company. The resume should be focused on the interview seeker's attributes applicable to that job.

3.3 Style and Editorial Considerations

Many so-called experts will advise that there is only one accepted style for resume presentation, and that the use of special paper or graphics and photos is almost mandatory. These are generally people in the business of preparing resumes for a living and their claims are just not true. While any reasonable style of presentation is acceptable, there are a few things to avoid:

DO NOT use italics in your resume or print it on a dot matrix printer. Both are harder to read, particularly for the quick scan reviewer.

DO NOT use various colored inks; they do not photocopy well. In a large company, your resume may be copied several times for distribution, and each one must be a clean copy to get the best review.

DO NOT telefax a resume unless specifically requested or supplemented by a mailed hard copy. Most telefax copies are hard to handle and to photocopy. On the other hand, modem-transmitted copies are likely to end up being printed on a decent laser or ink jet printer, so use this means if the company has made it available.

DO NOT fail to check the resume to ensure the spelling is flawless. Perfection is expected. Rely on a colleague for final proofreading even after spell-checking on a personal computer.

3.4 Irrelevant Information

The job seeker should not include irrelevant personal information or unrelated experience in a resume. The recent graduate who has little or no engineering experience to relate might be well served by listing some of the jobs held during school, both to show a sense of industry and to give evidence of provable good work habits. The new graduate is better served by including details of academic honors, technical hobby accomplishments, student projects, and thesis subjects.

The more senior engineer need not list any details of nontechnical employment. Earlier engineering jobs should not be covered in the same level of detail as those in the last five years, particularly if they are unrelated to the target job.

3.5 Objective and Personal Data

An objective is frequently cited as an important element in a resume. However, its inclusion is quite discretionary and might be counterproductive. It is totally useless to cite a personal objective of "a job of progressive responsibility leading to a position in senior corporate management," particularly if the candidate is a recent graduate.

The same applies to the more experienced engineer. An objective, if not stated in the terms of the target job, could be a negative discriminator. If the job is actually for a position performing laboratory stress tests and the applicant cites only an objective of computer modeling design stress, the reviewer may infer a mismatch, although both types of jobs may have been of interest to the engineer.

However, both an objective statement and certain personal data may be used by the engineer to select in or select out certain jobs. In the foregoing case, the person interested only in modeling, and with the option of waiting for the right opportunity, will wish to be screened out of offers to interviews that waste both parties' times.

The same use can be made of personal information which normally has no place in a resume. One's age, weight, height, ethnicity, physical condition, politics, and hobbies should be of no interest to the reviewer, have no legal bearing on the selection process, and yet may be used as unconscious discriminators if furnished. In a few instances the job seeker might seek such discriminators, positive or negative:

- If the job appears to require the judgment and experience normally associated with 20 years or more in the field, citing a graduation date or other age indicator could be a positive factor.
- A job involving substantial foreign travel or major relocations might be perceived as more attractive to the candidate who announces "No family responsibilities; able to travel extensively."

If there is a bona fide occupational requirement for physical activities supervising construction site activities, sports and fitness activities connoting robust health might sway a decision to interview.

The candidate who wishes to be interviewed only by firms not involved in weapons development, or by environmentally active employers, or by those who make unusual efforts to accommodate special needs can either state so directly or imply this by his or her association memberships.

It is up to the job seeker to decide on the value of such discriminators. No resume reviewer, in the contemporary legal climate, will explicitly demand such data be furnished before an interview.

3.6 References

Finally, a concluding section on references is frequently deemed obligatory in a resume. It is a waste of valuable space and is premature; references will be checked later in the employment process. More useless is the statement that "References can be supplied." In the unusual situation in which the applicant studied under a Nobel prize winner or is referred by the vice president of engineering for the company, that fact can be brought out more completely and tactfully in a transmission letter.

3.7 The Transmission Letter

If possible, the letter should be addressed to a specific individual in the Personnel or Human Resources (HR) department and a copy sent to the potentially interested engineering manager. The latter is likely to see far fewer resumes each week and to give each more scrutiny.

One caveat: The HR department should not be sidestepped in this process but used as a parallel source of contact. Procedures in many companies are quite structured, and bypassing HR may alienate a group whose support is needed to complete the interview process.

The letter can be used to provide additional personal information that could lead to an invitation to an interview. If the job seeker is currently located a good distance from the employment site, the reviewer may assume that there is little likelihood of acceptance of an offer that will involve relocation. This concern can be allayed by a statement such as

"I attended school in the Cleveland area and have always wanted to return to the quieter life-style . . ."

or

"I am a real ski enthusiast and the Denver area has a lot of appeal to me . . ."

or

"My husband's family is from Melbourne, so relocating to Florida has a definite appeal . . ."

The letter can also emphasize (1) the reason for a special interest in the type work involved in the advertised job, (2) a fact about the company that gives it special appeal to the applicant, (3) the candidate's reason for an apparent career change, and (4) names of friends working in the company with whom the candidate would like to work and who will act as internal references.

The idea is to give the reviewers some personal facts or views that will catch their attention, and that will make this particular resume more memorable. Honest statements of personal interest will come across more credibly; the letter should employ all the creativity the applicant has, but not resort to gross exaggerations.

3.8 The Follow-up

The majority of job seekers, and engineers are no exception, send a resume to a company and then sit back awaiting the call inviting them to an interview. This is generally a big mistake. Continuous follow-up is an important technique to ensure that the resume has arrived and is being considered and to restart a review for the original target job or another similar job. A significant number of tentative hiring decisions are not implemented for a variety of reasons, including the lack of interest or availability of the first candidates. In addition, in a large company, the same types of openings occur every several months. For that reason, the candidate whose resume was not in the first consideration group should call to see if it is truly being reconsidered or whether it is in a "deep file." Often such a follow-up call may provide some clues about a deficiency that can be remedied, making a resubmittal more productive.

Hint: Calls being placed during the day will often be answered by administrative assistants who can be very helpful, and will, if the extra time is taken, forge a person-to-person link. The candidate who believes that it is essential to talk to the "boss" should call after 5 P.M., when the boss is likely to be answering the phone personally.

4.0 THE JOB INTERVIEW

Interviews are the single most important factor in the job selection process. This is not to diminish the significance of the initial resume review, or of the reference checks and management reviews of all applicant material. However, most industry-related jobs, and many in the government and academia, are decided primarily on the person-to-person interchanges at an interview.

As stated in the preceding section, resumes are used first to screen out unqualified or minimally qualified persons for a specific job. Similarly, the job interview is used first to narrow the field of surviving candidates (assuming there are a number of paper qualified applicants). Therefore, the initial challenge for the applicant is to avoid being quickly deselected for want of proper preparation or acceptable interviewing skills. With a little help, any qualified candidate can pass the first screening and join the surviving best of the best. At that turning point, the interviews become a process of the company selling the candidates as well as the reverse.

4.1 Interview Preparation

One should prepare for an interview in the same way one would prepare for any important business meeting. The very preparation gives the prospective employer a first impression on how well the applicant will prepare for later assignments. These preparations should include (1) learning about the job and the employer, (2) making appropriate arrangements to get to the meeting, and (3) preparing personally for the interview.

An employer is almost always impressed by an applicant who has taken the time, and shown the ingenuity, to learn something about the company prior to the interview. This research will also aid the applicant in deciding what questions to ask. In addition to the information secured during the initial steps in the job search, the job seeker should

- Ask the person scheduling the interview for more details about the job or for a contact person to talk to in advance. Even a brief telephone preinterview can provide useful guidance.
- Request a copy of the company's corporate report, employee news-letter, and technology bulletins and absorb any facts relevant to the proposed job.
- Intensify and focus the initial library search and trade literature review as well as exploration of personal networking contacts.

The candidate should ensure written confirmation is received of the exact time, place, persons to see, and contact telephone numbers. Absent that, the candidate should mail, telefax, or electronically mail his or her understanding of the arrangements. Travel and meeting preparation is an important consideration for job interviews as well as business meetings in general. Unfortunately, many people give too little attention to this. The candidate should have a backup plan that includes consideration of delays due to heavy traffic, possible alternative routes, breakdown of a car, snowstorms, public transportation, availability of parking and its proximity to the plant or office, detailed directions to the specific entrance to use, the need to clear through security, getting a badge and presenting required credentials, and so on.

When the interview is to be conducted at distant locations, the backup plan should include more reserve time (travel to interviews the day before if at all possible), alternate airline flights or surface transportation (photo-copy and carry the applicable schedules), and city maps and information on local travel conditions (cabs may be better than a car rental for a congested city interview).

The company's interviewers have scheduled a specific time for the planned interview. If the candidate cannot meet that schedule, the company should be notified as soon as possible with a brief explanation. When a delay is inevitable, it is worthwhile to use an in-flight phone or a highway phone booth to advise your contact and reschedule.

Personal preparation for the interview should be done against a tailored checklist including the travel considerations just outlined as well as the following:

- Prepare a chronological record of all previous employers and addresses, salary history, supervisors' names, several business and personal references, and prior residence addresses. These may be required for an employment or security application prior to the interview; being prepared with a travel copy of this data reflects good planning.
- Ensure that references know the type job being applied for, refresh their memory about accomplishments (a copy of the resume might help), and confirm that their endorsement will be forthcoming.
- Bring photocopies of recent published papers or project details that are not classified or proprietary.
- Plan dress and personal appearance to fit conventional guidelines. If in doubt, err on the side of conservatism.
- Assume that Murphy's law will govern all baggage handling; carry on important papers and clothing items.
- Take along several pens, a pocket calculator, a ready list of phone numbers at the interview destination as well as at home port, and emergency travel agent numbers to change arrangements.

In addition to the logistics preparation, it is important to be psychologically prepared for the interview. Most employers will ask a number of questions during the first part of the interview, some technical and some personal, to get to know how the candidates respond on their feet. It may be wise to review some of the literature in the field of the advertised position, mostly as a refresher on nomenclature and specifications. It is not necessary or desirable to cram technically for the job if the applicant has a good working knowledge of the field and knows where and how to obtain required factual data.

It is important to demonstrate communication skills and the ability to deal with complex problems. Many standard interview questions are designed not to elicit a single correct response but to test the respondent's ability to think through and reply to complex issues. Typical questions are:

"What are your long-term goals?" "What do you believe it will take to succeed in a company like ours?" "What accomplishment of yours gave you the most satisfaction?" "Describe your strongest points and weaknesses?" "How do you balance cost concerns versus quality?" "Do you prefer team assignments or working as an individual?" "What would you do if faced with an ethics problem on the job?"

The novice interviewer should practice replying to questions such as those just given as well as prepare a list of questions about the areas of most interest to him or her. These questions not only demonstrate to the interview manager a serious interest in, and preparation for, a new job but also ensure that the applicant leaves the interview with the most important facts to assess a job offer. For many engineers, the most important questions include:

1. The nature of the typical job assignments in the first week, month, year

2. Identity of supervisors and colleagues involved in daily work, general procedures, and organization

3. The availability of training on the job and off, location of training resources, and financial support

4. Advancement potential and procedures, both in technical and supervisory progression ladders

5. Opportunities to participate in technical seminars, travel to conferences, publish papers, and support professional society membership and activities

6. Working conditions: office location, lab resources, support personnel, personal computer, and other equipment availability

7. Compensation issues: base pay, merit raises, bonuses, fringe benefits (vacations, holidays, insurances, pensions), and relocation assistance if applicable

8. Working hours, flex-time arrangements, emergency leave, family leave considerations, travel requirements and regulations, and spouse employment assistance

9. Preemployment agreements, including patent disclosure and assignment, confidentiality, noncompetition clauses, and freedom to consult

10. Amenities such as technical libraries, fitness programs, recreational activities, and dining facilities

4.2 The Interview Process

The interview starts at the front door. The applicant who has taken the time to prepare well, will arrive a little early, well rested and not under pressure. That atmosphere conveys a sense of organization and confidence and also provides the time to exchange a few cordial remarks with all the initial contacts, from security guards and secretaries to the initial interviewer who may be in the Personnel Department.

These contacts are important. The grapevine in most companies works well and fast. A late and catastrophic arrival coupled with curt greetings and rebuffs does not set the climate for a good reception or interview.

It is well to be prepared for some bureaucratic paperwork at the outset. The interviewing engineer might be pleasantly surprised to be directly escorted to one or more engineering managers, and some companies deal with all application formalities by mail or after the initial technical interview, but they are still the exception.

It is not wise to express impatience and self-importance at this point. Applicants who know they have a serious schedule problem should discuss this before the interview and make alternate arrangements. Otherwise, follow the lead of the staff in the Human Resources Department. They have a routine to follow, generally for a good reason, and they are important people in the ultimate decision process.

The interviewed engineer is also selling. Adopting an indifferent posture during an interview, whether to conceal nervousness or to project a "sell me" message is a guarantee of failure. The cognizant manager probably believes he or she has a fairly good position to offer and is looking for someone who will meet the challenge with enthusiasm, not indifference.

It is helpful to know two things:

1. It is the interviewer's responsibility to carry the conversational ball for the first half of the interview. The candidate can safely let him or her take the lead without appearing noncommunicative.

2. The interviewer is also likely to be nervous; he or she has something to sell and must have a successful placement to do the job.

This second factor can be used by the applicant who is close to nervous paralysis under the stress of interviews. A frank admission of this stress to the interviewer is likely to be met with extra accommodation efforts and will not be held against the applicant unless the job involves marketing or other duties where such stress response would be a serious impediment. In fact, the frank disclosure frequently leads to an incipient protege relationship that helps.

The applicant who has rehearsed some of the typical interview questions should easily find the rhythm of the conversation. Consider the following notes on personal mannerisms:

- Most interviewers expect a firm handshake; this is a problem for applicants from some Eastern cultures, but one that can be overcome with a little practice.
- Frequent direct eye contact is also a sign of credibility and confidence in our U.S. society.
- It is acceptable to pause before answering most substantive questions, and preferable to articulating numerous "well"s or other delayers. However, answers to less difficult questions (e.g., Why did you leave your last job?) should be answered more reflexively.
- Direct questions should be answered simply and qualified only as needed. Many engineers tend to overqualify their responses or answer questions in a chronological order that leaves the interviewer wondering if an answer will ever come. Time is important in an interview.
- Answers should be complete and correct, but not as extensive as in a thesis defense. The interviewer will ask follow-up questions if more is desired. He or she is typically looking for signs that the applicant is familiar with terms and specifications, published literature, hardware, software, and other tools required for the department's work.

It is not customary to use formal technical tests when interviewing engineers, particularly those with work experience. In fact, there is some legal danger for the employer who does so unless the tests have been properly validated. Nevertheless, many engineering managers may have their own standard quiz or problem analysis that they use for all interviews. If the applicant is totally ignorant in the quiz area, the best tactic is to acknowledge the fact and suggest a related subject for discussion in an area of strength. If the applicant has brought samples of past projects to the interview, this is a good time to review them to demonstrate depth of knowledge.

4.3 The Turning Point

There is usually a point in an interview when the prospective manager has made a tentative decision that the applicant is sufficiently qualified to consider for a job offer. If the time allotted for the interview has been established, the candidate may expect this at a point somewhat past the half-way mark.

The hiring manager now will be trying to sell the applicant and respond to his or her questions about the job. Having a prioritized list will pay off at this point. If the interview has not so far involved a tour, this is a good time to request a walk through the lab or office to see the potential work site and talk to a few future colleagues. The interview process can continue more informally in this environment.

There are a few areas the applicant may wish to treat with caution:

- Salary: It is best to let the employer make the first move in this area. Statistics show that employers offer more than most applicants think to ask for, particularly if the subject is brought up later in the selection process when the field has been narrowed down. Many companies will not discuss specific salaries during the interview. If the candidate has not been asked to provide salary history and wishes to ensure that both are in the same bandwidth, the topic can be addressed by asking about broad ranges in the context of promotions and advancements

- Security: The candidate may have had several bad employment experiences, with layoffs or furloughs due to contract terminations. If job security is a major concern, it should be discussed, particularly if the interview has disclosed that the job is contract specific.

- Deselectors: The advice on deselection factors with respect to resumes applies equally to interviews. The interviewer will normally avoid personal questions that could be the basis for a discrimination suit, for example, religion, ethnic background, family responsibility. The candidate should volunteer this information only if he or she wants to risk this data being used as a hidden selection factor.

A few important things the candidate should do are:

- Be as enthusiastic about the job as his or her nature allows; the hiring manager is looking for someone who really wants to join that department through desire, not default.

- Act in character, but remember, the interview process is a selling process. It's not a time to be overly modest.
- Be completely honest about factual data. Bad employment experiences or legal problems should not be volunteered, but neither should they be misrepresented if the issue legitimately arises.

4.4 The Close-out and the Follow-up

In many companies, the interview close-out will be with a personnel department staff member. This is a good time for the applicant to get details about the job, the policies, or benefits that the engineering manager might not have explained. It is also an excellent time to record the names and phone numbers of each person met during the interview for later follow-up.

The applicant should ask about follow-up and the anticipated schedule for a decision or additional interviews. The applicant should ensure that the Personnel Department staff knows how to make contact, particularly if the applicant will be traveling or at a temporary address in the immediate future. If the interview involved reimbursable travel expenses, the appropriate forms should be obtained and completed.

Every interview should be followed up aggressively. It should start with a thank you letter within days of the interview in which the applicant cites the part of the job that was particularly attractive. Not one in a hundred bother to do this, and it sets such candidates apart from candidates less interested. If no offer letter arrives within the expected time period, a phone call to the hiring manager is in order.

Hint: Busy executives have an effective telephone screening mechanism in their assistants. However, they frequently answer the phone directly early in the morning or later in the evening. A call placed at 7:00 A.M. or 5:30 P.M. might get through the screen. The persistent applicant should be aware that this is an intrusion; be brief and courteous.

The applicant can also use the waiting period to submit additional evidences of competency such as papers published, citations of excellence, awards. The majority err by doing too little follow-up; this is not a time to be shy.

If an offer letter is received, the employer's hiring process will take over. There may be some latitude to negotiate salary or special allowances, but many companies have fairly inflexible policies about benefits, preemployment agreements, and related policies. It is rare that an engineer will be offered an individual employment contract, the norm being a standard employment-at-will arrangement which either party can terminate at any time for any reason.

If an offer is not received, there are two things the applicant should be aware of:

1. In many large companies, similar openings occur every month or so. If the job and the company looked interesting, start the process over again in one to two months. Persistence can pay off.

2. Many people involved in the process of interviewing the applicant may feel bad about selecting another candidate to the exclusion of the applicant. It is worth contacting them to get advice on other jobs inside or outside their company, as well as advice on how to improve your presentation.

5.0 RECOMMENDED READING

American Association of Engineering Societies. *Directory of Engineering Societies.* New York: AAES, 1982.

Institute of Electrical and Electronics Engineers. *IEEE U.S. Membership Salary and Fringe Benefit Survey.* New York: IEEE, 1993.

Institute of Electrical and Electronics Engineers. *The Employment Guide for Engineers and Scientists.* New York: IEEE, 1991, 3rd ed.; 1992, 2nd student ed.

National Academies of Science. *Scientific, Technical, and Related Societies of the United States.* Washington D.C.: NAS, 1971.

Peterson's Guides, Inc. *Peterson's Guide to Engineering, Science and Computer Jobs.* Princeton, NJ: Peterson's, 1983.

U.S. Department of Labor, Bureau of Labor Statistics. *White Collar Pay: Private Goods-Producing Industries, March 1990,* Bulletin 2374. Washington D.C.: U.S. Government Printing Office, 1990.

3

Consulting and Private Practice

Richard G. Weingardt

1.0 BACKGROUND

The consulting engineering profession in the United States began its ascension right after World War II, growing in leaps and bounds to a multibillion-dollar a year industry. The trade association for consulting engineers, the American Consulting Engineers Council (ACEC), represents approximately two-thirds of the consulting engineers in private practice. The 5000 member firms of the ACEC had 1993 revenues of $12.6 billion and designed over $100 billion in constructed facilities. ACEC member firms employ 180,000 engineers and scientists, nearly 10 percent of the U.S. work force of engineers.

1.1 DEFINITION OF A CONSULTANT

A consulting engineer is an independent professional engineer who performs services for clients on a contract basis. Consulting engineers have no commercial or manufacturing affiliations that might bias their judgment. They have nothing to sell except service, time, and knowledge. Compensation consists solely of fees paid by their clients.

Consultants own and manage their own businesses. They operate as individual proprietors, in partnerships, or as corporations. Their organizations vary in size from the sole practitioner, to the principal with a few professional employees, to firms with a thousand or more engineers, technicians, scientists, allied professionals, and other employees.

Their services include investigations and analyses, preplanning, design and design implementation, research and development, construction management, and consultation on engineering problems. Consulting engineers are both advisors and problem solvers, developing concepts as well as complete plans and specifications.

They are qualified to render their services by education, technical knowledge, and experience. Consulting engineers are entrusted with protecting the public welfare, health, and safety. Accordingly, the law requires that they be registered professional engineers (P.E.s) and that they be licensed by the state to practice one or more branches of engineering.

1.2 Clients

A consulting engineering firm serves a wide variety of clients. They include individuals, industrial, manufacturing and commercial concerns, municipal, state, and federal governments, architects, other engineering firms, attorneys, contractors, developers, financial institutions, and others with a need for engineering services.

Fifty percent of the ACEC member firms have client bases that consist almost entirely of owners and governments. With these clients, the firms act as prime contractors. The remainder of the firms work mainly as "interpros." They are brought to a project through an "interprofessional" consulting contract. In these cases, consulting engineers work for other professionals, usually architects, prime design engineers, or architectural/engineering (A-E) firms.

1.2.1 Client Fees Consulting engineers work on an hourly or lump-sum fee basis. Their fees may be determined based on a percentage of the construction cost for the project they designed. Fees range from a few hundred dollars, for a few hours of service, to many thousands of dollars for large projects. Usually the cost of consulting engineering services are typically less than 1 percent of a project's total life-cycle cost.

1.2.2 Work Environment Consulting engineers usually work independently in their own offices, and occasionally in the client's office as an extension of the client's staff. Local, state, and federal governments hire consulting engineering firms to work closely with their in-house engineering staffs. Because their work involves an almost infinite variety of projects, consulting engineers bring with them a wide range of experience and knowledge that in-house staffs may not possess.

Contracting-out, as was described, avoids having to maintain a large, permanent in-house engineering staff. This practice is also widely used by private companies set up primarily to perform general services, like industrial or product design, who occasionally require a particular expertise, such as mechanical, electrical, or structural engineering. These companies or governments pay for the required, specialized engineering services on an as-needed basis, and when the job is done, the private engineers are off the payroll until another need arises.

2.0 MAJOR FIELDS

Consulting engineering is a truly diverse profession. Consultants are found in all engineering fields. The major fields are aerospace, agricultural, biomedical, electrical, chemical, civil, industrial, mechanical, mining, and petroleum. Several subdivisions or specialties of these disciplines also provide substantial employment opportunities for consulting engineers: automotive, environmental, geotechnical, structural, and software-computer engineering. In a 1993 business survey of its members ACEC found that their primary fields of practice were civil (40 percent), structural (14 percent), mechanical (12 percent), environmental (10 percent), electrical (8 percent), geotechnical (5 percent), surveying (4 percent), and all others (7 percent).

Most of this country's infrastructure—highways, bridges, water and sewer systems, public buildings and facilities—are designed by consulting engineers. The need for these services continues to grow, not only for designing new systems to meet the needs of a growing economy, but also to assess, maintain, and even rebuild facilities already in place. Somewhere in America every other day a bridge falls down.

The design and construction of food processing centers, solar heating and cooling, coal gasification, saline water conversion, specialty manufacturing facilities, treatment plants, and thousands of other similarly complex projects are normal everyday fare for consulting engineers. They may work alone or as part of a team. Frequently, these projects require more attention to zoning, machinery purchase and maintenance, markets, even financing and shipping issues, than to technical design and engineering. Consulting engineers contribute to such fields as health, sanitation, industrial production, transportation, public works, buildings, utilities, and communications.

From the time the sun rises and a person turns on the tap for a morning shower, until he snaps off the light before going to bed at night, every person who is a part of America's industrialized society benefits in some way from the service of engineers in private practice. The generating stations that provide the electricity for cooking, lighting, and myriad other appliances were probably designed by consulting engineers. The pure drinking water is very likely supplied by water systems designed by consulting engineers. Likewise most of the highways, streets, roads, and bridges have been engineered by consultants. Consulting engineers are heavily involved in the design of the office buildings, factories, and schools.

A major field for consultant engineering is in the operation of manufacturing or processing plants. Consulting engineers participate in projects that involve process engineering, production engineering methods, tooling, time and motion studies, and quality control.

Consulting engineers participate in the design of guidance systems for rockets, missiles, airplanes, and automobiles. They are involved in the design of conveyor systems, such as those for airport baggage.

Consulting engineers are requested to function as expert witnesses in court proceedings and to advise clients and attorneys on engineering matters involved in legal disputes. A number specialize exclusively in court work, particularly in the fields of valuation and rate making, and forensic engineering—reconstructing failures or even traffic accidents.

There are consulting engineers who engage only in patent work. Others are engaged in work related to financing and feasibility studies for financial institutions. Some consultants handle research problems and aspects of product development and the fabrication of devices, machines, instruments, and equipment. Others do testing of products and materials. Several are safety engineers, communications engineers, or acoustic engineers. And the list could go on.

3.0 CAREERS

Consulting is not for a person who hesitates to face new problems. The competent engineer who likes variety and enjoys the challenge of ever-changing problems can find a fascinating and satisfying career as a consulting engineer. Because major projects handled by consulting engineers include practically every kind of structure or facility that is planned, designed, constructed, or operated, all branches of engineering are involved.

The consulting engineering profession demands business and management ability in addition to engineering and professional talent. It offers a unique opportunity for self-employment. It is perhaps the only path open to an engineer with the spirit of an entrepreneur who wishes to become his or her own boss in full-time engineering work.

3.1 Career Paths

Many young engineers are employed by a consulting engineering firm right out of college, and they move up the ladder within the firm. They begin as a staff engineer, advance to project engineer, then into management and administration, and finally into ownership or partnership in the company. Other career paths to being in private practice are numerous. Some young engineers work for governmental agencies, contractors, manufacturers, or in research or education until they gain enough experience and investment capital to open up their own business. Some start their own consulting firm after working for other consulting engineers.

Rarely do recent graduates start their own consulting engineering businesses. The two main obstacles are the requirements of the licensure laws and the establishment of credibility. The licensure laws require that a graduate of an engineering college accredited by the Accreditation Board for Engineering and Technology work under direction for a minimum of four years as one of the requirements for becoming a registered professional engineer (P.E.). To establish creditability, a consulting engineer should have years of experience and/or expertise in a specialty with a proven track record.

4.0 MARKETING

Perhaps the most difficult aspect of private practice is not gaining engineering expertise, but rather gaining the ability to do effective marketing—the development of clients. To obtain commissions in the face of competition, consultants need to maintain a continuous sales effort, through a cogent marketing plan, to acquaint prospective clients with their talents. Some cling to the illusion that clients come to consulting engineers without any activity on the latter's part; one just needs to "hang out one's shingle."

Sales activities consist principally of contacts with prospective clients, supplemented by brochures and other devices of communication. The reputation of the firm, based upon its competence and experience, is critical. Every consulting engineer wants the maximum number of repeat engagements from the client he has served. Repeat engagements are a potent factor in building a reputation, for they signify that former work was completed to the satisfaction of the client.

However, while superior performance is the basis for repeat engagements, the consulting engineer also needs to maintain contact with former clients. Often there is a long period between a client's need for engineering services, during which the consultant should not rest his case entirely on previous performance. By keeping in touch with the client the engineer learns of coming needs and reminds the client, from time to time, of the quality of the previous relationship and current availability and interest in future work.

5.0 THE NEXT CENTURY

Science and technology will advance more in the next 25 years than in all of recorded history: a truly amazing thing to think about when you consider how far we've come since the Industrial Revolution.

Many new products, processes, and systems will evolve, and consulting engineers, because of their ability to produce in skillful and cost-effective ways, will be in the middle of it all. Several notable Americans, such as former Colorado Governor Richard Lamm and former U.S. ambassador to the United Nations Andrew Young, have called engineers "wealth creators and problem solvers par excellence; the protectors, of the very standard of life for everyone." Governor Lamm went so far as to say that the future economic well-being of the country will depend on its engineers.

Not only will consulting engineers help to develop new designs and products, they will have to continue to solve the problems of repairing what we have built in the past—and to build and maintain infrastructures to serve present and future generations.

The problem seems overwhelming. Nearly half of America's 575,000 bridges need replacement or repair. As noted earlier, a bridge falls down every other day in America. An estimated 15 gallons of water are lost for every 100 gallons consumed because of leaky pipes. Some 2000 of the nation's 4 million miles of highways must be replaced each year.

Consulting engineers will be needed to provide solutions to the environmental problems which arise from global warming (greenhouse effect), water shortages and contamination, the handling of hazardous wastes, waste management, and air pollution. Environmental engineering is one of the fastest-growing practice areas for consulting engineers.

5.1 Sustainable System Development

Sustainable system development is an area where consulting engineers have assumed a leadership role. A sustainable system from the engineers' point of view is one that is either in steady-state equilibrium or one that changes slowly at an acceptable rate. Sustainable system development will require that development, processing, transportation, and consumption of resources flow continuously as a closed-loop system rather than as a once-through system.

Don Roberts[1] stated that sustainable development will require adoption of an industrial ecology or artificial ecosystem patterned after natural processes.

The World Commission on Environment and Development (WCED), a United Nations entity, is concerned with sustainable system development. The goal of "meeting the needs of the present without compromising the ability of future generations to meet their own needs" was set forth in 1987 by WCED. WCED's activities address the issues of 1.5 billion people not having access to clean water, 2 billion with inadequate or no sanitation facilities, fossil fuels being depleted, and coping with problems associated with the increasing world population which has tripled since 1900 and which will double within 50 years.

Another organization concerned with sustainable system development is the World Engineering Partnership (WEP). The WEP represents 10 million engineers worldwide. It is spearheaded by many leaders from the consulting engineering profession. Its goals are to share ideas, innovations, and techniques that can make construction projects endure longer, have lower environmental impact, reflect better cost-benefit ratios, and influence sound regulatory agendas.

6.0 PROBLEM AREAS

The most serious problem facing the consulting engineering community, as of 1995, is that caused by the excessive rise in the number of legal proceedings brought against engineering firms. Before the mid-1950s, most consulting engineers did not carry errors and omissions (E&O) insurance.

It wasn't that they were more perfect then engineers are now; they just rarely got sued. The present-day litigious atmosphere did not exist.

With the advent of readily available E&O insurance for engineers, more and more consulting firms started being named in lawsuits for such things as faulty design, drawings, and advice. The engineers were not necessarily at fault, but they possessed the "deep pockets"; that is, their insurance could pay any court awarded damages.

Insurance cost and claims seemed to peak right after the late-1970s' collapse of the skywalk at the Kansas City Hyatt Regency Hotel. Shortly afterward many structural engineering firms went from paying 2 percent to over 10 percent of their gross billings for premiums for E&O insurance. It was not just structural engineers who were being affected. In the mid-1980s, no matter what discipline of engineering a firm practiced, nearly 50 percent of all consulting engineering firms in the United States were involved in one or more lawsuits concerning liability issues. Most of the lawsuits were frivolous and were settled out of court or dropped, but not without costing firms countless dollars in legal defense fees and many "sleepless nights."

With the enactment of tort reform legislation in several states and a softening of the insurance market, the problem has diminished slightly in recent years. This is probably because of the arrival of several new commercial insurance companies, as well as a risk retention group, Architects and Engineers Insurance Company (AEIC), organized by design professional themselves. Today, structural engineers can obtain E&O insurance for premiums in the neighborhood of 5 percent of their gross billings, and the number of lawsuits against all firms has dropped to 30 percent. Continuing efforts in tort reform is a most important ongoing activity for the engineering profession.

A second problem arises from the procedure of many municipalities, bound by legal statutes, to award contracts to the lowest bidder, disregarding the relative competence of the competitors. A third problem stems from the excessive government regulations that tend to inhibit the growth and expansion of engineering companies. A fourth occurs because the public relations efforts of the engineering community do not adequately portray the role of the engineer in society nor do they describe their many contributions. The public is unclear about the definition of the term engineer and is confused by its indiscriminate use. These problems and others cannot be solved or adequately addressed within the confines of the engineering industry or their professional associations. They have been discussed at engineering conferences for many years, and the problems still exist. To address these problem areas effectively, engineers need to become leaders in society. They should aspire to roles outside the narrow limits of their firms and their professional associations where they can influence or make decisions in problem areas that impact on their profession.

7.0 SOCIETY AND THE ENGINEER

Engineers, especially those in private practice, frequently report to almost every other kind of profession: lawyers, public administrators, bankers, accountants, and politicians.

Engineers have become managers—managers of other people's ideas. They act as technical experts. Consulting engineers design the bridges that others tell them to design. Very few engineers in private practice are decision makers.

By not being actively involved in society, community affairs, and politics, engineers become the victims of other people's decisions and legislation. For example, Massachusetts, Colorado, and Connecticut recently passed or proposed legislation to raise additional state revenues by taxing services. Consulting engineering services were included. However, the laws specifically exempted lawyers and doctors, both groups represented by strong lobbying budgets and political clout.

The nation's key to survival and economic strength is tied closely to modern technology, and technology is advancing too rapidly to leave the world's direction and major decisions totally in the hands of those not trained in problem solving or technology.

7.1 Engineer Status

Society values many nontechnical professionals and businesspeople more than the engineer, as is evidenced by the formers' higher financial compensations and by their presence in positions of power where they influence societal behavior. This is an imbalance that should be corrected so that those most capable of contributing to an advancing civilization will be attracted to the engineering profession.

Engineers must continuously refine and develop their leadership traits, especially their communications and presentation skills. They should find a nonengineer as a role model or a mentor, someone who can guide them through the often murky waters of business at large, the civic community, and the decision-making layers of local, state, and federal government. Most learn to become better engineers by finding a professional mentor, and the same thing can be done in nonprofessional areas to enhance our abilities to gain leadership positions.Engineers should broaden their perspective of their position in society. They must realize that their contributions to society should go beyond the application of advancing technologies to the enhancement and betterment of our way of life. They should become familiar with those elements of society whose actions impact on their lives and the lives of the populace as a whole, and they should act to ensure that these actions are beneficial.

7.2 Organizations

Influencing actions that affect the profession and our standard of living require that engineers become active in community and civil organizations, educational activities, politics, and public relations. The type of community groups one can get involved with are limitless. Community "think tank" groups, chambers of commerce, neighborhood building committees, or planning boards; even service groups such as the Lions and Kiwanis are beneficial because they broaden one's perspective.

7.2.1 Educational   Consulting engineers know what should be changed in college curriculum to arm graduates with the right business and design courses to make it in industry. By becoming a member of the local college advisory board, the engineer can influence the choice of courses. Engineers should lecture at schools and colleges on the field and its contributions to society. These presentations enhance the public's image of the engineer.

7.2.2 Political   Almost all federal or state legislators are lawyers or professional politicians. Very few are engineers. Engineers should seek to increase their numbers in these bodies. To paraphrase Plato, "If intelligent people do not get involved in politics, they will soon find they are being led by the less intelligent." Those who leave politics up to someone else may find that they have become victims of the system.

    To be involved in politics, one doesn't have to run for office, though this would be great. One can support worthy candidates and can influence legislation by communicating one's views to local, state, and federal legislators by letter or by personal visits. Applications can be made for appointment to state boards and commissions such as the state's long-range planning board or state engineering registration board. Most boards and commissions make or influence public policy.

    A coalition can be entered into with other professionals that will function to initiate legislative actions and lobbying efforts. In Colorado recently, consulting engineers headed a coalition of other professions that proposed tort reform to curtail unfounded liability lawsuits and to eliminate joint and severe liability. The effort succeeded. Colorado now serves as a national model for tort reform.

At the national level in 1974, the American Consulting Engineers Council, the American Society of Civil Engineers, the National Society of Professional Engineers, and several other groups of engineers and architects joined together to change forever how the federal government secures services for private practice professionals. The coalition (COFPAES, Council of Federal Procurement of A/E Services) introduced qualifications-based selection (QBS) procedures in a bill championed by Texas Congressman Jack Brooks. For the last 20 years the Brooks bill procedures have helped produce countless high-quality, value-engineered, and cost-effective public works projects.

8.0 PUBLIC RELATIONS

Engineers can truly be proactive as spokesmen for the engineering community. In spite of its importance, magnitude, and fascination, the engineering profession is little recognized and poorly understood by the public. The average man in the street has difficulty understanding the function of any engineer, for he is thoroughly confused by the misapplication of the title "engineer" to many tradesmen, mechanics, and skilled workmen.

The media—radio, TV, newspapers, magazines, and so on—offer the avenue through which information about the engineering profession can be disseminated. Specifically, guest spots on radio, appearances on TV, articles in the local newspaper, and talks at various club and community functions can all be used as vehicles to enhance the image of the engineer and to clarify the role of engineering in the community.

9.0 YOUNG ENGINEERS

Many of the future leaders of industry and society will come from the ranks of engineering undergraduates and those recently graduated. To prepare for their roles, they should

1. Supplement their technical training by taking courses or by self-teaching in nontechnical subjects such as law, government, politics, corporate and business administration.
2. Develop or improve communication skills.
3. Become active in community affairs.
4. Get involved in politics.
5. Find a mentor/role model.
6. Continue development of technical skills.

10.0 RECOMMENDED READING

Bennis, W. *On Becoming a Leader.* Reading, MA: Addison-Wesley, 1989.

Burns, J. M. *Leadership.* New York: Harper and Row, 1978.

Drucker, Peter. *Men, Ideas and Politics.* New York: Harper and Row, 1971.

Florman, S. *The Civilized Engineer.* New York: St. Martin's Press, 1987.

Guttman, Hans Peter. *The International Consultant.* New York: McGraw-Hill, 1976.

Kemper, John D. *Engineers and Their Profession.* New York: Holt, Rinehart and Winston, 1982.

Kuecken, John A. *Starting and Managing Your Own Engineering Practice.* New York, NY: Van Nostrand Reinhold, 1978.

Rubeling, A. "How to Start and Operate Your Own Design Firm," ACEC publication #1606. Washington, DC: ACEC, 1994.

Seiden, R. Matthiew. *Breaking Away—Engineer's Guide to a Successful Engineering Practice.* Englewood Cliffs, NJ: Prentice Hall, 1987.

Stanley, C. Maxwell. *The Consulting Engineer.* New York: John Wiley, 1982.

Weingardt, R. G. "Engineers and Leadership," *ASCE Journal of Professional Issues in Engineering,* Vol. 120, No.1, pp. 50-57, Jan. 1994.

ENDNOTE

1. Don Roberts, "Engineering for Sustainable Development," paper presented at the National Summer Meeting of the American Institute of Chemical Engineers. Seattle, Washington: Oct 1993.

4

The Entrepreneur

Orin Laney

1.0 INTRODUCTORY BUSINESS CONCEPTS

1.1 Engineering and Business

Too often, engineering is like being locked in a room where paychecks are thrown in over the transom and designs are slid back under the door. Engineers are often kept locked away to allow them to concentrate. Those engineers trusted to contact customers often discover that they enjoy comprehending a customer's needs well enough to diagnose his problems and propose a solution.

These first stirrings of an appreciation for business should be encouraged. Since the typical technical education does little to address the real-world operations of companies, many engineers flounder over simple business issues because they lack basic exposure to the principles of commerce.

Because the field of engineering is one where change and progress are normal facts of life, technologically based businesses must continually adapt or die. This dynamic environment has little in common with dry cleaning establishments or lawn care services. The typical literature available for the would-be businessperson must be read with a certain amount of care, for much of what is available does not translate well to technical activities.

This chapter spans many topics with which the fledgling entrepreneur should be familiar. The discussions are necessarily brief. There are tutorial introductions to some of the more important aspects of business, such as accounting and advertising. There is also a suggested deliberate approach to starting a first business.

1.2 The Small Start-up

Small start-ups are seldom the result of cold business judgment. Starting a business, particularly when you are short of funds and experience, is an intensely personal process that goes to the core of a person's self image. Temperament, willingness to learn and take risks, and tolerance for one's own foibles are easily as important as the product, because the entrepreneur is the single most valuable asset of the new enterprise.

The various routes to the decision to start a business include love for a burning hot idea, a desire for independence, and getting fired. Some people hate commuting or need to work at home to take care of someone else. The reason may be as simple as a lack of job openings, or even of personal salability, thus creating a need to create your own employment.

1.3 Venture Capital and Small Start-ups

The engineering world is permeated by a venture capital mythos, fueled by trade press reports of well-funded start-ups embarking on complex projects. Venture capitalists place considerable emphasis upon the individuals who will handle the day-to-day operations. A track record can be more persuasive than any product. Achieving the credibility, competence, experience, and contacts necessary to reach that state in life requires laboring in the trenches of your own business on your own capital. Venture capital is but one route of funding. Most first start-ups use whatever capital can be scraped up by the owners. Operation of a start-up is an important credential when and if venture capital is sought in the future.

2.0 LAUNCHING A START-UP

2.1 When to Begin

The best time to begin is when one feels inspired to do so. Nevertheless, inspiration comes in many forms. The salutary effect of getting fired is well known. In every recession, newspaper editors feel compelled to publish human interest stories about people who got laid off and went on to better lives. The real-life examples of stockbrokers who opened restaurants, junior lawyers who became photographers, and middle managers who tried their hands at farming sound a common theme of deeper satisfaction, and often one of realizing how confining their previous career choices were.

This sense of satisfaction is often couched in terms of personal growth. In other words, farming is not necessarily more satisfying than designing circuits, but there is personal power in opening up a world of your own choosing. In large measure, those who consider a layoff as a curse are indeed cursed, and those who look for blessings in it tend to find them.

2.2 Timing Versus the Economy

It is also fortunate that "inspiration" often arrives when times are bad. This forces you to count your pennies and learn to distinguish what you need to have from what you would merely like to have. Customers will be vocal about what they will and won't pay for. Start-ups that begin during a recession will have a running start when the economy turns around, providing an advantage over Johnny-come-lately competitors that pop up like mushrooms after a spring rain. For a time, these make money too, but when the economy cycles down again, a recession start-up will have already learned to operate efficiently. Fair weather start-ups have the double handicap of wasteful practices such as bloated staffs and budgets, and an institutional momentum for these practices that is hard to change quickly enough. A business that knows how to work in a recession can even pick up business as inefficient competitors fold.

This is not to say that inspiration is best forced upon you by circumstances or that it cannot come during good economic times. It is more likely, however, that an engineer will consider beginning a business when not distracted by heavy projects, steady raises, and sweet job offers.

2.3 Required Experience

There is some controversy over how much experience an engineer should have before starting a business. In truth, the primary effect of whether an engineer has 2 or 10 or 20 years of experience is the type of business the engineer prefers. Those of lesser experience tend to create specific products, while those of greater maturity tend to have a wider viewpoint and offer system-and enterprise-level solutions.

Reviewing classified advertisements for electronics engineers reveals that three to five years is a preferred range for experience. Several factors seem to prevail, the bottom line being enough experience to become valuable, but not so much as to become expensive. Engineers who start a business at or before this period tend to do so out of a sense of adventure. Engineers who have matured into more senior roles tend to be seeking personal fulfillment.

2.4 Qualifications

Not everyone ought to try running a business. Some individuals prefer a role that is defined for them. For every architect who goes independent, there are 10 more who would sweat every minute until another firm gave them a desk to sit at. Just as there is a particular type of mind that is best suited to accounting, another to engineering, and another to the literary life, there are certain personality traits that make an individual better suited for business. Fortunately, these qualities are often found in tandem with engineering ability, so that far from being mutually exclusive, they create a powerful combination for those who test themselves and discover entrepreneurial potential within themselves.

The primary impetus for running a business should not be a desire for wealth. While "the sky is the limit," getting there will require sacrifice. Many entrepreneurs, looking back, feel that the lessons of their early experiences, bruises and all, were the most valuable. The truth of the matter is that true entrepreneurs pursue business as a challenge in and of itself, and wealth is but one means of keeping score.

There is pleasure to be derived from such activities as creating new designs and making deals. Many engineers are delighted that not only do they get to play with enough equipment to build a starship, but they get paid to do it! The formal name for this is "psychic income." The happy individuals quoted by newspaper editors are thriving on the psychic income of having a direct hand in their own destinies. By comparison, their previous lives seem impoverished to them, and this even for those who experience a considerable drop in their monetary income.

True entrepreneurs are not born but made, discovering through circumstance that they have or can develop the abilities needed to run a business. Engineers represent an interesting class of potential entrepreneurs. They tend to be intelligent, but often narrow in their education and world view. They also vary tremendously in their communication and people skills. An outstanding asset of engineers as a class is an ability to learn quickly. Nimbleness of mind is probably the most important compensation for lack of experience. Engineers also tend to overexaggerate the applicability of their academic skills to many of life's problems. Knowledge of calculus does not reduce accounting to a trivial problem, for instance.

On the whole, engineers are prolific founders of new businesses. Their participation in the economy is especially important, because the fruits of engineering create new economic areas rather than simply expanding existing ones: anyone can open another car wash and employ dozens, engineers can pioneer whole industries that employ tens of thousands.

3.0 PREPARATION

3.1 Gaining Experience

The first responsibility of anyone aspiring to arrive at the point where someone would entrust them with several million dollars is to get experience. The first responsibility of a newly graduated engineer is engineering experience, because knowledge of the culture, vocabulary, and practice of engineering is the core around which a future business may be wrapped.

A new engineer can acquire the necessary technical experience most easily by working at a large company where the engineer is well supported by secretaries, technicians, senior engineers, and a drafting department and is exposed to clear lines of authority, formal signature requirements, and specialists in other disciplines.

Having acquired a solid grounding in the realities of engineering, the best vantage point for gaining useful business skills is at a small company, where an engineer is forced to handle things from which large companies insulate their technical staff. This often includes changing from filling out purchase requisitions to doing the actual purchasing or negotiating with customers directly rather than simply being handed a set of specifications to meet. Visibility into the detailed operation of a small business also provides the singularly important benefit of removing the mystery of it.

3.2 Seminars

Seminars constitute a short-duration, high-calorie means of gathering business start-up information. A typical approach invites a CPA to talk about accounting, an intellectual property attorney to talk about protecting your ideas, a marketing type about marketing your product, and a venture capitalist speaks on getting start-up funding. Often someone from the Small Business Administration is invited too.

This common seminar format offers both potential and peril because the individual topics are presented as disconnected pieces of a business. While each speaker may be an expert in his own field, this does not guarantee competence in others. The result is a certain amount of bad advice mixed with the good. For instance, the fact that a venture capitalist is invited to speak can create the mistaken impression that they are a preferred source of funding for a one person start-up. An accountant may salivate at the quantity of business that can be generated by selling to the federal government, but totally fail to appreciate the peculiar difficulties of this business area. Perhaps 50 percent of the information at a seminar will be incorrect. The problem is that the 50 percent that is incorrect for you will be different from the 50 percent for the guy next to you. Thus, the first lesson of the would-be entrepreneur is presented: you must exercise your critical judgment rather than accepting anything at face value.

Assembling the information on various facets of business into a complete whole is as important as the pieces. The seminar that one should attend without fail will feature a panel of successful entrepreneurs describing how they each made it. True entrepreneurs, as opposed to persons who merely work for themselves, tell incredible stories of near bankruptcies, cunning breakthroughs, around the clock work sessions, skullduggery attempted by competitors and suppliers, financial miracles pulled off with credit cards and bluff, and marketing victories that make you want to run out and start a business on the spot. Successful entrepreneurs tend to be shameless self-promoters, and they tell not so much the bare facts of what a CPA or an attorney does, as illustrate how to make those people work for you rather than the other way around. They speak of the process of running a business. The first type of seminar is like trying to understand an animal by examining the results of a dissection. The second is like watching one pace its cage, feeding and snarling.

3.3 Small Business Administration

The Small Business Administration (SBA) constitutes a seemingly obvious source of information for would-be business owners. As a taxpayer, you can get their materials for free, but there are some cautionary notes to keep in mind. One is that the scope of all possible small businesses is so vast that SBA materials are often general to the point of vacuousness. Applicability to your own immediate problems is sometimes not obvious. A deeper problem is simply that the definition of a "small business" for SBA purposes is very different from the typical start-up. The government definition varies by industry, but can include companies with up to 500 employees! The typical one- or two-person start-up is a different thing altogether, a "microbusiness" in size and a "seed" business in time. These are not serviced by the SBA in the way that organized, ongoing enterprises are, nor indeed can they be. The SBA should be considered a supplementary rather than primary source of information for small start-ups.

3.4 Incubators

An increasingly important trend is the availability of small business "incubators." Many are state sponsored and located near university campuses. Incubators provide start-ups with inexpensive rent, access to low-cost shared secretarial and accounting services, ready access to faculty consultation and student labor, and often eligibility for grant programs and tax incentives. Incubators are mostly new-product-oriented and carefully screen applicants for viability. The state government is the contact point to determine if there is a program in one's geographic area. The insights and information gained by studying incubator programs constitute an inexpensive and valuable source of learning.

3.5 MBA Degree

Of the various combinations of degrees, the MBA business degree and engineering technical degree mix especially well. Possession or nonpossession of an MBA is generally not a factor in whether to begin a business, but just as a formal engineering education greatly assists in high technical achievement, a formal business education greatly increases the upside potential of how far you can take a business. Many engineers remain stuck in consulting mode precisely because they lack the knowledge of how to proceed beyond this most simple form of business.

The MBA is a professional degree, and as such there is no admissions requirement for previous business training. Students are taken from all disciplines, but backgrounds that feature mathematics and rigor, such as economics and engineering, are favored. MBA courses are taught with a greater pace and emphasis upon conceptual understanding than undergraduate offerings in identical subject areas. Furthermore, courses are taught from the perspective of managing an enterprise rather than the undergraduate perspective of working for someone else.

The role of an MBA degree for eventual entrepreneurship is that it teaches the language and culture of business with a breadth that is difficult to gain through experience alone. The skills are general purpose and portable. Notwithstanding the time spent to earn the degree, an MBA can pay back the investment manyfold with avoidance of time and grief that would otherwise be spent at the school of hard knocks.

A trap for the future entrepreneur is going too fast from engineering to MBA school. Simply having an engineering degree does not make one an engineer. That requires engineering experience. However, it is hard to leave a career with good income, possibly after you have a spouse, a mortgage, and a few kids, to go to business school. There is no real resolution possible for the conflicting demands other than perseverance.

The MBA degree has been cheapened somewhat by schools that responded to rising demand by adding programs primarily to generate revenue. Avoid narrow, middle management credentials such as "masters of engineering management" or programs that are populated by middle managers that are trying to keep promotions coming on schedule.

4.0 START-UP MECHANICS

4.1 Organizational Forms

The procedure for beginning a business varies according to the chosen business form. One may choose a corporation, a sole proprietorship, or a partnership, and there are variations on each of these. Each has distinct advantages and disadvantages over the others.

4.1.1 Incorporation   A corporation is a business entity that is treated as if it were an individual. It can sue or be sued, enter into contracts, and so forth. A corporation is a legal entity unto itself, and thus, in theory, the individuals running it are insulated from the consequences of lawsuits, bankruptcy, and similar contingencies as long as they have properly discharged their duties. This insulating property tends to fail where the business is small enough that the management essentially is the enterprise. Corporations must handle a recordkeeping and paperwork burden that is more suited to larger enterprises. Several simplified variations, such as the "S" corporation, are preferred when small businesses wish to incorporate.

Corporations may be chartered on the state or federal level. The mechanics of doing either are not overly complex, but as there are specialized legal requirements, this task should be done with expert assistance. An attorney can be used, but for straightforward needs there are kits of forms that can be found in bookstores. There are also businesses that will handle the incorporation for you that advertise in places like *The Wall Street Journal*. The advice of a good accountant is recommended to assist you in determining your recordkeeping requirements and the relative tax advantages of the various forms of incorporation. A little effort will uncover specialized reading materials that will help to steer your decision of how, or even whether to incorporate.

4.1.2 Partnerships   Partnerships have distinct advantages and disadvantages. One advantage is that any partner can act on behalf of the entire enterprise, allowing any partner to run the entire business when the others are not available. One disadvantage is that any partner can act on behalf of the entire enterprise, making all the partners liable for the mistakes and financial losses created by any one of them. They are organizationally inflexible, as the addition or loss of a partner necessitates dissolving the previous partnership and setting up a new one that reflects the changes. By contrast, a corporation continues unchanged in legal form despite changes in personnel.

Since each partner has equal authority, any partner can order parts and equipment, accept or reject contracts, and hire and fire independently of the others—even in direct contradiction to the actions of the others. Overall, partnerships work well for parties that trust each other implicitly and have an established history of working together. Where these assumptions are not met, there are inevitable stories of partners who crash the business and leave the honest partners with the legal responsibility to make good on the debts or partners whose differing styles result in nasty disagreements without an ultimate authority to resolve disputes. While the partnership may evolve along lines of natural authority, a rogue partner can create a disaster. In forming a partnership, it is imperative to have an attorney draw up the partnership agreement. It should never be on a handshake basis.

4.1.3 Proprietorships   A sole proprietorship is the easiest form of business to create and run, and most suited to new, small enterprises owned by one individual. If circumstances eventually require it, the proprietorship can be converted to a corporation or partnership later. The essence of a sole proprietorship is that an individual deals as a person with the public at large. This may be done directly in the name of the proprietor (Jack Smith) or through a fictitious business name, often called a DBA (doing business as) or TA (trading as), for example, "Bob Klutz DBA Precision Bagel Foundry." If someone asks for "your DBA," your fictitious business name is what is meant.

Your fictitious business name must be officially sanctioned. No bank will issue business checks in a fictitious name without presentation of official authorization to do business under that name. Nor will the state issue a sales tax account number to an unregistered name. Registration typically involves travel to the county office and payment of a fee. A search is made to ensure that your chosen name isn't already taken or confusingly similar to an existing one. Public notice that you intend to adopt the name is normally required, and this is satisfied by publication of a notice in a newspaper that serves the locale where you intend to do business.

All businesses are regulated on city, county, and state levels. The registration and permit processes amount to three things: (1) to ensure that the laws are followed; (2) to ensure that the various levels of government and any other interested parties know who you are and where to find you; and (3) to ensure that taxes, license fees, and other charges are extracted from you. To begin a proprietorship, the place to start is at the most local level, namely, city hall if the city is incorporated or at the county level if it is not. The clerks are accustomed to answering questions and supplying forms to people starting a business for the first time. Expect a trip to the zoning department, where the allowable commercial activities for one's proposed place of business will be determined. In general, the laws cannot prevent earning a living regardless of location, but they do place limits on the manner in which business can be conducted.

In residential neighborhoods, for instance, it is common to forbid use of a showroom window and inventory of "stock in trade," for example, boxes of merchandise stacked in the garage and living room. Visits must be by appointment and few in number. Operation of heavy or noisy machinery or the creation of odors or loud or unusual noises will not be allowed. If you are subject to homeowner's association rules, the restrictions may be draconian. The basic intent is to operate the business in such a way that neighbors will not be impacted by it. Consulting, writing, designing, showing of samples, and similar small-scale activities are typically pursued under these rules.

At the state level, a sales tax account number will be obtained that authorizes collection of sales tax from retail customers and allows purchases without paying sales tax to wholesale suppliers. Some states will issue a tax number during a visit to their offices. This makes it possible to register a business name, pay a newspaper to publish a notice, obtain a city permit, open a business bank account, get a tax number, and be in business that afternoon. Some other states require tax registration by mail and can take up to six weeks to process the request.

Proprietorships with no employees are not required to obtain a federal tax I.D. number, since an individual already has a Social Security number for identification (a proprietor is by definition not an employee). However, the federal number is free and more professional appearing when requested by clients or when required by tax recordkeeping requirements, so this is something to be considered when time permits. When you first hire employees, a federal I.D. number will be required, in addition to worker's compensation insurance, a state unemployment insurance account, payroll withholding, and observance of various record keeping and report filing requirements.

5.0 FINDING BUSINESS

5.1 Print Media

Newspapers and magazines do not make a living from subscription fees. At most, subscription fees help to offset the costs of delivery. Commercial publications make money by selling advertising space.

5.1.1 Editorial Content   The editorial content (articles, reviews, etc.) of the publication defines the demographics of the typical subscriber. This content can be broad or narrow. If broad, it maximizes the total audience and will attract advertisers of broad appeal products, such as automobiles and cold remedies. The many specialty publications deliberately attract a narrow audience. These smaller subscriber bases are worth more per reader to advertisers of narrow appeal products targeted to that audience. Many specialty products cannot be successfully marketed in broad-appeal publications at all. Engineering consulting services, reagent-grade chemicals, and missile instrumentation each require targeted publications to achieve cost-effective exposure.

5.1.2 *Advertising Content*

In reviewing candidate publications, it is not the editorial copy (the articles) that should be given the most attention, but the advertising copy. Remember that the purpose of editorial copy is to attract an audience because that is what readers look at, but the purpose of the audience is to attract advertisers. Careful inspection of the advertising purchased by dozens or hundreds of other companies in the publication, most of which have advertising staffs far more expert and better financed than a small start-up, is the simplest way for a small, new advertiser to assess the suitability of a publication for a given product. The test is whether your product fits into the context of what is already advertised by others.

Look at several months of issues for each candidate publication. The advertisers can be segmented into several groups. The most important group for your purposes is those advertisers that appear issue after issue, but only in selected magazines. These advertisers have found their audience, and often only need repetition of modest ads to obtain the desired effect. Inspect their advertisements carefully to see if their offerings are similar to yours; in other words, if this is your audience too. Note whether they rely on 800 telephone numbers, accept credit cards, use a P.O. box or a street address, print their hours of operation, and so forth. They offer what their particular customer base expects. Offering less would compromise their legitimacy in the eyes of their customers, while offering more might be a waste of money for that audience.

To successfully insert yourself into this customer relationship will require that you meet these expectations. In other words, researching your prospective customer base is a fundamental piece of groundwork that should precede the decision to market a particular product.

Finally, look carefully for advertisers that appear once or twice and then disappear. This will be especially apparent in the smaller ads typically at the rear of the publication. Here you will find examples of bad layout and advertising copy, inappropriate products for the audience, badly conceived products, and so on. Contacting these companies can do much to explain why they discontinued advertising in the publication. Talking to the person that placed the ad is one thing, but sometimes you encounter things that explain enough by themselves, such as impossible layers of automatic phone attendant menus, people who are never available, or literature that takes forever to come when requested or is incomprehensible.

5.1.3 Selecting Publications   Even if you already receive publications that you feel are your natural forum, it is instructive to visit the library at a university (maximum selection) and browse through the periodicals. Unless your targeted field is very narrow and you know the publications serving it well, you will likely be surprised at how many variations there are to look at.

In each publication of interest, you will find an area called the "masthead." This states the name of the publication, gives the names of the editors, publishers, marketing directors, circulation directors, and the like. From it you can find the telephone number to reach an advertising representative. For publications of interest, call and ask for a "media kit." This will contain a sample issue, a rate chart, and information on the size and demographics of the circulation. You should also inquire at the library reference desk for various directories of periodicals. Explain your purpose—most librarians are delighted to introduce you to the tools that they themselves use.

5.1.4 Testing and Frequency   In placing your advertising, you will be asked to commit to four, six, or more insertions to gain a frequency discount. Notwithstanding that a single insertion has no discount, it is wise to test before committing to more, lest there be another billable insertion already at the printer should the ad prove unsatisfactory. The typical lead time between providing camera-ready copy and the appearance of the publication in subscriber homes is three months. Tabloid formats are as short as one month.

As a general rule, an untested publication should be tested with a single insertion of a successful ad, an untested ad should be run once in a tested, successful publication, and a successful ad in a successful publication should be tinkered with only minimally and incrementally and run as often as required to keep up customer interest.

5.2 Free Publicity

5.2.1 The News Release   News releases are a time-honored way to place information of new products before your audience. Editors print news releases for several reasons. One is that they may consider the information of genuine interest to readers. Another is that printing a news release acts as a demonstration of pulling power for you as a prospective advertiser. Editors receive many more news releases than they could ever print, and many are not truly newsworthy, such as price changes and announcements that so-and-so was promoted to vice president in charge of sales for North

Dakota. Of more interest are new products that distinguish themselves in some way from competitor offerings, industry news such as mergers and acquisitions, and noteworthy business successes (new start-up lands major order).

News release formats vary, but an example illustrates a typical approach:

Light Emitting Transistor Corporation
811 Eimac Way
Glowfet, PA 12345

FOR IMMEDIATE RELEASE   Contact: Varian Machlett
January 1, 1999   (215) 555-1212

JFET-LIKE DEVICE HAS BUILT IN FAILURE INDICATOR

Glowfet, PA—Light Emitting Transistor Corp announced a series of electrically rugged devices similar to N channel J-FETs. A unique feature is a red glow emitted during operation which serves as a failure indicator when it is absent. Staff scientists predict that

.

.

.

kilovolts. Another benefit is high tolerance for momentary
-more-

LIGHT EMITTING/2

overloads which would destroy typical semiconductor devices. Further research promises a quantum leap in performance both in

.

.

.

tolerates far higher temperatures than is possible with silicon transistors. Founded in 1998, the Light Emitting Transistor Corporation specializes in the development of semiconductor alternatives. Previously announced products include the thyratron—a replacement for SCRs, and the hexadecimalode—a truly versatile alternative to traditional logic gate implementations.

-30-

The basic features of any news release are a date when the release is allowed to be made public, the date of preparation, the name of a contact for further information, and the contact's phone number. A title follows, and it is echoed on continuation pages along with the page number. A

"-more-" tag is used to alert the editor that there are additional pages, and "-30-," "-end-," or some other mark is used to signal the end of the release.

Since the document is a release of news, it should not read like advertising copy. It will be edited rather than printed verbatim, so it is preferred to include as much explanation as is useful rather than attempting to boil it down yourself. The contents should include background information, which may include something about individuals, company history, financial backing, or other relevant facts. When photographs are included, they should be marked on the back with the company name, name of the product, and a brief description of what the photograph shows.

5.2.2 Articles   An article featuring your product can be very productive. If your product is unique enough and of sufficiently universal appeal, it may merit coverage as a single topic. Editors and subscribers demand balanced coverage, however, so an article is not a license to publish a thinly disguised long advertisement. A dispassionate comparison of various alternative products, including your own, is more likely to be accepted. A tutorial on the general subject of your product area that happens to use your product as an example is also an acceptable approach. The most instructive way to learn what is useful to a given publication is to study the articles in three or four issues as a minimum. Look for articles that you especially like and emulate their format. Many publications also offer author's guidelines that can be had for the asking.

5.2.3 Reviews   Giving away free copies of a product is a classic way of promoting sales. The critical issue is to place the samples in the right hands. A review editor can be one of the best places possible. Many consumer-oriented publications produce review articles that compare various products against each other. These are heavily relied upon by individuals who lack the time or knowledge to evaluate products on their own. A good review carries heavy weight and can equal the value of tens of thousands of dollars in advertising. However, a well-deserved bad review can all but end the value of advertising in that publication until your product improves. Contacting prospective publications that use the review format is the best way to learn of upcoming review topics and to be invited to participate.

5.2.4 User Groups   Consumer-oriented products may also be publicized by user groups. Reduced-price coupons and other offers are often used. Some groups are quite influential and have an effect far beyond their direct memberships. Others are merely local clubs. Discovering where user groups are is best done by scouring publications that list them. Mailing list brokers specializing in the personal computer industry and related areas can also provide up-to-date addresses. Many groups operate computer bulletin boards that can be discovered in BBS lists. Local groups are likely to invite you to speak and demonstrate your product in person. Many companies use these groups as forums for evaluating initial reactions and obtaining opinions of product value before national launches.

6.0 RUNNING THE ENTERPRISE

6.1 Wholesale Suppliers

Wholesalers often require a minimum order amount, and it is deliberately set beyond the needs of individuals. A wholesaler will want to see as a minimum a state sales tax certificate and business checks printed with your business name. To do business on credit, they will want bank and trade references. Fortunately, it is not necessary to have a well-appointed office with a receptionist, plants in the lobby, and art on the walls. The choice of surroundings tends to be an issue of customer contact, not supplier contact. Suppliers understand that businesses operate under all kinds of circumstances from all kinds of locations. Many successful businesses operate from greasy warehouses, basements, and small offices. If the orders are steady and the checks are prompt and clear the bank, that is what wholesalers care about.

Although salespeople, field representatives, applications engineers, and others who call on you in a supplier relationship will readily disregard your physical surroundings, your credibility will suffer if your business displays the earmarks of individuals attempting to pass as businesses merely to be able to purchase at wholesale. These include telephone calls answered "Hello?"; misspelled correspondence handwritten on plain paper; lack of a listing under the business name with directory assistance; lack of fax capability; and screaming children and a blaring television set in the background when you use the telephone.

6.2 How to Get Paid

The invoice is a fundamental document of commerce. It differs from a receipt in that it not only acknowledges that a sale was made, but does so in a manner that interfaces with your customer's payment system. Open account sales (sales made on credit) require invoices.

Commercial invoice forms involve three to five copies. To understand how the sales and payment functions are interrelated, it is illustrative to trace the use of a five-part invoice through a typical transaction. The transaction begins with the receipt of a purchase order, whether mailed, faxed, or telephoned in.

6.2.1 Creating an Invoice

When the order is shipped, an invoice is generated. A commercially printed five-copy invoice has individual layers that are color coded. In the customary color scheme, the top copy is plain white, and the second yellow. These two copies are mailed to the customer's accounting department upon shipment of the order. The next two copies are pink and green. These are retained in the seller's accounting department. The pink copies are inserted into a chronological file. The green copies go into the history files for each customer account, and these are in alphabetical order. The final copy is goldenrod in color and has the dollar amount column blocked out. It serves as a packing list and may be put in the box with the merchandise but is often placed on the outside using a clear, adhesive-backed envelope made for the purpose.

The contents of an invoice include the seller-issued invoice number; the customer-issued purchase order number; the date; the quantity, description, and dollar total for each line item; shipping instructions as applicable; shipping, tax, and other additional charges; and the invoice total. Informational items such as the salesperson's name may appear as well.

6.2.2 Receiving Inspection

When the package is received at the customer location, the receiving department accepts the package and checks it for obvious external damage. Then they use the packing list to verify that the contents listed on the packing list are inside the box. The individual contents may then be inspected for damage, conformance to specifications, and the like. The checked packing list and approval of the merchandise are then forwarded to accounting.

6.2.3 Accounting Review

The customer's accounting department matches the invoice copies received by mail with the purchase order and the packing list forwarded by the receiving department. Given both a demand for payment in the form of an invoice and proof that the items received correspond to a valid purchase order and were received in good order, the accounting department will approve and schedule payment. When the check is written, the white invoice copy is retained and filed as paid. The yellow copy is normally returned with the payment. The packing slip can be filed with the white copy if it contains useful additional information, but is often discarded at this step.

Meanwhile, the seller's accounting department periodically reviews the file of unpaid pink copies to find out which are overdue, enabling them to make timely phone calls to find out if anything is amiss or if the customer merely needs prodding. When payment is received, the returned yellow copy serves to match the check against the correct invoice. The yellow copy may then be discarded or filed as part of a file of bank deposit information.

6.2.4 Making the System Work

It should be apparent that this protocol interlocks the accounting systems of the buyer and seller in a rational way. While there are many variations to suit the circumstances of particular industries, in large measure the basic format is recognized worldwide. Sales of consulting services and other arrangements that may not generate a shippable item in and of themselves are often made to fit the system by sending the customer a schematic, progress report, or some other physical token of the work performed so that the normal cycle through receiving and accounting can be satisfied.

It should also be apparent that the system can be abused when businesses fail to match invoices to purchase orders and similar failures. Unfortunately, every small business is periodically approached by unscrupulous operations. The "toner phoner" scam begins with a phone call to check the model of your copier. Several days later a call from a business with a generic sounding name that seems to be familiar with your copy machine will "thank you for your past business" and offer you "a last chance" to get a case of toner "before the price goes up." If you prove that you aren't paying attention by agreeing to an order, a low-key stream of unordered generic items will begin to show up and be invoiced as well, such as copier paper, fluorescent bulbs, and cleaning supplies, all at unfavorable prices. It is dismaying how many businesses track every penny for production materials but leave the office supply budget to a secretary who is too busy to pay attention.

6.2.7 Accounting Automation

Computerized accounting systems eliminate some of the tediousness of record keeping that is apparent for the essentially manual system described. Notwithstanding that engineers are enamored of computers, there may be no sense in computerizing books unless the number of sales transactions demands it. Far more important than the automation of financial records is their adequacy. Accountants want "audit trails," meaning the ability to go back and find out where cash came from and where it went. Conquering this requirement outprioritizes any attempt to replace a professional bookkeeper (who is already using a computer) with an accounting package. Most businesses have enough to do without taking on this burden at the beginning.

7.0 APPROACHES FOR THE EMPLOYED ENGINEER

Many engineers dabble on the side. A small consulting project is a way to keep current, is good for the ego and the pocketbook, and can even look good on a resume. Nevertheless, most engineers who do this are snared in a trap of their own choosing. The trap is: they can't let go of a paycheck. Such engineers moonlight forever, or at least until some responsibility at work consumes so much time that the moonlighting has to be given up "temporarily."

The dream of growing a business on the side until busy enough to quit and gracefully transfer into self-employment is not realistic. There are not enough hours in a day to put adequate time into self-employment and keep up with a day job. Few persons ever successfully complete transition into self-employment by backing into it.

7.1 Small Side Business

However, there is a middle ground. There is nothing wrong with beginning a small side business with the explicit understanding that learning is its purpose and that it does not have to grow. This allows learning from the classic mistakes while one is small and has a cushion. It also demonstrates why full-time attention is needed to make the business flourish. Though a learner business, this still means getting a business license, business cards, and other trappings of a serious business. A combination fax/answering machine is another useful acquisition. Seeing these expenses and dealing with them should not be left as a shock for when one begins in earnest. To avoid legal troubles, a starter business should not conflict with one's employment agreement.

7.2 Consulting

For skilled professionals, consulting is the most common first approach to
self-employment. The reasons for this are simple: anyone can call themselves a consultant, and it doesn't take much cash. You can work from your
kitchen table. When discussing the things that make a successful business,
some otherwise competent engineers opine that an advanced technical
degree is one of the best things you can get. Within the narrow context of
consulting, this tends to be true, but technical ability alone is insufficient
for a successful business.

8.0 THE FINANCIAL UNIVERSE

8.1 Clerks

The finance and accounting community can be divided into four layers or
tiers. At the most fundamental level, you have clerks. These employees
handle cash and merchandise and generate a record of each transaction.
Sales clerks, shipping clerks, purchasing agents, and the like fall into this
category. Employees keeping time cards act as clerks for their own labor.

8.2 Bookkeepers

The next level is that of bookkeeping. A bookkeeper takes the records
generated in the course of business, enters the transactions into a journal of
financial activities, and then "posts" or enters the transactions into account
ledgers, such as one for sales, one for product returns, one for purchases of
resale inventory, a separate ledger account for office supplies, and so on. The
bookkeeper then uses this information to generate reports of daily or weekly
sales, payroll amounts, overdue receivables, and similar information.

8.3 Accountants

Accountants have the task of organizing and monitoring the work of clerks
and bookkeepers. The accountant passes on to management the measures,
such as return on investment calculations, balance sheets, and the like. The
accountant is in charge of the design of the paperwork system to ensure that
these tasks are properly carried out.

    If the accountant is on staff, it is standard practice to also have an outside accounting firm perform an annual audit. There are different branches of accounting, such as tax accountants, managerial accountants, and certified public accountants. Tax accountants are specialists, and CPAs are accountants who have passed the CPA exam. The accountant most often found on corporate staffs is the managerial accountant.

8.4 Financial Officers

Finance is mentioned primarily as a matter of completeness. Where the job of the accountant is to report to management, the chief financial officer is that management. If the job of the accountant is to ensure straight and level flight, the staff financial genius determines where the flight is headed. For instance, should the company raise funds via stock issue or debt, and how much? Does it make more sense to keep a division that is ailing and put in money to fix it, or sell it off, or close it? These are matters for the executive suite and are beyond the ken of accounting. Finance is a different world. *The Wall Street Journal* is about financial affairs and mentions accounting as a matter of related interest.

8.5 The Start-up Entrepreneur

If you are starting a business on your kitchen table, you can only dream about these levels of expertise. You will be your own clerk and often your own bookkeeper. Your forms will come off the rack at a stationery store. An accountant should be consulted about your recordkeeping needs, especially where taxes are concerned, and should inspect your books and prepare basic financial statements not less than yearly but preferably quarterly. The accountant should also remind you when various state and federal tax payments are due, possibly computing these amounts as well. For the daily demands of processing routine paperwork, you will find that the Yellow Pages lists bookkeeping services one letter of the alphabet away from accountants. While they cannot substitute for an accountant's advice, they are far cheaper for the mundane tasks that a college-educated, self-respecting accountant would just as soon pass on to others.

8.6 Using Outside Services

Some accountants have bookkeepers on staff as a natural extension of their services. This makes them a one-stop, full-service provider. However, some business owners prefer the unbiased opinion that comes from an accountant looking over work that is not his own. There is also an advantage in being able to sack either the bookkeeper or the accountant independently of each other and move on with a minimum of disruption.

9.0 DOUBLE-ENTRY BOOKKEEPING

Most consumers are familiar with single-entry bookkeeping, such as for their personal checking accounts. Deposits and checks are recorded in chronological order, and a running total is kept and compared against the monthly statement. This sort of bookkeeping works as long as all cash flows of interest pass through the account, and the cash being accounted for belongs to only one individual. As soon as either assumption is violated, single-entry bookkeeping fails.

Businesses are rather more complex, and require double entry bookkeeping. Double-entry bookkeeping treats the business bank account as just one of many reservoirs of monetary value that can be tracked. Examples of others are receivables, inventory, and business equipment, for starters. Double-entry bookkeeping also tracks multiple ownership claims, or liabilities. There will be inventory not yet paid for, paycheck amounts not yet issued, refunds owed, taxes collected but not yet remitted, and so forth. Each of these outside claims against a portion of the business assets must be added to the equity claim of the owner/entrepreneur.

9.1 Fundamental Concepts

The fundamental entries in double entry bookkeeping systems are called debits and credits, abbreviated "Dr" and "Cr." The two terms arise from Latin. The original sense of debit is "to owe," and the modern term "debt" has the same derivation. For credit, the sense is trust or belief. By convention, debits are entered into ledgers on the left, and credits to the right. The earliest double-entry bookkeeping systems used this convention when a merchant would first enter a description and price for an item handed over to a customer (the debit), followed by a notation of payment (the credit) by the purchaser. The merchant might mutter to himself, "I just handed you a pig so you owe me the pig until you pay, but I trust you to hand me twenty guilders."In modern usage, debits and credits represent increases and decreases in assets, respectively, or the mirror equivalent—decreases and increases in liabilities, respectively. The universal debits-to-the-left, credits-to-the-right format is maintained. Every transaction requires one debit and one credit (double entry), and the two must be equal in amount, that is, balance. There are instances where a debit or a credit is split into several pieces, but the same rule applies—the sum of debits equals the sum of credits for each individual transaction.

9.2 The Accounting Basis

The accounting basis can be either cash or accrual. Cash accounting recognizes revenues only when received and debts only when paid. Accrual accounting recognizes revenues as soon as they are owed to the business and debts as soon as they are owed to others. Cash accounting is the norm only for small enterprises that actually deal substantially in cash, or are not able to maintain detailed records. Accrual accounting is the standard for everyone else.

9.3 The Accounting Year

For tax reasons if no other, all accounting systems prepare statements at least once per year. Not all businesses use a calendar year. All tax authorities allow businesses to adopt fiscal years that end other than on December 31 when it makes good sense to do so. Many retailers, for instance, would find it artificial and distorting to split the Christmas season, their busiest of the year, between two accounting years. However, the calendar year is a logical choice for most small technological companies. The fact of employees and customers alike being absorbed in winter holiday activities usually creates a lull in business at that time of year, and the owner's personal tax reporting requirements remain on a calendar year basis.

9.4 The Accounting Perspective

Newcomers to accounting often sense an inversion of meaning from what they are familiar with, in that to a consumer, "credit" means receiving money, not having less, and debit or debt means giving money, not receiving it. However, the terms are applied by the bank or credit card company from the vantage point of their accounting systems—and indeed, loaning money to a consumer decreases their cash, and receiving debt payments increases it. A consumer who keeps a personal double entry accounting system realizes that the credit in the bank books is reflected as a debit in his personal set of books, and vice versa.

To continue the checking account example, banks like to assure depositors of their stability by stating an impressively large figure for assets. However, the majority of a bank's assets are deposits that are offset by corresponding liabilities representing the individual depositors. When these are subtracted out, many local banks are found to actually be small- to medium-sized businesses with modest investments in the buildings they are housed in and the equipment required to run the bank.

10.0 FINANCIAL STATEMENTS

The world has no shortage of business owners who cannot read financial reports and have even less interest in them. They tend to have lawn care businesses, install sheet rock in houses, and run fruit stands, and they see financial statements as a necessary evil to keep the tax collectors off their backs. No sophisticated enterprise can afford this type of attitude. Just as a real engineer is not content to stay at the "I turn this knob and this happens" level of understanding with his equipment, a real businessperson finds periodic financial statements highly interesting reading. These are the dials and gauges of the financial engine. Financial records and statements not only provide a history of what happened and diagnostics of why, but they also provide valuable clues for the future. Furthermore, a healthy interest in the financial position of your business does much to forestall laziness and chicanery among accounting personnel.

10.1 The Balance Sheet

The balance sheet, also known as a position statement, is one of the two most fundamental business statements, the other being the profit and loss statement. The balance sheet is a condensed inventory of every financial component of the business. As such, it is a "snapshot" of the business for the day on which it was prepared. However, businesses rarely change radically in the space of a few days, and the information in a balance sheet can be valid and useful for weeks or months after it was prepared.

10.1.1 Assets   The structure of a typical balance sheet follows a universal format. Listed first are the assets, and these are further divided into current and long-term assets. The current assets are those that are cash or are converted into cash in the normal course of business operation, usually within a year. Current assets include the bank balance, the total of accounts receivable, the value of inventory held for sale, and certain other items. Long-term assets include furniture, equipment, land and buildings, and other things intended for long-term use and not normally for sale.

10.1.2 Liabilities and Equities   The liability side of the balance sheet uses the same conceptual split. Current liabilities include trade payables and taxes due. The long-term liabilities include mortgage balances, stock held by shareholders, and the like. Stockholder capital is conceptually different from a loan, for it is permanently placed in the business and is not expected to be paid back directly. Hence, this item is referred to as an equity. The sum of liabilities and equities numerically equals the sum of the assets, that is, the categories balance, hence the name of the report.

Long-term debts like mortgages affect both current and long-term liabilities. Each month, the payment due appears as a current liability until paid, and the remaining long-term balance is adjusted downward to reflect that fact.

10.2 Profit and Loss Statement

The profit and loss statement, also known as an operating statement, is the other most fundamental statement. It also follows a widely accepted format. Listed first are the gross revenues. From the revenues, all the expenses are subtracted, category by category, until the net earnings remain. The first category subtracted out is the cost of goods sold, leaving the gross margin, that is, that portion of the sales total that directly contributes to profits. Next out are selling expenses such as commissions and advertising. Then general and administrative expenses that do not have a direct connection to sales are taken out, leaving the earnings before interest and taxes. Finally, taxes, interest, and similar charges that have no direct connection to revenue generation are subtracted out, leaving net income.

10.3 Relationship Between the Statements

Since the profit and loss statement (P&L) represents the business performance over an interval of time, and the balance sheet represents the state of the business at the end of an interval, it is standard practice to prepare a balance sheet and a P&L at the same time. The relationship between the two types of statements is fundamental. The P&L shows the financial flows of the business; the balance sheet shows the accumulations of those flows. The two must be read in tandem to get an accurate picture of the business, much as the instantaneous water level behind a dam and the rate of flow of the river feeding the lake are both required to forecast what the water level will be tomorrow.

10.4 Financial Ratios

Taken together, the balance sheet and operating statement provide the savvy manager with a great deal of information above and beyond the bare facts shown on these documents. Common engineering practice relies upon "figure of merit" computations to assess the relative performance of components and systems. So too, the financial community uses some obvious and not so obvious manipulations of statement items to generate various metrics of business health. As most of these involve division to normalize the results and make them independent of business size, they are collectively known as financial ratios.

The ratios are typically one of four kinds. Liquidity ratios measure the extent to which a firm is able to keep up with its bills, debts, and other short-term obligations. Profitability ratios measure the overall effectiveness of the business in creating profits. Leverage ratios measure the extent to which the business has been financed by debt. Activity ratios measure how effectively the firm is using its assets.

For instance, the "current ratio" is obtained by dividing the current assets by the current liabilities. It is a measure of the ability of the business to pay its debts over the next 30 days and is classified as a liquidity ratio. Suffice it to say, current ratios below 1.0 are a bad sign. Current ratios above 2.0 are usually a sign of health. The normal range varies considerably by industry. Statistics for various industries are published by the U.S. Department of Commerce, and it is always instructive to compare your business ratios against the industry averages.

A detailed discussion of financial ratios is beyond the scope of this chapter. The interested reader is directed to further study in the areas of accounting and finance. You are urged to be interested. Explanations applicable to your business should be forthcoming from your accountant. The business owner should not rely upon his accountant to choose and compute the appropriate ratios, but should learn to apply these tools directly: it is not the accountant who is running the business.

10.5 Accounting Credibility

If accounting is the language of business, a universal assumption is that accounting information exists and is reliable. This is one of the least believable assumptions for many small businesses. The fact is that many bookkeepers are incompetent and some CPAs are better able to derive sense from chaotic books than others. It is imperative to create a good paper trail of invoices, purchase orders, check stubs, and other primary documents. It is wise to keep xerographic copies of checks received for payment and copies of deposit slips. A truly competent CPA will read your balance sheet and P&L like a novel and have questions, explanations, and suggestions within minutes of reading them. Do not settle for a relationship where you drop off a collection of documents and weeks later your reports are mailed back.

11.0 CONCLUSION

Establishing and maintaining a business depends on a great deal more than just technical expertise. New entrepreneurs must learn to manage their own time and those of their employees efficiently. They must develop an appreciation of what motivates people and how to interact with colleagues and prospective clients in a world that is much broader than the engineering universe. The challenge of operating a business is a growing experience that expands and nurtures the whole person. It is often difficult and at times traumatic, but it is seldom unrewarding.

The liberal arts courses foisted on unwilling technical undergraduates age well if nurtured with a newspaper subscription here, an opinion magazine there, and a good political argument once in a while. Of all those who begin new enterprises, those who are most successful and content are those who employ their zest for learning over the whole range of human activities, and not merely within their technical niche.

12.0 REFERENCES

Hawken, Paul. *Growing a Business*. New York: Simon & Schuster, 1987.
Brown, W. Dean. *Incorporating Without a Lawyer Series*. Knoxville, TN: Consumer Publishing, 1995.
Stone, Bradford. *Stone's Uniform Commercial Code in a Nutshell*. St. Paul, MN: West Publishing Co., 1993, 3rd Edition.

5

Pensions and Retirement Planning

George F. McClure

1.0 INTRODUCTION

It may seem superfluous for a young engineer, just embarking on an engineering career, to be concerned with retirement planning. But the task is easier when time is on your side. Time is your ally in accruing and investing assets for retirement, and the earlier the task is started, the easier it is to reach your retirement goals.

Someone saving $100 per month in a tax-deferred retirement account, between the ages of 25 and 35, would have $184,000 at age 65, assuming an 8 percent growth rate, even if no more contributions were made after age 35. A young engineer making a pretax contribution of $300 per month into a company's tax-deferred retirement savings plan, starting at age 25 and continuing until age 65, with the same 8 percent growth rate, would have over a million dollars in the plan when retiring.

Pensions were first offered to employees about a century ago, as an incentive to stay with the company for the long term. The retirement age of 65 years was established early in the twentieth century, when the average lifespan was less than 60 years. In 1900, only 4 percent of the U.S. population was age 65 or above. Thus, few workers lived long enough to retire, and, if they did actually retire, fewer still lived long enough to collect significant pension benefits in retirement. In periods of wage and price control, such as in World War II, companies were able to make pension benefits more generous as a substitute for increasing current employee income. Today, life expectancy for 65-year-olds is approaching 20 years. A recent survey of working Americans showed that most expect to spend 23 years in retirement.[1]

While fewer than half of the workers in the United States have jobs that provide any retirement plans or other pension benefits, most engineers and scientists are employed by companies that do offer retirement plans. This chapter covers many of the points of pensions and retirement planning that engineers and other professionals should be aware of early in their careers, when there is ample time to take steps that will ensure a comfortable postcareer retirement.

2.0 PENSION TYPES

2.1 Defined-Benefit Pension Plans

Defined-benefit pension plans are promises by the employers to pay a stated benefit, based on a formula involving number of years of credited service times a percentage of final average pay. Some provided for a higher percentage credit for later years of service; in any case the use of final average pay as a calculation component provides employers an incentive to encourage these workers to leave service early to control pension costs. Most pensions are fixed in amount at the time of retirement, or even earlier if the pensioner left the company before his retirement occurred. The average job tenure of an engineer in the United States is under 7 years, and the average worker in the future is expected to have eight jobs in his lifetime. Thus, it is more likely that a worker will have a number of small pensions in retirement than that he will have one large one. Studies comparing a worker changing jobs every 10 years to a worker staying at one job for 40 years show that the mobile worker will typically accrue about half the pension credit of the long-term worker at the same salary levels.

2.2 Defined-Contribution Pension Plans

Defined-contribution pension plans give the employee full control of his or her pension funds but require continuing attention to investment options to achieve needed growth if adequate funds are to be available in retirement.

Over 30 million workers are covered by defined-contribution plans. Ironically, by restricting themselves to very safe investment options, such as certificates of deposit or guaranteed investment contracts, many workers investing in defined-contribution plans do not achieve the growth needed in their retirement funds to live comfortably when they reach retirement. Pension portability may be achieved, under pending legislation, by converting a defined-benefit into a defined-contribution lump sum under the control of the plan holder.

2.3 401(k) Plans

The popular 401(k) salary reduction plan, in which the worker contributes pretax dollars to a retirement fund and a fraction of the worker's contribution may be matched by employer contributions, is an example of a defined-contribution plan. Automatically portable, because the amount in the employee's account is always defined, 401(k) plans permit tax-deferred growth of the funds contributed, with taxes paid only when the funds are withdrawn. There are limits on the amount contributed annually by the employee and the employer. The sum may not exceed 25 percent of income, or $30,000, whichever is less, while the employee's pretax contribution is limited to $9420 per year (adjusted for inflation) but typically may range between 10 and 15 percent of salary based on discrimination tests to prevent highly compensated employees from having a disproportionate share. Part of the allowed contribution may be after-tax dollars, based on the discrimination tests. A vesting period may be required for the employer contributions to be fully credited to the employee's account. Upon separation or retirement, the pretax portion of the proceeds of the plan may be rolled over into an individual retirement account (an IRA, further discussed shortly). The after-tax contributions are returned to the employee at that time but cannot be rolled over. The earnings on the after-tax contributions, however, are themselves tax-deferred and can be rolled over.

2.4 403(b) Plans

Workers employed by a college or other public institution are not eligible to participate in 401(k) plans, but are covered by a 403(b) plan that works much the same way. The limit on contributions is currently $9500 per year or 20 percent of salary, whichever is less.

2.5 457 Plans

457 plans are designed for employees of state governments or to the management of nonprofit organizations. Participants contribute a portion of their salaries on a pretax basis, but all contributions are owned by the employer and are subject to the claims of the employer's creditors.

2.6 Individual Retirement Accounts

Any worker may contribute up to $2000 of his earnings each year to an IRA, a retirement account that grows tax-deferred until the funds are cashed in for use in retirement, at which time the tax due is paid. For a nonworking spouse, $250 per year may be contributed. If the worker is not actively participating in a pension plan (and neither is a spouse who files a joint tax return), then the $2000 is deductible from taxable income. If either participates in a pension plan, then there are salary limitations defining deductibility. The full amount is deductible if adjusted gross income (AGI) is $40,000 or less, reducing to none deductible at $50,000 AGI. However, the growth of the IRA funds is always tax deferred, even when the contribution is made with after-tax dollars. The advantage of the tax-deferred earnings status can be seen by comparing a contribution of $2000 per year for 30 years and for 40 years, where no taxes are deducted, and deducting a nominal 28 percent of earnings each year for taxes. (See Table 5.1.) The growth rates assumed are the long-term rates for the Standard & Poor's 500 stock index (10 percent per year) and for managed equity funds (15 percent per year).

Table 5.1 Tax-Deferred Advantage of IRA

Condition	Pretax	Post-tax
$2000/year, 30 years		
10% growth	$328,988	$195,858
15% growth	869,490	383,086
$2000/year, 40 years		
10% growth	885,185	420,440
15% growth	3,558,181	1,101,426

The tax deferral permits the dollars that would otherwise be paid out in tax each year to remain and compound, resulting in gains from 68 percent to 220 percent higher than if taxes were paid each year over the periods shown.

The important point to remember is to start early on investing for retirement, so that compounding over time can work in favor of the worker, to build the best nest egg for a comfortable retirement, later. The same advantage applies, of course, to all tax-deferred retirement accounts. The disadvantage is a 10 percent penalty for early withdrawal of these funds, before age 59 1/2.

2.7 Keogh Plans

Keogh plans are tax-deferred retirement accounts available only to persons with self-employment income. This can include part-time or sideline income as well as partnerships or even income earned from sitting on boards of directors.[2] Keogh plans can be set up as either defined-benefit plans, to yield a specified income each year in retirement, or defined-contribution plans.

2.8 Simplified Employee Pension Plans

Simplified Employee Pension (SEP) plans can be set up by self-employed individuals without difficulty, using standard forms available from financial institutions. The holder keeps the form on file. The maximum contribution is 15 percent of earnings per year, with a ceiling of $30,000. These contributions are pretax dollars. The individual directs the investment of SEP funds. The SEP lacks the flexibility of the Keogh, but also lacks the stringent annual reporting requirement that a Keogh plan entails.

2.9 Profit-Sharing Plans

Profit-sharing plans permit variable contributions by employers, up to 15 percent of total employee compensation, to grow tax-deferred. The employer determines the amount of the contribution each year and the investments to be used. Contributions may be made even in years when there are no profits.

3.0 TAX-DEFERRED ANNUITIES

Annuities are insurance contracts that are purchased to provide a fixed income for a defined period of time or for life. In tax-deferred annuities, the purchase funds are contributed in advance of the start of the payout period. These funds are permitted to grow tax deferred, with the tax being paid on the taxable part of the payout when received. A primary advantage of annuities is that there is no limit on the size of the investment to receive this preferential tax treatment, but commissions and marketing expenses must be paid, reducing the net amount of the funds available for growth, and there are usually penalties imposed by the company for early withdrawal of the funds. Various investment options are available, including fixed income and variable annuities. For the latter, performance is not guaranteed but, as in stock mutual funds, depends on the performance of the investment portfolio. A second advantage of annuities is that you cannot outlive your money; payout from a life annuity will last as long as you do.

3.0 TAX CONSEQUENCES

3.1 Tax-Qualified Plans

Only plans approved by the Internal Revenue Service (called IRS-qualified plans) are eligible for the tax-deferred treatment on earnings. IRS-qualified pension plans, profit-sharing plans, 401(k) plans, Keogh plans, 403(b) plans, and retirement plans for government workers weigh in the determination of eligibility to make a pretax IRA contribution.

3.2 Payout Requirements

Payouts can begin without penalty at any time as a stream of payments, at least one per year, planned to last your IRS-projected lifetime. Otherwise, payouts from IRAs may begin as early as age 59 1/2 without penalty and must start by age 70 1/2. These payouts must be calculated to remove from tax-deferred status (and pay the tax on) all retirement assets over a period equal to your life and that of your beneficiary.

3.3 Penalties

A 10 percent penalty for early withdrawal (before age 59 1/2) applies to tax-deferred accounts except for those disabled. A 15 percent penalty for excess distributions applies against tax-deferred funds in excess of $150,000 withdrawn during a single year. A 50 percent penalty applies to amounts not withdrawn that should have been. For example, if you should have been withdrawing $8000 from your IRA to pay tax on and only withdraw $6000, then you will have a penalty equal to half of the $2000 shortfall, or $1000. This penalty is in addition to the tax due. There is an incentive to leave as much in the tax-deferred account as long as possible, to maximize growth. However, if your investment performance is so good that you are in danger of the equal annual payouts over your lifetime exceeding $150,000, then you risk the 15 percent penalty on the excess, and you may want to start withdrawing the funds earlier.

Withdrawing the funds to pay the tax does not mean that you cannot reinvest the balance of the withdrawn funds not needed for living expenses in an after-tax account, for further future growth.

4.0 RETIREMENT PLANNING

4.1 Income Requirements

Income (purchasing power, after allowing for inflation) requirements in retirement are typically less than in the years before retirement. The children are out of college. There is less expense for commuting (auto maintenance, insurance, gas, tolls, and parking), business lunches, and maintenance of business clothing. The home typically is paid for, so there is no mortgage payment in the retirement budget. The 15 percent of income that was probably being contributed to a salary reduction retirement plan is no longer required. Expenses for education, entertainment, and travel will likely increase. The consensus is that a replacement ratio of 70 to 80 percent of preretirement income is adequate for beginning retirement, depending on desired life-style: amount of travel desired and whether a golf club membership, several autos, and a summer home are kept.

Some retirees plan to move to low-cost communities in the Sunbelt for retirement and may convert part of their equity in the old home to savings if a smaller home is purchased in the new location.

Checklists and computer spreadsheets are available for detailing the budget requirements in retirement. In addition to the income needed starting in retirement, there are several events that should also be considered:

- If retirement starts prior to age 65 for either spouse, significant health insurance costs may be incurred. This has not been the case for most career workers where the employer benefit package includes group health insurance and major medical plans. However, while some employers offer retiree health insurance, health care costs can be expected to continue to rise and the retiree may have to pay a larger portion if not the full cost of medical insurance premiums. At age 65, enrollment in Medicare will reduce the premium cost. But even after age 65, since Medicare is shifting more cost to the individual, Medigap insurance is becoming more expensive.

- If retirement starts prior to age 62, no Social Security benefits can be received, except for disability, until age 62, when the benefit will be 20 percent less than at age 65. These ages start increasing for those born after 1937. A nonworking spouse is entitled to receive half the worker's benefit when age-eligible; this steps up to the full worker's benefit on death of the retired worker.

- Provision for continued retirement income after death of one spouse should be analyzed. Most industrial and military pension plans provide for continued payment of a fraction of the pension to a beneficiary spouse after death of the pensioner. This is typically a 50 percent pension for the lifetime of the surviving spouse. The primary pension is reduced to cover the cost of this joint and survivor benefit, typically by 10 to 20 percent, depending on the age of the spouse.

The retirement income requirement should be figured three ways: (1) prior to age 62 (or other later age at which Social Security benefits will be drawn), (2) at age 65 for each spouse, when Medicare health coverage is available, and (3) for the life of the surviving spouse.

4.2 Computation Aids

Features on retirement budgeting are published at least annually in *U.S. News and World Report, Money Magazine,* and *Smart Money.* Occasional retirement planning tips appear in the "Your Money Matters" feature printed on Fridays in *The Wall Street Journal.* The Sunday *New York Times* runs a feature called "For Your Account" in the business section, frequently reporting on changes in laws and other financial matters affecting retirement planning.

Publications of the American Association of Individual Investors[3] cover aspects of both retirement planning and investment. Annuity and insurance evaluations have been published by *Consumer Reports.* Mutual fund performance is covered in several publications, most exhaustively in the Morningstar[4] subscription service, available in libraries, but also in

Forbes' annual August 15 issue, *Money Magazine, Smart Money,* and *Consumer Reports.*

There are several computer software packages available to help with the budget requirement and investment analysis needed for retirement planning. Mutual fund companies such as T. Rowe Price and Fidelity offer low-cost financial planning diskettes for PCs as well as free printed material on retirement income requirements that can be converted into a spreadsheet. Over 500,000 copies of the free T. Rowe Price Retirement Planning Kit have been distributed over four years; it permits you to select various rates for investment return, income tax, and inflation and to evaluate performance of your retirement funds under those conditions. Shareware spreadsheet templates are also available.[5] More elaborate packages such as Wealth Builder, Smart Investor, and Managing Your Money can be purchased. For an updated list contact the IEEE-USA Pensions Committee.[6]

Access to stock quotes and business news is available after the markets close from several on-line information services, including the Dow-Jones News/Retrieval service and America Online.[7] America Online maintains a special section, sponsored by the American Association of Individual Investors, that includes tools for portfolio management. One feature is automatic daily updating of stock and mutual fund prices in the subscribers' portfolios, performed when first logging onto the service after the market's closing prices are available.

5.0 STRATEGIES FOR RETIREMENT INCOME

Having calculated the income requirement for starting retirement, your next step is assessing how to satisfy that requirement in a way that permits reasonable safety and growth for your retirement nest egg. Other considerations include providing a hedge against inflation by stepping up payouts later in retirement to maintain roughly the same purchasing power that you start with, scheduling tax payments on tax-deferred retirement funds to comply with the law, and ensuring that your nest egg will last as long as you do.

5.1 Components of Income

Income may include wages from a part-time job; a fixed stream of payments from one or more defined-benefit pension plans; a Social Security benefit with an annual cost-of-living adjustment; rents and royalties; dividends and interest income from stocks, bonds, money market funds, and certificates of deposit outside your IRA; and withdrawals from your IRA (likely invested in similar securities, either directly or through mutual funds). Record keeping is important, to be sure that IRA funds are withdrawn and tax due is paid at a rate that satisfies the IRS. This rate is designed to withdraw and pay tax on all the funds over the lifetime of the owner of the IRA and his beneficiary, usually the spouse. If both die before the full tax has been paid, the balance of the IRA goes into the estate of the beneficiary, and income tax is due on the whole amount. Federal estate taxes are also due, at progressive rates starting at 37 percent on an estate valued between $600,000 and $750,000. If the estate is large, estate taxes at the maximum rate of 55 percent are due on the excess over $3,000,000. If the assets pass through a will, probate costs will also be incurred.

5.2 Inflation Protection

Since most defined-benefit pension plans use fixed annuities to provide the benefit to the pensioner, few have any provision for cost-of-living adjustments (COLAs) after retirement. Social Security, government pensions, and military pensions do have COLAs, but these are subject to stretchout by the Congress as a weapon in the fight for deficit reduction. Interest income from bonds has no inflation protection; rather, the market value of the bonds will fall during periods of inflation when interest rates rise.[8]

Dividend income from stocks generally keeps pace with inflation as corporate earnings rise; over the long term, stock prices will also rise with earnings. Therefore, income stocks are a useful inflation hedge in a retirement portfolio. The total long-term gain in the Standard & Poor's 500 stock index is over 10 percent, with inflation running at under 5 percent.

The value of tangible investments, such as income real estate, can generally be expected to keep pace with inflation, as rental income rises. Rent receipts, therefore, are a form of retirement income that can be expected to maintain purchasing power.

5.3 Asset Allocation

Since the only thing certain about markets is that they will fluctuate, it is prudent to diversify retirement assets. One rule of thumb is that the percentage devoted to bonds should be equal to 100 minus your age. Obviously this simplistic rule of thumb will have to be modified to reflect your goals for growth and safety, your comfort with investments in which the principal amount may go down occasionally as well as up, the interest rate and inflation rate environments, and the income requirements that you place on your retirement nest egg. The basis of asset allocation is modern portfolio theory that has shown that uncorrelated investments can be combined so that the overall risk in the portfolio is less than the risk any one holding poses. Some computerized portfolio analysis programs include this function, providing recommendations on the mix of stocks, bonds, money market funds, and illiquid investments for your portfolio.

Lack of diversification has acted to the detriment of many holders of 401(k) plans, who must make choices in the investment of these funds during their working career, but who have devoted most of their holdings to fixed return investments, such as guaranteed investment contracts, that emphasize safety of principal over growth. This has been a mistake, since these funds must be invested to grow over the years before retirement if the nest egg is to be adequate for retirement needs. Equities have a risk of falling in value and are shunned by some for their retirement portfolio. However, as shown in Table 5.2, returns in two unmanaged group of stocks, the Dow Jones Industrial Average of 30 stocks and the Standard & Poor's 500 Index, have far outperformed fixed income investments over the 50 years ending in June 1991.

Table 5.2 Average Annual Total Returns Through June 30, 1991

Years	Dow Jones Industrial Average	Standard & Poor's 500 Index
1	4.63%	7.38%
5	13.01%	11.88%
10	16.49%	15.52%
20	11.11%	11.35%
30	9.53%	10.18%
40	11.14%	11.81%
50	11.51%	12.31%

One way to handle the asset allocation problem in your IRA is to invest in mutual funds that perform the asset allocation function for you. These funds are invested in a mix of stocks and bonds, varying the mix percentages as market conditions change. The Morningstar fund rating service[9] lists 31 such mutual funds, one of which rates their highest five-star rating for high performance with low risk although managing assets of over $8 billion.

Since stocks will provide a greater return than bonds or money market funds over a period of more than five years, it is probably prudent to keep as much of a retirement portfolio invested in stocks as the owner is comfortable with, assuming that these stocks do not represent funds needed for current spendable income in the near term. It is important to know your own threshold for risk in making the allocation. Many people can sleep in spite of a 10 percent drop in the value of their invested assets, but fewer can tolerate a 20 percent or a 30 percent drop, even though the portfolio value may reach a new high three to five years later.

6.0 PITFALLS IN PENSION PLANNING

There are factors beyond the control of the individual that you should be aware of in making your retirement plans. Some of these are the following.

6.1 Job Changes Short of Vesting Periods

The vesting period for defined-benefit pension plans is generally five years. A worker who changes employers in less than five years does not vest—that is, he is not entitled to any pension credit. A bill before Congress, endorsed by IEEE, reduces this period to three years.

6.2 Reversions

Defined-benefit pension funds contributed by an employer may grow beyond the funding requirements if there is favorable investment experience. In this case, the employer can stop making payments as long as the funding exceeds requirements. He can also remove some of the excess funds through a process called reversion. In reversion, the pension plan is terminated, funds are set aside to satisfy the liabilities of the fund to all present planholders, and the balance of the fund reverts back to the plan sponsor. The law provides for a 10 percent tax penalty on the withdrawn amount to be paid by the employer, to discourage reversions. The risk, from the standpoint of the individual vested in a pension plan, is that the plan in which he participates and on which he is counting as a component of his retirement plan, will be terminated, with either no replacement plan or a less generous replacement plan.

6.3 Underfunded Pension Plans, Bankruptcies, and Pension Protection

Underfunding of defined-benefit pension plans by employers has been a long-term concern. Defined-benefit pension plans are underfunded when the amount of the employer (plan sponsor) contributions plus earnings growth are not sufficient to satisfy the actuarially projected liabilities of the fund. Some pension plans that were considered to be adequately funded when interest rates averaged 8 or 9 percent are no longer fully funded when interest rate projections fall to 5 or 6 percent. The shortfall is the unfunded liability of the plan.

The Pension Benefit Guaranty Corporation (PBGC) was established by the Employee Retirement Income Security Act (ERISA) in 1974 to provide insurance protecting pension beneficiaries in companies that went bankrupt or had unfunded pension liabilities and therefore were unable to keep their promise of a defined-benefit pension to those vested in the plans.

PBGC insures that beneficiaries of defined-benefit pension plans receive at least a portion of their pensions (up to a maximum of about $29,000 per year) in the event of default by the employer. Forty million Americans in 85,000 company pension plans are covered by this insurance. Pension fund insurance premiums paid to PBGC by employers provide a fund intended to cover this guarantee. These premiums total about $800 million per year. However, the growing extent of corporate bankruptcies has increased the potential liability of the PBGC to as much as $51 billion if companies already underfunded fail and if PBGC is to cover all the shortfall as required by law. This is well in excess of the premium income and represents a threat that taxpayers may have to make good on the difference. The bankruptcies of Pan American World Airways and Eastern Air Lines, for example, saddled the PBGC with $1.6 billion in unfunded pension liabilities.

As the premiums charged employers by PBGC have risen, with congressional approval, because the overall liability increased, some employers who do not have shortfalls in their funding have more incentive to terminate the defined-benefit plan and replace it with a less expensive defined-contribution plan. Defined-contribution plans are automatically funded as the contribution is credited to the employees' accounts; therefore defined-contribution plans do not require a PBGC guarantee.

The Employee Benefits Research Institute, speaking for employers, regards the problem as overstated, since 85 percent of pension plans have funds equal to 100 percent of their liabilities, and 37 percent have assets in excess of 150 percent of liabilities for accrued benefits in 1992.[10] But even though single-employer pension plans in the United States overall have over $900 billion in assets to cover $750 billion in benefit obligations, funds from one employer's overfunded plan cannot be used to make good the pension promises of another employer whose plan is underfunded. The most severe underfunding is in the auto and steel industries. Pending federal legislation to improve pension funding is opposed by the National Association of Manufacturers.

6.4 Nonportable Defined-Benefit Plans

When employment conditions change and force workers to change jobs, those who are vested in defined-benefit pension plans usually must leave their pension credit fixed at the old company, with no opportunity to increase the amount of the pension before they reach retirement age and start drawing the pension. A worker leaving a job with an early pension credit at age 35, then working elsewhere until age 65, finds that when he starts drawing the 30-year-old pension its purchasing power has eroded significantly. If the inflation rate is 4 percent per year for 30 years, then the purchasing power when the pension finally begins will be only 31 percent of the value it had the day he left that company. This pitfall can be corrected by making the defined-benefit portable, as a bill now in Congress does, permitting the employee to roll over the lump-sum present value into his IRA when he leaves the company. A real (deflated) interest rate is used to compute the present value. If that is done, the earnings growth of the lump sum over the succeeding 30 years will more than offset the erosion due to inflation and the worker's retirement purchasing power will be preserved. In the example, the lump sum will be 41 percent of the cost of an annuity at age 65 that would provide the earned lifetime monthly pension payments. If this sum in the IRA grows at 8 percent per year over 30 years, the final value will be 10 times the amount rolled over.

   As an example, if the benefit at age 65 is worth $100,000 ($417 per month for 20 years), the lump sum rolled into the IRA 30 years sooner would be $41,200 (present value computed at a 3 percent discount rate). If this grew at 8 percent, it would amount to $415,000 after 30 years, at age 65, with a purchasing power equivalent to $128,000 if the inflation rate was 4 percent over 30 years.

6.5 Forced Early Retirement

The current trend to downsize corporate America and to increase outsourcing[11] to meet intermittent demands for special skills has resulted in numerous companies reducing employment by 10 to 15 percent. While some of this reduction can be handled by attrition, most of it, especially the elimination of layers of middle management, require the dismissal of employees, by early retirement incentives or layoffs.

Older, higher-salaried employees who may be eligible for retirement benefits are the usual targets for offers to leave the company. Incentives offered by the company, such as departure bonuses or richer pension offers, are one-time costs offset by long-term savings in salaries and associated benefits. From the companies' viewpoint, these departures will reduce payroll and open up additional promotion opportunities for younger, lower-salaried workers.

From the government's viewpoint, staying on the job would be preferable, bringing in tax revenue from the high salaries paid these senior workers and delaying the insolvency of the Social Security system by the additional payroll tax receipts.

From the individual's viewpoint, the prospect for forced early retirement is another variable in the retirement planning equation. Many workers leaving high-paying jobs find that jobs paying equivalent salaries are not readily available or require an unplanned relocation if they can be found. This means that plans for further savings in the 10 years or so prior to normal retirement may be disrupted, leaving the individual to face early retirement with less financial resources than he had planned for his normal retirement.

A study of early retirement offers in the Midwest revealed that fewer than 10 percent of workers who were asked to leave received an offer of additional early retirement benefits, and only one-third of the offers containing incentives included any increase in the pension; the rest offered a one-time bonus.

6.6 Integration of Pension Benefits with Social Security

Employers pay a payroll tax to Social Security equal to that deducted from the workers' pay. In recognition of this employer contribution, the law permits employers to take credit for a part of the Social Security benefit, up to 50 percent depending on income level, and to subtract that amount from a defined-benefit pension payout. About half of the professional workers in the United States who are vested in a defined-benefit plan are subject to this

Social Security integration pension reduction. In calculating the benefits available to you in retirement, it is necessary to determine whether you will be subject to this integration, so that you do not count on receiving a higher total of pension and Social Security income than you will actually receive.

6.7 Source Taxation

About a dozen states that impose income taxes on workers within the state also have a statute that permits them to tax pension income (considered as deferred compensation earned in the state) even when the pensioner has moved away from the state. In planning any relocation for your retirement years, you should be aware that you could have dual state taxation on your pension if both your old state and your new state impose income taxes. If you move from a source tax state, such as California, to a state without an income tax, such as Texas or Florida, you may owe tax on your pension income to the source tax state even though your new state of domicile does not impose income taxes. After several attempts over the years, a bill to outlaw source taxes was finally signed into law early in 1996.

6.8 Type of Pension Plan

While the historic pension plans have been of the defined-benefit type, which require the employer to take action necessary to ensure that the promised benefit is delivered, these have been supplemented and in some cases replaced by defined-contribution plans, as described in Section 2.2. These plans put all the responsibility for achieving investment performance that is needed to embark on a financially comfortable retirement on the employee.

6.9 Preserving Pension Assets

There is an attraction, when changing jobs, to taking the proceeds of the 401(k) or profit-sharing plan, paying the tax and penalty for early withdrawal, and using the remainder to fund moving expenses, to make a down payment on a new house, or to fund the children's college education. This exchanges a long-term benefit, the opportunity for tax-deferred growth of retirement funds, for an immediate problem solution. Once tax-deferred funds are cashed in, they cannot be replaced in the same tax-advantaged status. It is far better to take out a short-term loan to fund moving or education expenses than it is to cash in retirement funds. While such loans, under present tax law, are not tax deductible unless in the form of a home mortgage (home equity loan), the tax-deferred growth of the undisturbed retirement plan assets offsets the cost of the loan until the loan is paid off, and can still be extended further in the future. None of this is possible if the retirement funds are diverted to solve present needs for funds.

6.10 Perils in Transferring Defined-Contribution Funds

Many workers terminating employment find that they have a sizable nest egg in the tax-deferred 401(k) or similar plan to which they have contributed during their employment. These funds should be preserved for retirement and transferred to the next employer's account for the worker or to the worker's IRA. Because of a 1990 change in law, this transfer must be made very carefully if an immediate tax liability is to be avoided. While an individual can transfer funds from one IRA account to another, can receive a check payable to himself to do this, and has 60 days in which to complete the transaction without penalty, transfers from employer accounts do not have this latitude.

Trustee-to-trustee transfers are required in moving funds from an employer account to an IRA. The IRA must be established first and the check made payable to the trustee of the IRA, not to the individual even if the IRA, once established, is to be self-managed by the individual. Failure to follow this procedure subjects the transferred proceeds to 20 percent withholding. If the beneficiary of the account is under 59 1/2 years old, there is an additional deduction of a 10 percent penalty on the amount of the withholding.

While the IRA owner can borrow funds to replace the amount of the withholding, then file for refund of the amount withheld on his next income tax return, many of these 401(k) accounts contain six-figure amounts and the withholding could amount to $25,000–$50,000 or more. Clearly, careful planning of such a transfer to avoid the withholding is an essential strategy in preserving the retirement assets while avoiding unnecessary interest expense and penalties.

All financial institutions are familiar with the details of the requirements for funds transfer and have the information the account holder needs. Ironically, while this cumbersome process was the result of a change in law to provide additional tax revenue to fund an extension of unemployment insurance eligibility, tax revenue is generated only from transfers by those who are uninformed of the consequences of using the wrong procedure.

7.0 FUTURE OUTLOOK

While today's retirees are financially more comfortable than any previous generation, owing in part to increases in real estate values as baby boomers increased the demand for housing and in part to liberalized Social Security benefits, there are indications that future retirees will have to begin planning and saving much earlier for their retirement as demographics change and as the trend to defined-contribution retirement plans and away from defined-benefit retirement plans continues, making the individual more responsible than ever before for investment performance to fund his retirement. In this concluding section we look at the structural problems surrounding some of the issues facing retirees in the future and summarize the advance planning required to ensure a comfortable retirement.

7.1 Social Security

While the Social Security Act was characterized as Old Age Insurance when it became law in 1935, it is not an insurance system in the sense that each worker's account covers payments to that worker in retirement. Rather, it is a system of transfer payments in which contributions by younger workers fund the retirement benefits paid out to older workers.

The system was expanded several times, to provide supplemental benefits for dependents of retired workers for surviving dependents in case of death (1939), to increase the number of workers covered and to expand benefits by 77 percent concurrent with the first tax increase (1950), to add disability insurance for workers (1956), to permit early retirement at age 62 with reduced benefits (1956 for women, 1961 for men), to add Medicare for those over age 65 (1965), to add annual cost of living increases (1972), and to add the Supplemental Security Income program replacing other programs for the needy elderly, blind, and disabled (1974).

By 1977 the Social Security system was in financial trouble, causing the benefit formula to be revised and taxes to be increased significantly (1977) and disability benefits to be reduced (1980). In 1983 the retirement age for full benefits was adjusted upward from 65 to 67, starting after the year 2000 and, for the first time, income tax was levied on half the benefits of retirees with relatively high incomes. In 1994, the tax levy was extended to 85 percent of the benefits of higher-income recipients.

While the system operates on a pay-as-you-go basis, funds received in excess of current needs are recorded in three "trust funds," for Old Age and Survivors Insurance (OASI), disability insurance (DI), and Medicare's hospital insurance (HI). These funds are lent to the government through special-obligation U.S. Treasury bonds until required. In 1981, Congress permitted the three trust funds to borrow from each other in the event of a deficit. Projections indicate that the HI fund will be in deficit before 2000 and the OASI fund (Social Security) will start running a deficit no later than 2010.

More than 95 percent of all working Americans are covered by Social Security. For most, their Social Security taxes are larger than their income taxes. Retirees get back all their own contributions to Social Security in three or four years and then receive others' contributions for the remainder of their lifetime. The very first recipient of Social Security, a woman who received benefits starting in 1940, had paid $22 into the system and received benefits totaling $20,000 before her death at age 99.

Seventy percent of all workers start collecting Social Security benefits before age 65. The maximum worker's benefit at age 65 is about $1000 per month for a worker paying the $34,000 maximum earnings tax over the working lifetime. A nonworking spouse is entitled to a 50 percent benefit at age 65, stepping up to 100 percent on the death of the working spouse. The benefit is reduced by 20 percent if started at age 62; this age will increase as the age for full retirement increases.

Problems with funding of the Social Security system include the growing number of recipients, their longer lifetimes, and the reduced number of workers contributing to the system. Now, 31 million people, 12 percent of the U.S. population, are age 65 or older. By the year 2025, 60 million people, 19 percent of the U.S. population, will fall into that category. Life expectancy at birth for a male born in 1910 was 48.6 years; by 1920 it was 54.6 years, and by 1930 59.7 years. By 1990, life expectancy for men at age 65 had increased to 16 years; for women to 19.2 years. In 1989, there were 3.4 workers contributing to the system for every retiree. By 2010, there will be 3.0 workers, and by 2030 only 2.0 workers per retiree, based on current projections.

On a pay-as-you-go basis, the payroll tax for Social Security and Medicare would have to grow to 22.2 percent by 2060, nearly a 50 percent increase over today's rate, to keep the system solvent.[12] There may be intergenerational conflict, as the young workers object to the burden placed on them to fund the retirement of their elders. While the Social Security trust funds will grow from $1 trillion in 2000 to $12 trillion by 2030, by 2025 payouts will be running at $3.5 trillion per year, and will have exceeded income since 2010. Drawing on the trust funds requires that the Treasury have the funds to redeem the special-issue bonds that trust funds are invested in. However, unless the government budget has a surplus, there will be no funds with which to redeem these bonds.

Older baby boomers will probably receive their Social Security, but younger baby boomers may not. As the pressure builds to reduce Social Security payouts after 2010, the retirement age will likely increase further, all benefits will become taxable, and a means test may be applied to limit full payouts to those who have made the least provisions for their own retirement. The succeeding Generation X baby busters should not count on receiving the full amount of Social Security payments, as currently projected, for their retirement.

Various proposals have been offered to permit individuals to partly opt out of Social Security, either by receiving income tax credit for the tax paid to fund Social Security, and putting the resulting tax savings in their IRA, or by splitting the system into two components, a transfer payment component that everyone eligible would receive and an annuity component, with the amount of the benefit keyed to the previous salary history level of the annuitant. The latter approach is followed by some European countries.[13] Neither approach seems likely to solve the serious underfunding problem that will emerge by 2030.

7.2 Other Government-Sponsored Retirement Plans

The U.S. government has two trust funds set up to cover 7 million civil service and military workers' retirement costs. Federal government pensions do include some Cost of Living Adjustments (COLAs), typically providing adjustments lower than the increase in the Consumer Price Index, so that these retirees have some inflation protection in retirement that most retirees in the commercial sector lack. As with Social Security, these trust funds operate on a "pay-as-you-go" basis and are now underfunded by more than $1 trillion. The shortfall is growing by 2.2 percent per year, from $1.32 trillion in 1988 to $1.44 trillion in 1992.

By 2010, money needed to fund the annual benefit payments to federal retirees will nearly triple from current levels, to $160 billion per year. The liability is growing faster than funds are being set aside. Perhaps for this reason, civil service workers in lower grades are not being offered early retirement incentives as a part of the downsizing initiative under the reinventing government program.

The older Civil Service Retirement System did not have a tie-in to Social Security and did not require employees to contribute additional funds to their own retirement. The newer Federal Employee Retirement System is coupled to Social Security and requires employee contributions to reach an acceptable pension income level. Members of the military are being offered "early-out" incentives consisting of bonuses linked to length of service to help in the force reductions made necessary by the collapse of the Soviet Union and the end of the Cold War.

Some of the best federal pensions are reserved for members of Congress. The average lifetime pension for a former member of the House of Representatives is $1.5 million; for a senator it is $2.0 million.

Over half of the states have underfunded pension plans for state employees. For 28 states the underfunding amounts to $55 billion. A dozen states are more than 25 percent underfunded. The largest underfundings are in West Virginia, Maine, Louisiana, Oklahoma, Indiana, Connecticut, Illinois, and Michigan in order, from largest to least underfunding.

7.3 Pressure on Pensions from Health Care Costs

Rising health care costs, by consuming an ever-increasing share of the corporate benefits budget, are also impacting pensions. The Financial Standards Accounting Board in its Rule 106 directed that employers providing retiree health insurance have to account for the lifetime costs up-front on an accrual basis, rather than using pay-as-you-go accounting. This accounting change reduced U.S. company profits by a total estimated by the General Accounting Office at $412 billion. The effect was most severe in the automobile and steel industries, where there are more retirees than current employees. This accounting change amounted to a one-time charge for General Motors of $20.8 billion and reduced its net worth by more than 80 percent.

The cost of providing health benefits to retired workers rose 11 percent in 1992, to an average $2760 per person per year, based on a poll of nearly 2500 employers.[14] The number of employers providing health benefits to retirees eligible for Medicare has fallen 20 percent in five years, to 46 percent of employers in 1992. Even fewer provide any health benefits to retirees before age 65. More than 90 percent of employers with retiree health benefits provide prescription drug coverage, but only 31 percent cover dental care and less than 20 percent cover vision care. All three coverages are part of many corporate active employee health benefit plans. Government plans may provide active employees with minimal dental care and discounted, rather than covered, vision care, through a referral network.

The health care reform proposal by the administration in 1993 included a payroll tax of 7.9 percent for all employers of 75 or more workers to fund health insurance premiums. This employer "mandate" has become the most hotly contested provision in the debate on alternative health care plans. Where this tax is more than the current health insurance cost paid by employers, it will, if included in the bill finally enacted into law, put pressure on salary levels and on other benefits to contain the employers' overall labor cost. There will be further incentive to reduce pension costs, resulting in further terminations of generous pension plans, to be replaced by less expensive plans or by no plans at all.

7.4 Personal Savings and Investment Planning

The worker entering the work force today is expected to have eight jobs during his career. Pensions will have changed from "golden handcuffs," that formerly ensured that a worker would spend his entire career working for the same company, to simply deferred compensation that the individual worker must be proactive in managing as it accumulates so that his retirement income will be adequate when it is required.

The trend in pension plans is away from defined benefit and toward defined contribution. The PBGC insured 120,000 defined-benefit plans in 1974 compared to 85,000 today. The reason is the greater cost to employers of the defined-benefit plans, especially for older workers. On average, the cost is at least 6 percent of payroll. In a 401(k) defined-contribution plan, the employer may match half of the first 6 percent of the employees' contributions, limiting the company exposure to 3 percent of payroll if all employees participate.

The trend toward defined-contribution plans and away from defined-benefit pension plans will put increasing responsibility on the individual to manage his retirement assets so that the growth needed for a comfortable retirement can be attained. Individuals will have to become savvy investors, rather than putting their retirement funds in CDs or GICs, especially when interest rates are very low. In 1993, when low interest rates caused many homeowners to refinance their mortgages, retirees unhappy with 3 or 4 percent returns moved their funds into riskier investments, such as mutual funds. The influx of new money into these funds bid up stocks so that the average U.S. stock fund gained 12.54 percent for the year, compared with the 10.06 percent total return of the S&P 500 with dividends. The average foreign stock fund grew 39.4 percent, while even low-risk utility funds achieved returns of 13.13 percent for the year.[15]

Recent studies cited in congressional testimony cast doubt on the ability of baby boomers to fund their retirements, based on their low savings rates and the lack of a windfall in the form of increased values from home ownership such as were experienced by their parents. Savings rates in the United States have long been below 5 percent, compared with double digits in Europe and Japan. One study at Princeton University[16] concluded that it will be necessary for the boomers on average to sharply reduce present consumption and at least triple their savings rate, if there will be a pension, or quadruple it if there will be no pension, to accumulate adequate funds to provide retirement security. A married boomer couple with $75,000 earnings, for example, would need to save the percentages shown during each age decade of their working career to stay on track for retirement:

Table 5.3 Savings as a Percentage of After-Tax Earned Income Needed for Retirement, per Decade

Age Group	25–34	35–44	45–54	55–64
With pension	1.7%	8.9%	19.5%	17.1%
With no pension	8.2%	14.1%	23.1%	20.9%

It can be seen that the savings rate for this income level peaks at 19.5 percent of after-tax income during the age 45–54 decade for retirement even if there will be a pension, or 23.1 percent if no pension. While savings rates this high are found in Japan, they are very rare in the United States. The Princeton study found that, if retirees are to maintain the same life-style as they had before retirement, total retirement savings at age 65 should fall between 2.5 and 6 times the annual household earnings before retirement, if the primary earner is covered by a pension plan, or 4 to 8 times earnings, if there is no pension.

Strategies for improvement now to permit a more comfortable retirement later include supporting pension portability legislation (to gain control of your previously earned pension funds in time to grow them further before they are needed), maximizing contributions to salary reduction plans where available, and contributing to an IRA. All these are tax-deferred investments, where growth typically will be 50 percent higher than if taxes were paid each year on the annual gain in value. Thus, the compounded growth will also leverage on the (unpaid) tax component. Even when the initial contribution to an IRA is not tax deductible under current law, because of the income level and pension plan eligibility of the taxpayer, investing after-tax dollars each year is still a good strategy if the funds have 5 to 10 years to grow, tax-deferred. Likewise, if the discrimination tests for your company-sponsored salary reduction plan limit the amount that you can contribute pretax, as a "highly compensated employee" it is still valuable to contribute any excess amount up to the legal maximum as posttax dollars, since all growth is tax deferred. At this point, you typically will be saving 15 percent of income plus $2000 per working spouse in your tax-deferred plans. If self-employed, you can have a defined-benefit Keogh plan tailored for you to put away up to half your earnings in a tax-deferred pension account.

If you have still further funds available to devote to retirement, tax-deferred fixed or variable annuities permit pretax investments of any size, with taxes paid on growth only as the funds are withdrawn, usually in retirement. There are usually penalties in annuities for early withdrawal, so these should be funds that can be left alone for at least five to seven years. By investing in equities, variable annuities have achieved higher rates of return than have fixed annuities, thus providing a greater inflation hedge. The same idea applies to funds in a 401(k) or IRA: returns from an investment in the Standard & Poor's Index of 500 stocks provides returns about double those from corporate and government bonds over a period of 10 years or more.

Retirement planning is the individual's own responsibility. This has always been true, but is even more important today as the complexity of retirement taxation compounds with the problems of achieving necessary investment performance. A long-standing truism, that the purchase of a home is the largest financial transaction the average person will ever have, is being overtaken by the size and importance of tax-deferred retirement accounts. Today, the transfer of a 401(k) account, where the individual has taken the maximum salary reduction for the life of the program, is likely to be the individual's largest financial transaction.

8.0 RESOURCES

1. Merrill Lynch, "Retirement Builder—Guidebook to Planning Financial Security," April 1991, complimentary.
2. Aetna Life Insurance and Annuity Company, "Retirement Made Easy or... What to Do If Uncle Winthrop Doesn't Leave You $50 Million," complimentary. Request from Aetna, RW1F, 151 Farmington Avenue, Hartford, CT 06156; telephone 203-273-0123.
3. Fidelity Investments. "Common Sense Guide to Planning for Retirement," complimentary; telephone 800-544-8888. "Retirement Planning Guide," complimentary; diskette, "Fidelity Retirement Planning

Thinkware," for PC and compatibles only, $17.50; order these two items from 800-457-1768.

4. T. Rowe Price, "Retirement Planning Kit," 1989 (paper), complimentary, call 800-541-5142. PC Version 1.1 (not available for Macintosh) is $15.00. Call 800-541-4005 to order. Other complimentary publications also available from T. Rowe Price, 100 East Pratt Street, Baltimore, MD 21298-6581:

"IRA Planning Kit"

"Deciding What to Do with Your Company Retirement Money"

"Retirees Financial Guide"

"Asset Mix Worksheet"

"SEP-IRA Kit"

"Profit Sharing and Money Purchase Plan Information"

5. Charles Schwab, "The Charles Schwab Guide to Maximizing Your Retirement Plan Distribution," complimentary. 101 Montgomery Street, San Francisco, CA 94104; telephone 800-526-8600.

6. IEEE Financial Advantage Program, including Chase Manhattan Vista funds, with normal 4.75 percent sales charge waived for IEEE members and holders of shares in the IEEE Balanced Fund. For information, call 800-GET-IEEE (800-438-4333).

7. IEEE Annuity Investment Program, contact Seabury & Smith, 800-829-8763.

8. "The Retirement Planning Projector," shareware disk #1875 from PC-SIG, 1030D East Duane Avenue, Sunnyvale, CA 94086; telephone 408-730-9291. Features templates (living expenses and investment performance) for Lotus 1-2-3 and 23-page text file user's manual; runs on PC-compatibles.

ENDNOTES

1. Gallup Poll conducted for the Employee Benefits Research Institute, Washington, D.C.

2. Donna S. Carpenter, *The Price Waterhouse Retirement Planning Adviser* (New York: Pocket Books, 1992).

3. American Association of Individual Investors, 625 N. Michigan Avenue, Chicago, IL 60611, publishes the monthly *AAII Journal*, the bimonthly *Computerized Investing*, and other publications, including *The Individual Investor's Guide to Computerized Investing, The Individual Investor's Guide to No-Load Mutual Funds, Quarterly No-Load Mutual Fund Update, Investment Home Study course, Investing Fundamentals Videocourse, Mutual Funds Videocourse*, and *AAII Stock Investor*. It has 58 local chapters

around the United States that present speakers at monthly meetings and arrange annual educational conferences featuring investment topics for subscribers.

4. Morningstar, *Morningstar Mutual Funds,* 225 W. Wacker Drive, Chicago, IL 60606, 800-876-5005. Subscription: $395 per year.

5. "Retirement Quick Monitor" calculates additional savings needed to retire, given retirement income, expenses, and present savings. Three shareware programs, available from Public Brand Software, P.O. Box 51315, Indianapolis, IN 46251; telephone orders: 800-426-3475.

6. IEEE-USA, 1828 L Street, NW, Suite 1202, Washington, DC 20036; telephone 202-785-0017.

7. Dow Jones Information Services, Princeton, NJ; telephone 800-522-3567, ext. 264. In New Jersey, telephone 609-520-8349, ext. 264. America Online, 8619 Westwood Center Drive, Vienna, VA 22182-2285; telephone 800-827-6364.

8. For a good, understandable discussion of the relation between interest rates and bond prices, see Burton Crane, *The Sophisticated Investor* (New York: Simon & Schuster, 1963).

9. Morningstar, *Morningstar Mutual Funds.*

10. "The Sky Isn't Falling," *Financial World,* January 18, 1994.

11. Charles Handy, *The Age of Unreason* (Boston: Harvard Business School Press, 1991).

12. Dorcas R. Hardy, *Social Insecurity: The Crisis in America's Social Security System and How to Plan Now for Your Own Financial Survival* (New York: Villard Books, 1991).

13. Michael J. Boskin, *Too Many Promises: The Uncertain Future of Social Security,* A Twentieth Century Fund Report (Homewood, IL: Dow Jones-Irwin, 1986).

14. Survey by Foster Higgins, New York, released December 6, 1993.

15. "Mutual Fund Gains Put Investors on Top of the World," year-end survey, *The Wall Street Journal,* January 7, 1994.

16. B. Douglas Bernheim, "Is the Baby Boom Preparing Adequately for Retirement? Summary Report," Princeton University, Princeton, New Jersey, January 15, 1993 (prepared for Merrill Lynch & Co., Inc.).

PART 2 ENGINEERING AND THE LAW

6

Professional Engineering Licensure and Registration

Robert W. McClure and Richard A. Schwarz

1.0 INTRODUCTION TO LICENSURE

The Tenth Amendment to the Constitution empowers the states to grant licenses for the practice of engineering within their borders. The only federal restriction is that they observe the provisions of the Americans with Disabilities Act.

The rationale for regulation of the practice of engineering is expressed in the preamble of the engineering registration act for the state of Delaware.

> WHEREAS, because the field of engineering is highly technical and complex and the recipients of professional engineering services do not normally have adequate expertise by which they might be able to evaluate the services rendered by a professional engineer; and
> WHEREAS, because of these complexities, the qualifications of a professional engineer should be established and evaluated by other engineers; and
> WHEREAS, it is in the best interests of the public property, health, safety, and welfare that the evaluation of an engineer and the control of the practice of engineering be vested in members of the engineering profession; and ...

The form of the registration act varies among the states, but over the 1970s and 1980s a commonality of requirement for demonstrating competence has evolved. There are no formal reciprocal licensing arrangements, but there is a similarity in the licensing requirements by individual states that facilitates licensing in another state once an engineer has been licensed in their first (home) state. This action of becoming licensed in other states is called *comity*. States may have special requirements for licensing that reflect conditions unique to the state. For example, California requires an in-depth knowledge of earthquake's lateral forces for its structural engineers license.

The practice of engineering is complex. The general public cannot evaluate either the competence of engineering proposals or that of the engineers offering the proposals. The state licensure laws are enacted to protect the interests of the public by reserving the title "Engineer" or in some states "Professional Engineer" to those individuals who have met the state's requirements; that is, those individuals who have demonstrated to the state that they can practice engineering safely in the interest of the public. Registration boards are required by law to police the use of these titles.

Anyone is eligible for licensing if they can demonstrate to a state board that they possess "minimum competence", where minimum competence is defined as the ability to practice engineering in a manner which will protect the safety, health, welfare, and interests of the public.

2.0 PROFESSIONAL REGISTRATION IN THE UNITED STATES

2.1 Background[1]

Wyoming was the first state to regulate the engineering profession. It passed an engineering registration law in 1907 and established the Wyoming Board of Engineering Examiners. Seven state boards founded the Council of State Boards of Engineering Examiners (CSBEE) in 1920 primarily to address the issue of comity, that is, licensure from state to state. The following year, the CSBEE proposed a "model law," addressing the issue of national uniform licensing for engineers. National was added to the Council's name in 1925. During the 1920s additional states joined the Council. The National Council of State Boards of Engineering Examiners (NCSBEE) was incorporated in South Carolina in 1938 with 40 state boards as members and with 60,000 registered engineers. By 1948, the 48 states plus Alaska, Hawaii, and Puerto Rico constituted the Council. These boards reported 125,000 registrants.

The National Bureau of Engineering Registration (NBER) and the Engineers Council for Professional Development (ECPD) were established in 1932 as committees of NCSBEE. The function of the NBER was to establish and formalize the qualifications for licensing to practice engineering, while that of the ECPD was to set standards for accreditation and to evaluate and accredit the curricula of engineering colleges that met these standards.

By 1937, 107 schools had been accredited. The ECPD was renamed the Accreditation Board for Engineering and Technology (ABET). The ABET is currently performing engineering college curricula accreditations.

The model law was revised in 1943 to incorporate the concept of "engineer-in-training." In 1949 the engineer-in-training (EIT) exam was 8 hours, with 50 to 70 percent of the material devoted to common basic subject matter, such as math, chemistry, physics, and engineering.

In 1958, the First International Conference on Engineering Registration Organization was held in New York City. A major revision to the model law eliminated the eminence clause, and the grandfather clause added provisions for corporate licensure and exemptions for utility employees.

A national EIT exam was first administered in 1965. During fall 1966 and spring 1967, 24 state boards administered the first national uniform Principles and Practice of Engineering (P&PE) examinations in chemical, civil, electrical, and mechanical engineering. These four disciplines are currently the subjects of the four major examinations known as the "P.E. exam." In 1967, the acceptance of the national uniform exam(s) along with the revised (early 1960s) model law established the basis for making comity a reality. The Council's name was shortened to the National Council for Engineering Examiners (NCEE). The NBER Committee became the Committee on Engineering Registration (CER). A national certification program was begun by NCEE in 1970. Several issues were addressed by including mandatory continued professional development and limited (industrial) exemptions.

By 1988, all 50 states and 5 territories were utilizing the national exams. The "model law" that had evolved over the years is used in most states to guide legislatures writing laws concerning fundamental requirements for registration such as education, experience, and examination. Universal comity has become a reality—a remarkable feat considering how diverse the states are, each with its own individual needs and each very protective of its authority.

In 1989, the Council name was changed to NCEES, National Council of Examiners for Engineering and Surveying. The Council Headquarters are in Clemson, South Carolina. Despite the efforts of the NCEES, only about one-third of the engineers in the United States are registered.

3.0 PRESENT REGISTRATION MODELS

3.1 The U.S. Model

The registration process in the United States is similar, but not identical, in all 50 states and 5 licensing jurisdictions.

3.1.1 Education   In many states, four years of acceptable practice are required instead of six or more years, for graduates of engineering colleges whose programs are ABET accredited. There are a few states that will only license graduates of ABET accredited programs. However, most states still allow the four year educational requirement to be met by non-ABET accredited programs, by engineering technology programs, and/or by related science programs. A few states do not require a degree. These states allow substitution of additional years of experience for the educational requirement.

3.1.2 Examinations   Most states require 16 hours of examination, 8 hours of the Fundamentals of Engineering (FE), which can be taken shortly after graduation or during the senior year, and 8 hours of the Principles and Practice of Engineering (P&PE), which cannot be taken until all experience in the Practice of Engineering requirement has been met. All states offer exactly the same examinations on exactly the same days. The FE examination and the most commonly requested P&PE examinations are offered in April and October of each year. The less commonly requested P&PE examinations are offered only in October of each year. The FE and P&PE examinations are prepared by and scored by the NCEES.

The *FE examination* is designed to assess an engineering program graduate's competence in general and discipline-specific knowledge, skills, and abilities. About 50 percent of the examination content is common to all disciplines and 50 percent specific to the discipline-selected by the candidate. Passing the FE examination permits a candidate to use the title "engineer-intern" (E.I.) in most states.

The *P&PE examination* is designed to assess an engineer-intern's competence in the practice of engineering. It is a discipline-specific examination to evaluate the knowledge, skills, and abilities gained during the first few years of practice. All states give the same set of P&PE examinations. Most states offer P&PE examinations twice per year in

Chemical engineering
Civil engineering
Electrical engineering
Environmental engineering
Mechanical engineering
Structural engineering

and offer more specialized P&PE examinations once per year in

Aeronautical/aerospace engineering
Agricultural engineering
Control systems engineering
Fire protection engineering
Industrial engineering
Manufacturing engineering
Metallurgical engineering
Mining/mineral engineering
Nuclear engineering
Petroleum engineering

As with the FE examination, most states accept the results of the P&PE examination taken in another state as equivalent to passing it in their state.

Many states also require some form of locally prepared examination covering state-specific statutes governing the practice of engineering in that state, and in some cases, an examination on the ethical practice of engineering.

3.1.3 Experience   State laws often define the "practice of engineering." The following definition is taken from the NCEES model law:

The term, Practice of Engineering, within the intent of this Act, shall mean any service or creative work, the adequate performance of which requires engineering education, training, and experience in the application of special knowledge of the mathematical, physical, and engineering sciences to such services or creative work as consultation, investigation, evaluation, planning, and design of engineering works and systems, planning the use of land and water, teaching of advanced engineering subjects, engineering surveys and studies, and the review of construction for the purpose of assuring compliance with drawings and specifications; any of which embraces such services or work either public or private, in connection with any utilities, structures, buildings, machines, equipment, processes work systems, projects, and industrial or consumer products or equipment of a mechanical electrical, hydraulic, pneumatic, or thermal nature, insofar as they involve safeguarding life, health, or property, and including such other professional services as may be necessary to the planning, progress, and completion of any engineering services.

Engineering surveys include all survey activities required to support the sound conception, planning design, construction, maintenance, and operation of engineered projects, but exclude the surveying of real property for the establishment of land boundaries, rights-of-way, easements, and the dependent or independent surveys or resurveys of the public land survey system.

A person shall be construed to practice or offer to practice engineering, within the meaning and intent of this Act, who practices any branch of the profession of engineering; or who, by verbal claim, sign, advertisement, letterhead, card, or in any other way represent themselves to be a professional engineer, or through the use of some other title implies that they are a professional engineer or that they are registered under this Act, or who hold themselves out as able to perform, or who does perform any engineering service or work or any other service designated by the practitioner which is recognized as engineering.

The minimum engineering experience, often as an engineer-intern, required for licensure is four years in the practice of engineering. Some registration boards require this to be under the supervision of a licensed engineer and/or that it demonstrates progressive assignments in responsibility and degree of difficulty. The evaluation of a candidate's description of his practice of engineering is made by members of the registration board who practice in the area claimed by the candidate. Thus, "acceptable to the board," although subjective, is the result of expert opinions by engineers practicing in the area involved. Most boards permit a candidate to appeal the decision of the experience review committee.

3.2 Canadian Model

The Canadian model differs from the U.S. model in that much more reliance is placed on the educational process. Graduates of engineering colleges whose programs are accredited by the Canadian Engineering Accreditation

Board (CEAB) are granted a license after acquiring two years of experience and passing an examination in business law and ethics. The North American Free Trade Association (NAFTA) agreement requires that each country treat foreign applicants exactly as it treats native applicants. These differences are being discussed by the Canadian Council of Registration Boards and the U.S. National Council of Examiners for Engineering and Surveying. At this time there has been little progress in accommodating the two approaches. U.S. border states offer examinations at convenient locations for Canadians who elect to meet their state registration requirements. Some states will also accept the education of a Canadian applicant who graduated from a program accredited by the CEAB as equivalent to the education received by a graduate of an ABET accredited program.

3.3 The Mexican Model

The Mexican model is in a state of flux. There are ongoing discussions between the Mexican organizations and their U.S. counterparts. The United States is proposing that Mexico adopt a model similar to the U.S. model, using the same examinations prepared and scored by NCEES and instituting an educational program accreditation process similar to that used in the United States.

4.0 ORGANIZATIONAL INVOLVEMENT

Many organizations have an active interest in the registration and licensing of engineers. They are briefly described along with their participating activity in the following.

4.1 National Council of Examiners for Engineering and Surveying

The NCEES members are representatives from the registration boards of the 50 states and the 5 U.S. territories. Its chief function is to prepare and grade the engineering and surveying examinations required for state licensure in engineering and surveying. NCEES is involved in many other areas such as comity (reciprocity requirements), continuing professional competency, international trade agreements, uniform laws, communicating with the engineering profession as well as the general public, engineering education, and so on.

The NCEES provides model laws to state legislatures for guidance in reviewing and rewriting state laws with a goal of all states having similar requirements. The NCEES also has a records verification program in place to aid comity applicants. This program keeps a master file and serves as a clearinghouse for educational transcripts, base state registration(s), references, and employment history. In most cases, the council record provides the necessary background information required by registration boards.

The NCEES is working with the states to achieve uniformity of requirements for continuing professional competency. Some states already have laws in place or are seeking legislation establishing requirements for and evaluation of continuing professional competency. NCEES is an active member of the United States Council for International Engineering Practice (USCIEP). In this capacity, it promotes the establishment and adoption of uniform registration laws and procedures internationally. To date, the USCIEP has met with Canadian and Mexican officials.

4.2 Accreditation Board for Engineering and Technology

ABET, established in 1932, was formerly called the Engineering Council for Professional Development (ECPD). It is a federation of 27 engineering professional technical societies that represent more than 1.8 million engineers. ABET's function is to evaluate the curricula of engineering colleges and to accredit those colleges whose programs meet established standards.

An engineering degree granted to an alumnus of an accredited college is a valuable asset. Some states will not license an individual who did not graduate from a college with an ABET accredited program. Most states require additional years of experience from graduates of nonaccredited programs.

ABET officers are elected from and by a board of directors. The directors are nominated by a group of participating societies. Discipline-specific programs are reviewed by and accreditation action is recommended by three committees, called commissions. These are the Engineering Accreditation Commission (EAC), the Technology Accreditation Commission (TAC), and the Related (science) Accreditation Commission (RAC).

Program accreditation is for a finite period of time. The present maximum period is six years, with many programs receiving accreditation for only three years based on deficiencies uncovered during the evaluation. The academic institutions request accreditation and pay for the costs associated with the accreditation process. Program evaluations are by experts in the particular discipline. Program evaluators are unpaid volunteers. They are trained by the society they represent. The evaluators spend about a person-week preparing for an on-campus visit, two days conducting interviews on campus, and another week writing up and reviewing their visit report. There is concern within ABET that the amount of volunteer time required restricts the number of volunteers, especially those from industry, and some steps are being considered that may reduce these time demands. Visitors generally review over 100 programs each year. Most visits occur in the fall. Final accreditation recommendations are made by the EAC of ABET in July of the following year to the president of ABET who notifies the institutions shortly thereafter.

4.3 Engineering Societies

Engineering societies are members of ABET, and they participate in the establishment of standards for accreditation of their discipline in engineering college programs. They train and provide volunteers to visit and evaluate these programs. The societies encourage their members to become licensed. Many of them have committees whose only concern is licensing and registration. Several of these societies have issued policy or position statements.

4.3.1 Institute of Electrical and Electronics Engineers[2]   The IEEE encourages its members to become licensed engineers. The Licensure and Registration Committee of the United States Activities Board meets twice a year to review registration and other related professional matters. The Committee contributes to the preparation of examinations and monitors examination performance. The Committee has developed an Entity Position Statement on licensing and registration which was approved by the IEEE United States Activities Board. The following is quoted from that statement.

> We strongly encourage individuals to pursue licensure and registration, not only as a means of meeting legal requirements for protecting the health, welfare, and safety of the public, but also to ensure that they can be prepared to meet the needs of international, national, and state engineering practices.

4.3.2 National Society of Professional Engineers   The NSPE is a national organization with branch organizations in each state. The state branches lobby their respective state governments and the national organization which maintains a presence in Washington, DC, interacts to represent their interest with the federal government. State registration laws are strongly influenced by the local branches of NSPE. The following is quoted from the 1993 – 1994 NSPE Policies and Procedures.

1. Engineering Registration
"Registration as a professional engineer" is the statutory process through which a person meets the legal requirements sufficient to be permitted by law to practice engineering in that jurisdiction. Licensing and registration are the terms used, often interchangeably, in the state statutes to establish these requirements.

State registration laws for design professionals are predicated upon and justified only as a means to protect the public health, safety and welfare. The public interest is best served by the registration of all qualified individuals within the engineering profession.

4.3.3 American Society of Mechanical Engineers The following is quoted from the ASME Policy on Professional Engineers Registration, paragraph II.

The American Society of Mechanical Engineers endorses registration as being in the best interest of the public and the profession. The American Society of Mechanical Engineers recognizes that the licensed or registered engineer should be identified by the P.E. abbreviated title after his or her name and acknowledges that identification is in the public and professional interest. The awareness by the public and by the engineering community engendered by registration and licensing will enhance engineering as a single and noble profession.

4.3.4 American Society of Civil Engineers The following is quoted from the ASCE Policy Statement on the Registration of Engineers.

The American Society of Civil Engineers (ASCE) strongly supports efforts to protect the public health, safety and welfare through the competent practice of engineering, through professional registration. ASCE strongly endorses lifelong learning and continuing professional development as requisites for continued competence in the practice of civil engineering.

4.3.5 American Institute of Chemical Engineers The AIChE Code of Ethics & Institute Policies has a section which addresses individual registration. An excerpt from that section reads

. . . Registration is one avenue to define an engineer's level of competence, and it does provide assurance to the public that those with the title "Registered Professional Engineer" or "Licensed Professional Engineer" have met certain minimum requirements at one point in their careers.

In consideration of these facts, AIChE recommends that its members become registered in their respective states as soon as possible after entering the profession.

5.0 CURRENT ISSUES IN REGISTRATION

5.1 Recovering Disenfranchised Engineers

Many engineers elect early in their professional career to ignore licensure because their area of employment neither recognizes nor rewards possessing a license. Consideration is presently being given to restructuring the P&PE examination to more specific, subdiscipline areas of practice so that the registration process will be more relevant to their area of practice.

5.2 Government and Industrial Exemption

Exemptions from professional registration are given to individuals working in government and industry. Rationale for these exemptions is being reconsidered by the states. States may follow the lead of Minnesota and not allow any exemptions in the future.

5.3 Professional Ethics

Professional engineers, like medical doctors and lawyers, are granted the right to practice their profession for life. Engineering is a broad profession ranging from the design of bridges to the development of waste treatment processes to the design of electronic traffic control and emergency communications systems. No one expects every engineer to be competent in all areas of practice. In fact, it is left to the individual engineer, through the code of ethics he ascribes to, to determine which engineering tasks he is competent to perform and to only practice in his areas of competence.

Adherence to the code of ethics and the law enforcement function of the state registration boards should minimize abuse; however, infractions by unethical practitioners do occur. Unethical practice may take either of two forms: outright dishonesty or practice in an area outside of one's competence.

The execution of a vigorous and active law enforcement policy by the state boards is clearly the most effective means of policing the profession.

5.4 Continuing Education

Some professions require continued education as a means for assuring continued professional competence. This does not appear to be effective. The selection of the course material is somewhat arbitrary and their applicability to the practitioner in many cases questionable. The IEEE-USA has adopted a position paper that encourages its members to avail themselves of all opportunities to improve themselves and to increase their competence; however, it does not support continuing education as a mandatory requirement for practice as a licensed professional engineer. Enhancement of an individual's capability through continuing education should be the personal choice of each engineer. Competence can be maintained by the experience gained through active professional practice.

In 1994, only Alabama and Iowa had as a legal requirement continuing education for licensed engineers; however, Michigan, Minnesota, Oklahoma, South Dakota, Utah, Vermont, West Virginia, and Wyoming had enabling legislation.

6.0 PERSONAL BENEFITS OF BEING REGISTERED

Individuals who have chosen engineering as a career should have as one of their priority goals the obtaining of a license to practice engineering for the public, to become a professional engineer (P.E.). There are several personal and professional benefits that accrue to a licensed engineer. These benefits are described in the paragraphs that follow.

6.1 Title

Only engineers granted licenses by a state can legally use the title engineer, call themselves P.E., and refer to their services as engineering. This is analogous to the legal use of the term "medical doctor" (M.D.) by state-licensed physicians who practice medicine.

6.2 Certification

Consulting engineers working on projects that affect the public must have P.E.s sign and seal their drawings. Public utilities must submit their plans and drawings to public agencies to receive authorization to proceed. These public agencies require seals and signature by licensed engineers as an indication of the individual's competence to prepare the documents. These agencies do not recognize the engineering baccalaureate, additional education, and even experience as sufficient evidence of competence.

6.3 Career Advancement

A career path may change either voluntarily or involuntarily. An individual's lack of a P.E. license may place limits upon his or her career path. Some routes will be closed. Only P.E.s can consult in private practice. Many utilities and consulting firms require registration as a qualification for management and senior positions. The license to practice provides additional credibility to testimony given by a P.E. as an expert witness in court.

6.4 Personal Credential

A P.E. license is a credential that attests to the competence of the engineer. It commands the respect of fellow engineers, and it demonstrates the pride one has in being an engineer and in committing to the high ethical and personal standards of professional engineers. As previously noted, most technical societies like ASCE, AIChE, IEEE, ASME, NSPE, and others encourage their members to become licensed.

6.5 Job Insurance

State registration boards, at present, grant exemptions to industry and government to the use of the term "Engineer" and allow the practice of engineering by nonlicensed individuals. Most state boards are considering revoking these exemptions in the near future.

7.0 CONCLUDING REMARKS

Physicians need to be licensed to practice. The medical profession is held in high regard because it ensures that only competent practitioners are able to call themselves medical doctors, M.D. Engineering has not exercised that same type of oversight over the individuals who call themselves engineers and the profession suffers for it. Licensure and the use of the title P.E. is a safeguard to the public. The public should be educated to recognize that the P.E., like the M.D., is a title granted to individuals who have committed to practice their profession only in ways that ensure the safety and health of the public. State boards should actively enforce the legal prohibitions of misuse of the title "Engineer" and should revoke all exemptions to licensing for the practice of engineering.

ENDNOTES

1. Oliver B. Curtis, Sr., *The History of the National Council of Engineering Examiners,* private printing, 1988; Library of Congress 88-61899.
2. IEEE-USA Professional Guidelines on Professional Engineering Registration, August 1994.

7

Intellectual Property

Howard L. Rose

The subject of intellectual property rights requires a discussion far greater than can be covered in a single chapter or, in fact, in a single or several volumes. So Chapter 7 will discuss and answer some of the more common questions raised by engineers and scientists and other technical personnel and writers (referred to throughout as "engineers") concerning this area of the law. This chapter, it is hoped, will serve as a road map to direct you to the right place in your consideration of what you may want to do with your idea. Once that is decided, it would be prudent for you to consult a professional knowledgeable in the area.

The first question that must be considered is: What does a patent, trademark, copyright, or mask protect? Briefly, a patent gives the inventor or his or her assignee the exclusive right to make, use, sell, or lease the subject matter of the patent for a period of 17 years. These rights will be discussed in greater detail later in this chapter. A trademark gives the owner the exclusive right to the use of a name, a logo, or both, and a copyright the exclusive right to copies of his or her work. The basis for the patent, trademark, and copyright laws is found in the U.S. Constitution as follows:

Article 1, Section 8, Clause 3: The Congress shall have power ... to regulate commerce with foreign nations, and among the several states, and with the Indian tribes.

Article 1, Section 8, Clause 8: The Congress shall have the power ... to promote the progress of science and useful arts by securing for limited times to authors and inventors the exclusive right to their respective writings and discoveries.

The U.S. Patent and Trademark Office (PTO) examines applications for patents and trademarks and has been established as an office in the Department of Commerce, while administration of copyrights has been assigned to the Library of Congress.

1.0 PATENTS

As stated in the Constitution, inventors have "the exclusive right to their ... discoveries."

The Congress has established an elaborate set of laws, and the PTO has established an equally elaborate set of rules and regulations to determine what is an inventor's "discovery."

The law provides that

Whoever invents or discovers any new and useful process, machine, manufacture or composition of matter, or any new and useful improvement thereon may obtain a patent therefore, subject to the conditions and requirements of this title. (Title 35, U.S. Code)

Note the use of the phrase "whoever invents." As a result, patent applications in the United States must be filed in the name of the inventor(s), whereas in most countries the application can be filed in the name of the assignee.

Pursuant to this just-quoted provision of the law, patents are granted for new and useful improvements in mechanical, electrical, chemical and biochemical categories, and plants and designs. Each of these categories is subdivided into structure and process patents. Thus, we may have a novel drug, for instance, and a novel process for making the drug. Usually, the PTO will not permit both of these inventions to be issued in a single patent and require "division" between the two so that two patents will issue if the requisite requirement for novelty is met independently by both categories of invention.

These requirements result from the fact that the language used by Congress in establishing the patent laws cast the wording in the singular form "new and useful improvement," not "improvements."

Design patents are also available for novel designs of utilitarian products—not artistic endeavors which are covered by copyrights. Design patents are good for 14 years.

Plant patents can be obtained for asexually reproduced plants that are a distinct and new variety of plant. Standard patent terms apply.

The first logical step to be followed by an inventor upon initiating the patent process is to conduct or have conducted a preliminary patentability search. Such a search can be conducted either on a computer with a proper program or in the public search room at the PTO at no entrance fee. The patents are classified by various categories and may be searched by hand. Foreign patents are searched in the patent examining groups, not being available in the search room.

Such a search is not conclusive evidence of patentability since patent copies are missing (5 to 15 percent) from the files in which the search is conducted and some patents are not properly classified and do not appear where the search is conducted. It is estimated that such a search is about 75 percent correct. Raising the percentage to, say, an 85 percent certainty (about the best that can be done) often costs more than preparing the application.

It should be noted, as will be apparent by what follows, that literature should also be searched, a far more difficult task without a computer than searching the patents.

The various provisions of the patent law, however, should be carefully examined both before a decision to initiate the first step in the patenting procedure, a search, and after conclusion of the search to determine if the inventor should continue pursuit of a patent.

The provisions of the law that should be consulted are reproduced in the paragraphs that follow.

35 U.S.C. §102. Conditions for patentability; novelty and loss of right to patent
A person shall be entitled to a patent unless—
(a) the invention was known or used by others in this country, or patented or described in a printed publication in this or a foreign country, before the invention thereof by the applicant for patent, or
(b) the invention was patented or described in a printed publication in this or a foreign country or in public use or on sale in this country, more than one year prior to the date of the application for patent in the United States, or

(c) he has abandoned the invention, or

(d) the invention was first patented or caused to be patented, or was the subject of an inventor's certificate, by the applicant or his legal representatives or assigns in a foreign country prior to the date of the application for patent in this country on an application for patent or inventor's certificate filed more than twelve months before the filing of the application in the United States, or

(e) the invention was described in a patent granted on an application for patent by another filed in the United States before the invention thereof by the applicant for patent, or on an international application by another who has fulfilled the requirements of paragraphs (1), (2), and (4) of Section 371(c) of this title before the invention thereof by the applicant for patent, or

(f) he did not himself invent the subject matter sought to be patented, or

(g) before the applicant's invention thereof the invention was made in this country by another who had not abandoned, suppressed, or concealed it. In determining priority of invention there shall be considered not only the respective dates of conception and reduction to practice of the invention, but also the reasonable diligence of one who was first to conceive and last to reduce to practice, from a time prior to conception by the other. (Amended July 28, 1972, Public Law 92-358, Sec. 2, 86 Stat. 501; November 14, 1975, Public Law 94-131, Sec. 5, 89 Stat. 691.)

35 U.S.C. §103. Conditions for patentability; non-obvious subject matter

A patent may not be obtained though the invention is not identically disclosed or described as set forth in section 102 of this title, if the differences between the subject matter sought to be patented and the prior art are such that the subject matter as a whole would have been obvious at the time the invention was made to a person having ordinary skill in the art to which said subject matter pertains. Patentability shall not be negated by the manner in which the invention was made.

Subject matter developed by another person, which qualifies as prior art only under subsection (f) or (g) of section 102 of this title, shall not preclude patentability under this section where the subject matter and the claimed invention were, at the time the invention was made, owned by the same person or subject to an obligation of assignment to the same person. (Added November 8, 1984, Public Law 8-622, Sec. 103, 98 Stat. 3384.)

Section 102(a) limits knowledge or use by others to this country where such knowledge does not appear in a patent or publication anywhere in the world. Note that this section applies where the events occurred before the person's invention.

Section 102(b) denies a patent if the events described occurred more than one year before the filing of a patent application in the United States.

By treaty, to be described, the U.S. filing date may in fact be the filing date in another country so long as the filing abroad occurred a year or less before the prohibiting event.

The public use must be in this country and must be "on sale." The "on sale" term has been interpreted to cover solicitation of orders even though the product has not been completed. The law on this subject is complex, but stated simply, if the development of the product has proceeded to the point where it is almost complete and it is known that it can be completed in a reasonable length of time without further invention, it can be considered "on sale."

Section 102(c) is also the subject of much litigation. What is abandonment? There are many grounds for abandonment. One of these is set forth in Section 102(d). Another ground is putting a discovery aside and simply not pursuing it for a period of time. Also, there may be deliberate concealment or suppression, perhaps to protect an existing product.

Section 102(d) provides that a U.S. patent is barred if a person entitled to the patent but required by law to file first in the United States has filed a patent application or inventor's certificate abroad or for those not required to file first in the United States filed abroad more than one year before the U.S. filing date. A person subject to U.S. law must obtain a license from the PTO to file an application abroad based on a U.S. application if the foreign filing is to occur in less than six months after the U.S. filing.

Section 102(e) provides that a person shall not obtain a patent if the invention was patented before the present inventor made his invention. The material relating to Section 371(c) concerns filings in the United States based on a foreign application for an invention made abroad.

Section 102(f) is self-explanatory, but its impact is modified by the second paragraph of Section 103, to be discussed shortly.

Section 102(g) gives rise to the U.S. interference practice. The United States is the only major country that has such a practice, all others awarding the patent to the first applicant to file.

An interference proceeding is an attempt to determine who actually was the first inventor. The procedure is long, complex, and expensive and is explored in greater detail later in this discussion.

Section 102 requires that prior materials ("prior art") can be applied only if those materials are for substantially identical inventions. Section 103 provides much broader and highly subjective grounds for refusal to grant a patent on an application. Under Section 103 a patent can be refused if in the opinion of the PTO the contribution by the applicant is not significant relative to what was already known. The term "obvious" is used in the statutes and by patent examiners. The test is based on what one with "ordinary skill in the art" would do if faced with the requirement to provide a solution to a problem. Would replacing a screw with a rivet in a particular situation be inventive—probably not, but it could be. And that's where the tug-of-war between the patent examiner and the applicant and/or his attorney begins.

If the parties cannot agree, and the patent examiner finally rejects the application, the applicant can appeal, a procedure to be discussed subsequently.

The second paragraph of Section 103 softens the provisions of Sections 102(f) and (g). It became apparent to industry and eventually to Congress (1984) that engineers and scientists working side by side or at least in a close relationship cross fertilized one another, and it was often difficult to distinguish between where one left off and the other began or how much overlap existed. Thus, where there is to be or is a common assignee of the patents to be issued, the work of a co-worker cannot be used as prior art unless the earlier work constitutes a statutory bar under Section 102. This paragraph thus eliminates the necessity, particularly of an assignee, to determine who did what. Under the prior law a mistake in such a decision led to or could lead to invalidity of an issued patent.

Once a decision has been made based on the facts known to the inventor as a result of the inventor's knowledge of his or her field and the results of a search, if conducted, that the invention is patentable (there are unpatentable inventions, particularly under Section 103), the next step is to file a patent application.

Such an application is composed of a specification, claims, and where appropriate, drawings. The specification should set forth the prior state of the field of the invention and its deficiencies, the fact that these deficiencies are overcome by the present invention, and a detailed description of the "best mode" of practicing the invention. More on "best mode" later. The claims set forth what the inventor considers to be his invention, and infringement of a patent can occur only if the claims read on the infringing device. The fact that the specification discloses what another party is doing is of no moment if the claims do not "read" on the other party's device.

Once an application has been filed, it will be directed to a group in the PTO that has cognizance of the specific subject matter of the application and is assigned to the "expert" in that particular field in the group. Applications are required to be processed in the order in which received. There are exceptions to this rule, the exceptions being instituted upon filing of a petition to make special alleging certain specified factors. Specifically, petitions based on "Applicant's age or health, or the invention will materially enhance the quality of the environment or materially contribute to the development or conservation of energy resources."

The commissioner of patents may advance the processing of an application to expedite the business of the office or upon a determination that the invention is of particular importance to a branch of the government.

The examiner searches through his files of U.S. and foreign patents and such literature as he may have. At that point the examiner can allow the application, reject it, or require an "election of species" if it is believed that more than one invention or species is being claimed in the application. If there is an allowable claim generic to the various species, up to a specified number, then the examiner cannot require such an election, but he can still require division where it is considered that two inventions are being claimed.

The examiner may reject on prior art or under Section 112 of the law, in the latter case on several grounds, such as the specification does not support the claims, the specification or claims are vague and indefinite, something is inaccurate, the claims are incomplete and/or not properly structured, or the language of the claims is functional and does not define a step in a process or method. In a claim to a structure, a claim reciting "means" for performing the function is acceptable. There are still other rejections based on this section of the law.

The applicant can respond to the examiner if the examiner has rejected the claims for any reason or required division or election of species. The applicant can correct that on which there is agreement with the examiner, including amendment of the claims, or argue that the rejection is wrong. The specification cannot be amended unless there is an obvious minor error (typo) or an addition to the specification is supported by the claims as originally filed.

The examiner can then allow the application or issue a final rejection. The applicant can request an interview with the examiner and attempt to convince that person that he is wrong. If all else fails, the applicant can file an appeal with the Board of Patent Appeals and Interferences.

If the applicant fails to obtain a reversal of the examiner's rejection, an appeal can be taken to the Court of Appeals for the Federal Circuit (the "Federal Circuit") or to a U.S. district court whose decision, if adverse to applicant, can be appealed to the Federal Circuit.

A further requirement for prosecution before the Patent Office is the filing of an information disclosure statement in which the applicant cites to the PTO any prior art known to the applicant. This citation is to be made within three months of filing of the application and updated as additional information is acquired. Failure to disclose pertinent information known to the applicant will often result in the patent being held invalid. There are also penalties assessed by the PTO for inexcusable late filings of the statement.

The application must set forth the "best mode" (the preferred embodiment) of practicing the invention at the time of filing the application. If the best mode is not disclosed, the patent is invalid. It is foolish to withhold the best mode for any reason, since if the patent is sued on discovery by the defendant, it will usually turn up the fact that best mode was not disclosed and the patent will be held invalid.

There are several other procedures that can occur in the PTO that must be discussed. The interference procedure is not only an attempt to determine the first inventor but also to determine which inventor was most diligent in pursuing the invention. If A invents first and is diligent in pursuing his invention, that is, reduces it to actual practice or by filing an application in the PTO, A will win the interference. If the first to conceive the invention is not diligent and a second inventor who invented later but was diligent to a reduction to practice before the first inventor, the second inventor wins. An inventor may not initially be diligent, but if diligence is started before a second party invents, the first party will win. The interference procedure is usually quite expensive, involving taking of depositions, preparing exhibits, and so on. Appeal procedures are available.

A patentee may file for reissue of a patent. If the patentee files within two years of the issue date of the patent, the claims of the original patent can be broadened to cover more than the original claims. To achieve this result, the patentee must allege inadvertence, accident, or mistake in not having presented the broader claim earlier, that is, during prosecution of the application. The PTO is very stringent in the requirements for proof of inadvertence, accident, or mistake.

A patentee may also file for reissue of narrower claims. This effort is usually the result of discovery of additional prior art that limits the original claims.

In both broadened and narrowing reissues, the PTO can cite new art and reject the application, which can in effect destroy the original patent.

In the case of a broadened reissue, persons who were practicing the invention and only now infringe the patent because of the broadened claim have intervening rights that may permit them to continue the practice of the invention.

There is now available a reexamination procedure. If it is believed that a patent is invalid, a party can file a request for reexamination with the PTO at a considerable cost. New prior art is usually presented and arguments submitted as to why the patent claims are invalid over this new art. If the PTO does not agree, it will not institute reexamination proceedings and part of the fee is refunded.

If the PTO decides to proceed with reexamination, a rejection of some or all of the claims may be issued and the patent owner can respond as in any pending application. If the Patent Office finds nothing patentable, the patent is invalid and of no effect. The more usual case is that some claims will be lost or will be amended to define over the new references cited. In the latter case a reexamination certificate is issued indicating any amendments made to the patent.

Reexamination often occurs in conjunction with a suit for infringement at the direction of the judge.

The patent owner may also file for reexamination if that person or entity wishes to cite new prior art and hope the PTO agrees that the new art does not invalidate the patent or agrees to certain amendment to the claims.

Upon the issuance of a patent, PTO issue fees are required, and as with filing fees are different for a small entity from a large entity. Maintenance fees for patents are due at the end of $3\frac{1}{2}$, $7\frac{1}{2}$, and $11\frac{1}{2}$ years. The fees increase at each benchmark and are different for small and large entities. If the fees are not paid, the patent lapses.

None of the fees are stated here since they change (increase) with great regularity.

A word of caution. All responses by a patent applicant to actions taken by the PTO are required to be filed within specified time periods. If the responses are not filed within the specified period, a late response can be filed upon payment of an extension fee unless the response is filed later than the allowable statutory time period of six months. Even then a late filing may be accepted if a valid reason for the late filing is documented and certain fees are paid.

The United States is a party to two international conventions relating to patents: the International Treaty for the Protection of Industrial Property and the Patent Cooperation Treaty (PCT).

The former treaty gives applicants of countries that are members of the treaty one year after filing in their own country the right to file an application in another member country and obtain the benefit of the filing date in their own country. Thus, prior art that became such in that intervening year cannot be used against the application in the foreign country.

Filing under the latter treaty (the PCT) must also be made within one year of the filing in the original country but delays the requirement to file in foreign countries that are members until 20 months after the original filing in the host country or 30 months if an international patent search is requested within 19 months of the original filing.

If foreign patents are to be filed, there are two cardinal rules that must be followed. First, as has been indicated, the foreign application must be filed within one year of filing the original application. Otherwise, anything published in the interim between the United States and foreign filings may bar the patent. The second rule is that filings in most industrial nations (not the United States) are barred if the invention is made known to anyone outside of the organization or individual to which or to whom the invention belongs. The exception is the right to engage an outsider or an outside firm to help in the building or development of the invention, but even then only if such party is not a potential customer. There are usually no other exceptions.

The PTO provides for public use proceedings upon a showing by one having knowledge of a pending application that the invention forming the subject matter of the application was in public use or on sale more than one year before the filing of the application. Hearings and other proceedings are held to determine if in fact such sale or use occurred.

Once a patent has been obtained, the owner has the exclusive right to make, use, sell, or lease the invention. The owner may license others to practice any one or all of these exclusive rights. The license may be exclusive, in which case the owner cannot practice the right(s) licensed, the license may be a sole license, in which case the owner and the licensee are the only two who can practice the invention, or the license may be nonexclusive, in which case anyone who is licensed may practice the invention. The license may be for a period of years only and/or may apply only to a specific territory. Blanket licenses are not required. The owner of a patent may also sell (assign) the patent to another party, usually with a right in the assignee to sue for past infringement and to sue in its own name.

As indicated, the U.S. government requires three maintenance fees over the 17-year life of a patent. Most foreign countries require annual annuities which escalate and, of course, are subject to changes in foreign attorney's fees and the currency exchange rate. Some of the annuities for late years in the life of a patent can become quite large.

Patents may be assigned, but such assignments are not valid against a purchaser for value without notice that the patent has been previously assigned to another party unless the assignment has been previously registered in the PTO.

Royalties are based on just about anything upon which the parties can agree. The royalty can be a percentage of the net sales price of the product or on the method of production of the product. The royalty can be so much per pound, a ton, or other weight, it can be a fixed price per unit with or without a cost of living or consumer price index escalator. The royalty can be based on a percentage of profit on sale of the product or on a percentage of the reduction in cost of manufacture of a product or reduction in the cost of producing the product by the process of the patent.

Assignments of patents are very common under employee contracts. The employee usually is required to assign his inventions to his employer. The employee must be careful that the assignment agreement does not require assignment of patents acquired on applications filed before employment commenced. Also the agreement to assign even during the period of employment should not go beyond that which the employee is hired to do or that which his or her employment brings the individual into contact. Also the agreement to assign usually requires assignment for a period after employment terminates of inventions related to the employment. This period should be closely restricted. This subject is discussed in more detail subsequently.

An assignment of rights should convey all rights under the international treaties and the right to sue for past infringement. These rights should be assigned regardless of the reason for the assignment unless the rights assigned are only pertaining to a specific country or region and the agreement should be tailored accordingly.

The question of patent infringement and resulting damages is extremely complex, and a detailed discussion is beyond the scope of this chapter. Some discussion of this subject, however, must be undertaken.

A first question that must be answered in any suit is: Is the patent valid? The defendant will raise just about any conceivable defense that comes to mind. The attack will be on prior art (usually new), failure to disclose best mode, failure to file a proper information disclosure statement, false statements to the PTO, and improper inventorship to name a few. Both sides will take pretrial depositions and hire expert witnesses to testify at trial.

Assuming that the patent survives the question of validity, the next issue is whether the claims are infringed. Of course, one must also establish lack of a right to practice the invention in the alleged infringing party if such a right is alleged. Infringement can be direct, that is, the claims read directly on the device, process, and so on, claimed to be infringing or under the doctrine of equivalents. This doctrine states in effect that if an alleged infringing device, process, and so on does the same thing, in the same way, with the same results, infringement may occur. One test sometimes used is to write a claim, eliminating from the claim in the patent that which is essentially nonessential and does not impair the validity of the claim. Infringement may then be found. A step in a method or a clause to a part of the structure cannot be eliminated, only some relatively minor detail in a clause or step may be so stricken.

Damages, like royalties, have a wide variety of permutations. Damages may be based on an industry standard percentage of royalties if one exists, based on profits or fixed rates per pound. If willful infringement is found, the defendant may be assessed treble damages, postfiling interest, and, in extreme cases, attorneys' fees. In one reported case royalties on sales were well under $10,000,000 while the final judgment was far in excess of that amount. The court may also order destruction of the infringing product.

A court may also issue a temporary restraining order, a preliminary or permanent injunction, denying the defendant the right to continue to practice the invention or sell already existing products. Such remedy is usually not available unless the patent on which suit is brought has previously been held valid. Also, if a trade secret or confidential information is used without a right, such orders of the court may issue.

Notice to the public that an article is patented is given either by marking or by direct notice to an infringing party. By marking is meant that the patented article has affixed thereto or to its packaging the word "Patent" or "Pat." together with the number of the patent. Failure to so mark a product prohibits the collection of damages for infringement occurring prior to notification of infringement by the patent owner.

Infringement of a process patent may occur by sale of an article produced by the process. This doctrine has been extended to manufacture in a foreign jurisdiction. Thus, if an article is manufactured in a foreign country by a process patented in the United States, importation of the article constitutes infringement of the U.S. patent and is actionable in U.S. courts.

Articles that infringe a U.S. patent can be impounded at the border by an action brought under Section 1337 of the customs laws of the United States. Briefs are filed and hearings held to determine validity and infringement questions.

Another word of caution. A written or public allegation of infringement can trigger a declaratory judgment action. The alleged infringer may bring suit in federal court in an effort to have the patent(s) declared invalid or not infringed. Be certain you are ready to go to trial if need be when you make a written or public statement of infringement.

The vast majority of patents are litigated in federal courts. If, however, the patents are the subject matter of a contract, the case may end up as part of a suit on the contract in a state court. Try not to let this happen. Some very strange results can occur, and no appeal to the Federal Circuit may be available.

As a general rule, patent applications filed in the United States are kept secret as long as they are pending. Filing in a foreign country, however, usually produces publication in 20 months after the U.S. filing date.

Copies of U.S. patents can be purchased from the PTO.

2.0 TRADEMARKS

The word "trademark" as generally used is really a generic name for trademarks and service marks. Trademarks apply to goods, and service marks apply to services. The quality of the product or service can be significant selling points.

The value of a trademark resides in its association with specific goods, goods of a certain type, quality, consistency, and value. To paraphrase a statement that was allegedly made by a high official of the Coca-Cola Company many years ago, "If every Coca-Cola plant in the world were to be destroyed tonight, I could raise $100,000,000 tomorrow morning on our trademark." The value of a trademark thus resides in the confidence the public has in the product or services.

There are three primary types of trademarks, common law, state law, and federal law, and these may encompass a word, a logo, or a color.

A common law right usually arises through continuous use of a mark until it has acquired in the minds of the public an association with a particular product, known as "secondary meaning." Usually the mark will have ™ after it, and it is enforceable in state courts or federal courts if the necessary requisites for a suit in a federal court have been met, diversity of citizenship, amount, and so on.

A trademark registered under state trademark laws may be enforced in the state issuing the mark. A ™ should also be used in such case.

The federal registration is the most powerful of the marks and can be enforced in any federal court where infringement occurs. The prerequisites for a federal registration of a trademark are use in interstate commerce by applying the mark to the goods and/or their containers or enclosing instruction manuals with the goods. Advertisements alone do not satisfy the requirements for use in interstate commerce of a trademark.

Advertisements in publications in bulletins, brochures, and so on shipped in interstate commerce, letterheads, used in correspondence in interstate commerce, and the like, however, may satisfy the requirements for use of a service mark in interstate commerce.

An application for federal registration includes a statement of the owner of the mark, the goods to be protected, the dates of first use in commerce and in interstate commerce, the manner in which the mark is used, a drawing of the mark, specimens of the mark as used at the time of filing, and a statement by the applicant (which can be an individual or any other legal entity) that the applicant is believed to be the owner of the mark and have the sole right to register it for the goods claimed.

A recent amendment to the trademark laws permits the filing of an Intent to Use application. Such application is treated as any other application through an opposition period explained subsequently. Once the application receives a Notice of Allowance, a Statement of Use must be filed within six months of such notice. Extensions of such requirement for another six months are liberally given, but thereafter extensions are given only upon a satisfactory showing of a need for a continued period to bring the product to the market. Failure to file a Statement of Use within the permitted time frame leads to abandonment of the application.

Trademarks are registerable on a principal register and a supplemental register.

A mark to be registerable on the principal register must not be (Section 2 of 15 U.S.C.) descriptive of the goods (they can be suggestive) and must not be sufficiently similar (confusingly similar) to another mark such that the sources of goods can be confused. Further, the mark cannot be deceptive, disparaging, false, suggestive of connection with another, a flag, coat of arms, or insignia of the United States, a state, a municipality or a foreign country, functional, geographically descriptive or deceptively misdescriptive, immoral or scandalous, matter protected by law, the name, portrait, signature of a living person without that person's consent or a deceased president of the United States without the consent of the widow or widower.

The most common rejection of an application is related to confusing similarity to another mark.

Concurrent registrations of similar or even identical marks is permitted under certain circumstances. Thus, if the trademark attorney in the PTO determines that registration of the second mark or concurrently filed mark is not likely to cause confusion as to certain limitations on the mode or place of use of the mark or the specific goods involved (as a far-fetched example, a radio transmitter and hand soap), concurrent registration of the same or which would otherwise be confusingly similar marks may be permitted.

The law also provides for collective marks and certification marks. Certification marks are marks that the owner anticipates that someone other than the owner will use. The mark "UL" is a prime example in our industry of such a mark. A collective mark is a mark used by members of a collective group or organization and is intended to indicate membership in an association, union, club, or other organization.

The supplemental register was established pursuant to the Convention for the Protection of Trademarks and Commercial Names, signed in Buenos Aires on August 20, 1910. The register records marks capable of distinguishing applicant's goods but not registerable on the principal register. Those marks prohibited as set forth on page 136 cannot appear on the supplemental register. Marks recorded on this register are not subject to opposition. A trademark owner who feels that its mark will be damaged by issuance of such mark may protest its issue.

Section 2(f) of the Act provides a mechanism for obtaining registration (unless expressly prohibited by the prior paragraphs of Section 2) if the mark has been used extensively by the applicant such that the mark has become distinctive of applicant's goods in commerce. The PTO will usually accept as proof of distinctiveness the substantially exclusive and continuous use of the mark by applicant in commerce for a period of five years prior to the claim of distinctiveness. (See the remarks that follow relative to the supplemental register.)

Thus, a mark that might not otherwise be registerable under Section 1 of the Act (the provision providing broadly for registration of marks) may be registered under Section 2(f).

A trademark can be on, for instance, the box in which the goods are packaged since such use can provide a designation of the goods or more particularly the source of the goods. Goods for protection of an automobile from theft may be sold in a box in the form of an automobile or a smoke detector in a box emulating a burning house. In such instances the boxes provide a clear identification of the goods and the source and are registerable.

Registration on the supplemental register may not be used to stop importation of goods bearing the mark. The value of such registration is to hold the mark while the registrant attempts to have the mark acquire secondary meaning so that it may be registered on the principal register or at least to stop others from interfering with the registrant's use of the mark. See the subsequent discussion of "palming off."

Once a trademark application has been filed it is examined, and it may be allowed at the examining stage or rejected for any one of the reasons cited earlier or the PTO trademark attorney may require a change in the statement of goods (a very common requirement), a new classification of goods (to be described shortly), or division of the goods into a number of different classes or the like. If the trademark attorney requires listing in more than the number of classes that the initial fee covered, an additional fee is due.

Quickly, since the United States is a member of the Paris Convention on Trademarks, the international classification of goods is used. Goods are broken down into 34 classifications, services into eight classes. Certification marks are broken down into two classes, goods and services, and collective marks all fall into one class.

Once a trademark attorney in the PTO believes a mark is registerable it is published for opposition. Any party that feels it will be injured by issuance of the mark can file an opposition. The party does not have to have a registered mark or a pending application for registration of a mark. As an extreme example, if the Coca-Cola Company did not have a registered mark it could still oppose an attempt by a third person to register that name. The language of the statute, 15 U.S.C., Chapter 22, Section 13, briefly is, "Any person who believes he would be damaged by the registration of a mark upon the principal register may . . . file an opposition."

The opposition proceeding is rather complex, can become quite expensive, and is commenced by filing a Notice of Opposition within 30 days of publication of the mark in the weekly issued *Trademark Gazette*. A common law mark is an asset in such proceedings as is a state registration.

Under Section 14 of the Trademark Act, a registration may be canceled after issue.

Diverting for the moment, if appropriate affidavits or declarations are filed, a mark may become incontestable. These are known as filings under Sections 8 and 15 of the Act. The filing under Section 8 must be made within the year preceding the sixth year of registration and provide a showing that the mark is still in use or give acceptable reasons why it is not currently in use (a fire that burned down the plant, for instance). If such is not filed, the registration is canceled.

Under Section 15 of the Act the mark must have been in continuous use for five consecutive years and is still in use (Section 8), provided that there has been no final adverse decision to registrant's claim of ownership, and there is no pending proceeding involving such right.

Once this latter affidavit or declaration is filed, the mark is incontestable unless fraud or the like in its procurement or in filing of the foregoing declarations is proven.

Another ground for defeating a mark is discussed shortly relative to licensing.

A mark may be lost because it becomes the generic name of the product. The word "aspirin" is a classic example of the loss of a mark because the mark became the generic name of the product.

The term of a trademark acquired prior to November 16, 1989, is 20 years. Marks issued on or after November 16, 1989, have a term of 10 years. Marks may be renewed every 10 years thereafter. Registrations under the Acts of 1905 and 1881 remain in force for their original terms and then may be renewed under the current Act. Registrations under the 1920 Act cannot be renewed unless required to support foreign trademarks. Applications for renewal must be made at least six months before expiration.

A mark must be assigned along with the goodwill of the business to which it pertains, or it may be lost. As with patents, the assignment may be void against a subsequent innocent purchaser for value unless the assignment is recorded in the PTO.

A refusal to register a mark by the trademark attorney to whom the application has been assigned or failure to achieve the desired results in other final proceedings before the PTO may be appealed to the Trademark Trial and Appeal Board (TTAB). If unsuccessful, appeal may be made to the Federal Circuit. Alternatively, appeal may be made by civil action in a district court. If an adverse party to a proceeding resides in a foreign country, the civil appeal must be taken in the Federal District Court for the District of Columbia.

Once a mark has been registered, notice of registration of the mark is given by a statement that the mark is registered or an R in a circle, ®, may be applied to the goods. If such notice is not given, damages do not occur unless the defendant in such a suit had actual notice of registration.

Unlicensed use of a registered mark is actionable in federal courts. If the infringement is by a publisher that is innocent, an injunction against further use shall lie, but there shall be no damages granted.

Infringement by other than an innocent party may permit recovery of profits, damages, costs, and attorney's fees by the owner of the mark. The plaintiff must prove only the defendant's sales. The defendant must prove all elements of costs to reduce profits. The court may assess up to three times the actual damages proven at trial. The court has wide discretion in the award of damages. The court may also require destruction of the offending articles.

Importation of goods with infringing marks may be stopped at the place of entry. False designation of goods is also actionable.

As previously indicated, the United States is a member of several conventions. Pursuant thereto the PTO shall place upon a register foreign marks supplied by the international bureaus. This register, which contains complete information concerning the marks, is a continuation of the register provided under Section 1(a) of the Act of March 19, 1920. No such mark shall be registered in the United States until it has been granted in the country of origin. Such application for registration must be filed within six months of filing of the application for registration in the country of origin. These same requirements apply to U.S. trademark filings abroad. Registration in the United States of such a mark is subject to all the legal requirements for filing in the United States and as in the country of origin of the mark.

A notice of caution: if a trademark is licensed to a third party, the license must permit the owner of the registration to inspect the goods to insure that the quality of the goods meets the standards established by the owner of the mark. This provision is required to ensure that a licensee does not damage the mark by producing inferior goods or providing inferior services. If such a provision is not included in the license, the mark can be lost.

Copies of trademarks can be purchased from the PTO.

3.0 COPYRIGHTS

Copyrights are intended to protect from copying literary and artistic works and include such things as architectural, audiovisual, literary, musical, dramatic (including accompanying music), pantomimes and choreographic pictorial, graphic and sculptural works, and motion picture and other audiovisual works. The law deals differently with many of these items, as will become apparent below.

The key word in the law of copyrights is copying. A completely independent creation of the same work is not copying, and a copyright does not protect against such independent generation of a work. The copyright law also includes sound recordings, computer programs, and masks used in making computer chips.

Under many situations, a copyright is the least difficult federal intellectual property right to obtain. Forms for filing for copyright protection with instructions are prescribed by the copyright office and may be obtained from that office.

One must be cautious if a work contains old, new, and/or derivative materials, for instance, and in these situations a professional should be consulted. The more difficult aspect of copyrights relates to what protection is obtained. The doctrine of fair use permits copies to be made for certain purposes. In the field of the visual arts, sound recordings, motion pictures, video broadcasts, and the like, the law provides compulsory licenses with exceptions upon exceptions. Some of these various aspects of the law are touched on in the paragraphs that follow, but only briefly, since a detailed discussion of such is well beyond the scope of this chapter.

The United States is a party to the Berne Convention. A work is a Berne Convention work pursuant to prescribed rules such as in an unpublished work the author(s) is a national of a country adhering to the Convention, or, if published, was first published in a nation adhering to the Convention. If the work is an audiovisual work, the legal entity or individual must be domiciled or have residence in a member country, if related to a building the structure must be in a member country.

The U.S. law also provides a definition for each of the categories mentioned earlier. In addition, the law provides for different types of origination. For instance, a collective work has a number of contributors while a compilation is a gathering of preexisting materials usually produced by others than the compiler but with the copyright owner's permission.

Materials copyrightable under the Berne Convention contrary to prior U.S. law do not require a copyright notice; this is discussed in greater detail subsequently. We deal initially with the U.S. law.

A work is copyrightable in the United States apart from the Berne Convention, if unpublished regardless of the author's nationality or domicile. If the work is published, it is copyrightable in the United States if on the date of publication the creator is a national or domiciliary of the United States or of a country that is a party to a copyright treaty to which the United States is a party, the work is first published in the United States or in a country that is a party to the Universal Copyright Convention, the work is first published in the United Nations or Organization of American States, or the work comes within a proclamation of the President.

It is important to note that if the U.S. law, Title 17, applies, the rights under the Berne Convention do not.

The rights granted under a copyright vary with the type of work. The exclusive rights to public display of motion pictures or other audiovisual works, musicals, dramatic and choreographic works and the like are provided by the law. The exclusive rights to reproduce and to distribute such works also apply, as well as production of derivative works.

An important feature of the copyright law is that only the author of a work of visual arts has the right, regardless of ownership, to claim authorship to prevent use of his or her name as the author of works he or she did not create or of works he or she created that have been distorted or mutilated or to prevent distortion or modification of the work.

The duration of a copyright for visual arts created on or after the Visual Artists Rights Act of 1990 is the life of the author. Such works created before 1990, but the title to which has not been transferred, shall be as above. These rights may not be transferred, but they may be waived.

There are numerous exceptions to the owner's or artist's rights in copyrighted works.

A first of these exceptions set forth in Title 17 is the doctrine of fair use. Under this doctrine, use of a work for "criticism, comment, news reporting, teaching (including multiple copies for classroom use), scholarship or research, some secondary transmissions" is not considered infringement. Also, under certain circumstances, small segments of a copyrighted work may be used if not in a competitive environment, or for competitive purposes but perhaps to make a point, and provided the copyright is acknowledged. A professional must be engaged for guidance in this area.

A compulsory license is given for secondary transmissions by cable companies, and they must pay royalties for such. The law provides numerous exceptions to the exclusive rights in the form of compulsory licenses with fees, but numerous rules and exceptions to the exceptions are also established.

The compulsory licenses, in addition to cable TV and satellite transmission, are available for coin-operated phonograph players and for making and distributing phonorecords. Displays of useful articles in a work are protected only to the extent that the useful article is protected. The exclusive rights in computer programs do not extend to copying for archival purposes or as an essential step in utilization of the program.

Fees for uses of copyrighted materials under compulsory licenses are established by a federal body.

The ownership of a copyright can be a difficult question to resolve. A trap that many people and companies fall into is the engagement of an independent party to prepare copyrightable material for them. The Supreme Court has held that under such circumstances the term "work made for hire" must appear in writing at some place in the record or the person preparing the work, rather than the purchaser, owns the work unless an independent assignment is incorporated or separately executed.

Further, the ownership of the individual works included in a collective work remains with the creators of the individual items. Copyrights may be transferred as other property, but such transfer does not transfer rights in material objects. A transfer of a copyright is invalid unless in writing and signed by the owner or his duly authorized agent.

A transfer of a copyright can be recorded in the copyright office and serves as constructive notice of such transfer.

The term of a copyright except as noted early in this chapter is for the life of the creator and for 50 years after his death. If the work is a joint work, the 50 years is based on the last to survive. Anonymous works or works created under a pseudonym and works made for hire have a term of 75 years from first publication or 100 years from creation, whichever is shorter.

The duration of works in their first term on January 1, 1978, endure for 28 years from the date originally secured but under certain circumstances can be extended for 47 years. There are other terms for copyrights created still earlier for those that have been transferred, and the law should be consulted to determine which term applies.

A notice of copyright may be applied to any work created under the Act. Thus, a "C" in a circle, the word "Copyright" or "Copr." may be used followed by the date of first publication and, if appropriate, the dates of further publication followed by the name of owner. The notice should be applied where it is likely to give reasonable notice.

The notice applicable to phonorecords of sound recording uses a "P" in a circle and is otherwise as above. Such notice denies a defendant the claim of innocent infringement.

It is not necessary to register a copyright. However, within three months of the date of first publication, deposit with the copyright office of two complete copies of the work is required, if a recording, two copies of the record. If the work is not published, only one copy need be recorded. These copies may be used to satisfy or at least partially satisfy the deposit requirements when and if copyright registration is requested.

At anytime during the life of a copyright, the owner may request registration in the office.

No action will lie for infringement of a federal copyright until it is registered except for actions in Berne Convention works where the country of origin is not the United States. An action can be instituted if a request for registration has been refused if the Register of Copyrights is notified of the action.

Upon a finding of copyright infringement, injunctions against continued infringement may issue and the infringing items can be impounded and/or destroyed. Damages and profits are available also. It may also be considered a criminal offense to willfully and for purposes of commercial advantage infringe a copyright.

States and their employees are not immune from infringement of a copyright. Importation of copyrighted materials is prohibited and is actionable.

As indicated, the Act now provides for protection of chips and resulting products. A semiconductor chip product as defined has "two or more layers of metallic, insulating or semiconductor material intended to perform electronic circuit functions." A "mask work" is a series of related images "having or representing the predetermined, three dimensional pattern of metallic, insulating, or semiconductor material present or removed from the layers of a semiconductor chip product; and in which series the relation of the images to one another is that each image has the pattern of the surface of one form of the semiconductor chip product."

The protection afforded by the Act is acquired if certain rules are followed relating to Section 908 of the Act or first commercially exploited in the United States or a country that is a party to a treaty affording protection to mask works. A type of "fair use" is afforded but is limited for the most part to "teaching, analyzing or evaluating the concepts or techniques embodied in the mask work."

The mask work may be registered if registration is applied for within two years of commercial exploitation of the work. Notice of registration is given by an "M" in a circle or *M* and the name of the owner. A civil action can be brought for infringement.

There is one further area of the law that is appropriate to this chapter but does not fall under the patent, trademark, or copyright law. This area is known as "palming-off" and arises from consciously producing a product that is sufficiently similar to another party's product (trade dress) that the public cannot or cannot readily distinguish between the two products. Such conduct is actionable in civil actions.

This chapter has not touched on a very important area of copyright law relating to computer programs. It may be copyright infringement to decompile a program and use the decompilation to produce an infringing product. In a recent decision it has been held to be fair use to disassemble a program while engaging in reverse engineering and producing a program from the material thus collected. Initiation codes may be copied where this is the only way to gain access to a computer.

It appears that the courts agree that for disassembly not to be infringement, it must be necessary to gain access to the parts of the program that are not protectable. Such disassembly has been held to fall under the fair use doctrine. The statute sets forth four fair use criteria for determining fair use.

The situation is confused by the fact that the courts do not agree on application of those tests. The second and third circuits disagree on the application of the tests or in fact on the tests that must be undertaken to distinguish between protectable and unpatentable parts of a program and that disassembly has occurred.

It suffices to say that this area of the copyright law is in flux and is the subject of much litigation. It behooves the computer programmer to consult an expert in this field to get the latest update on this ever-changing battleground of the law of copyright.

Also the registration of computer programs is an anomaly since it is only necessary to make record of a sufficient part of the program to be able to identify it. For instance, it is possible, with permission, to file, say, the first and last 25 pages of a reasonably extensive program to obtain protection or in a program that has a well-defined core of novelty to eliminate enough of this core to prevent ease of copying. The copyright office or a professional in this area of the law should be consulted before such a procedure is attempted.

A word to all engineers, scientists, and computer programmers, particularly the recent entries into these fields: before accepting a position with a new company, read carefully all documents you are expected to sign as an employee before accepting the position. The claims by companies on your intellectual property rights vary greatly from company to company, with some restricting their claims closely to your responsibilities while others retain all claims, regardless of its applicability to you and the requirements of your job. Also observe closely the period the company claims in your intellectual property conceived after leaving the company's employment. Many companies establish a six-month period, others even longer. One further area that should be of concern is a noncompete provision that may be broader than justified.

All these matters are usually treated in an intellectual property agreement that you will be required to sign; read it carefully and understand it fully before signing.

This chapter is at best a very brief summary of the laws relating to intellectual property in the United States. In all instances a professional in the field of interest must be consulted to avoid the many legal traps and pitfalls that await the unwary.

4.0 ADDENDUM

The General Agreement on Tariffs and Trade (GATT) has been adopted by the United States and various provisions of the U.S. patent, trademark, and copyright laws have been amended. The following is a discussion of such changes, not only as a result of GATT, but also as a result of the North American Free Trade Agreement (NAFTA), which has already been adopted.

The major changes in the patent law provide a 20-year term from date of filing and priority rights based on activity in any country of NAFTA and the World Trade Organization (WTO) under GATT. The 20-year term may be extended for up to 5 years for delays resulting from appeals, interferences, and placing the application under a secrecy order by a government agency.

Patents may be obtained on sexually as well as asexually reproduced plants. The term is 18 years from date of filing.

It would appear that the U.S. law permitting filing within a year of public disclosure will continue to apply and will apply also to WTO and NAFTA countries.

Invention certificates filed in foreign countries will have the same effect in the United States as those filed in the United States.

A provisional application can now be filed to establish priority. Such an application requires an adequate disclosure and drawings—but no claims. A provisional application provides for priority of invention but does not start the running of the 20-year period if a regular application is filed within one year of the filing of the provisional application.

As has been indicated, the agreements also affect trademarks. The United States can no longer register marks relating to "wine and spirits" that contain misleading geographical indicators.

Currently, a trademark can be canceled for nonuse for two years. The term will be extended to three years.

The field of copyrights will be heavily impacted by the new laws. There are numerous changes relating to sound recordings, restored works, computer programs, and others. Member countries must provide rental rights in computer programs. Copyrights that have lapsed under U.S. law but not under laws of another member of WTO will be restored and will lapse concurrently with its foreign counterpart. Also, a copyright owner of a restored work must give a notice of intent to enforce.

The changes required by GATT become effective on June 8, 1995.

The foregoing is at best a thumbnail sketch of what will or may happen under GATT and NAFTA. Not all changes are discussed, and certainly there may be changes in what is discussed. The PTO has issued final rules implementing the new laws relating to the 20-year term and provisional applications.

On or about August 15, 1995, the United States Patent Office issued rules pursuant to which patent applications filed in the U.S. Patent Office on or after January 1, 1996, will be published 18 months after filing, provided that Bill No. 1733 pending before the House of Representatives becomes law. The purpose of this change in the law is to eliminate submarine patents, that is, patents that are issued many years after the application is filed and that may have an impact on an already established industry or market.

5.0 REFERENCES

Bureau of National Affairs. *Patents, Trademarks and Copyright Laws.* Washington, DC:.

Hazard, John W., Jr. *Copyright Law in Business Practice.* Boston, MA: Warren, Gorman & Lamont, 1989.

Stobb, Gregory A. *Software Patents.* New York: John Wiley, 1995.

Superintendent of Documents. *37 CFR—Code of Federal Regulations for Patents, Trademarks and Copyrights.* Washington, DC: U.S. Government Printing Office.

8

Legal Aspects of Employment

Larry P. Malfitano

1.0 BACKGROUND

Historically, the term "employment" denoted a relationship created when one person was required by another to perform certain services, and the latter had the right to control the manner in which the services were to be performed. What is known today as employment law originated and developed out of domestic relations law. Before the Industrial Revolution, when society was more agrarian, a substantial amount of labor was commonly performed by family members. In that context, the "employee" was treated in certain respects like a member of the family. With the coming of the Industrial Revolution, however, the employee was no longer treated as part of the family, but rather as one who was freely able to contract for services.

With the passage of time, laws developed to define and regulate the employment relationship. Today, the employment relationship is dominated by laws and the legal process. Federal and state laws govern wages and hours, labor-management relations, equal employment opportunity, employment discrimination, occupational safety and health, and a variety of other subject areas. Additionally, the employment relationship is affected by common law doctrines; that is, legal principles not enacted by Congress or state legislatures, but inherited from court decisions and precedents.

2.0 THE APPLICATION PROCESS

The employment relationship normally begins with the consideration of a prospective employee's application for employment. Most employers require that an applicant for employment complete a standard job application form. The job application form and the application process are important in that they set the framework for the entire relationship.

2.1 The Job Application and Interview

Most job applications require the applicant to verify that the information being provided is accurate and complete. The job application may contain a provision indicating that failure to accurately and completely respond to the application's questions will result in dismissal from employment. Likewise, misrepresentations made during an employment interview may also seriously affect subsequent employment.

Employers are restrained by federal and state laws from making certain inquiries in connection with prospective employment. For example, federal law prohibits any inquiries that directly or indirectly relate to the applicant's age, race, creed, color, national origin, sex, or disability. These prohibitions pertain to both a written application and any pre-employment interviews.

2.2 Pre-employment Physicals and Protections for Disabilities

The Americans with Disabilities Act (ADA) regulates how employers can deal with applicants and employees with disabilities. The ADA is intended to assure equality of opportunity, full participation, and economic self-sufficiency to disabled individuals by prohibiting discrimination in employment. The ADA prohibits employers from discriminating against any qualified individual on the basis of that individual's disability. Significantly, a "qualified individual with a disability" is one who, with reasonable accommodation, can perform the essential functions of the job held or sought by that individual.

The ADA prohibits employers from conducting a pre-employment medical examination. It also prohibits making inquiries of a job applicant as to whether an individual has a disability or as to the nature and severity of the disability. An employer may, however, inquire as to the ability of an employee to perform job related functions. An employer may also condition an offer of employment on the results of a medical examination if all entering employees are subject to a similar examination regardless of disability and the information obtained is treated as confidential. To successfully defend against discrimination charges brought under the ADA, an employer must be able to demonstrate that (1) an alleged discriminatory qualification, test, or selection criteria is job related and consistent with business necessity and (2) performance cannot be accomplished by reasonable accommodation.

2.3 Background Checks of Applicants and the Negligent Hiring Doctrine

There is an obvious reason for employers to investigate job applicants: employers want to hire the best qualified workers. Employers, however, are also under a legal obligation to investigate potential employees. If an employer fails to satisfy this obligation, the employer risks significant legal liability. For example, if an employer hires an employee without checking that person's background and abilities, and that employee, while carrying out his job, later harms a third party, the employer may be held liable for negligent hiring. The common law doctrine of negligent hiring provides that an employer is liable for the hiring of an individual where a reasonable investigation of the individual's background would have revealed a propensity for the applicant to cause injury to others.

Under the common law doctrine of negligent hiring, even if an employer does not have actual knowledge of an employee's background, the employer may still be held liable if it "should have known" that the employee had a history or propensity for conduct that could result in injury to others. However, if the employer conducts a reasonable background search that does not reveal any damaging information, the employer will not be held liable for negligent hiring. If no background inquiry is made, the employer will not be liable for negligent hiring, so long as a reasonable search would not have revealed information sufficient to place the employer on notice of the employee's unfitness.

2.4 Consumer and Credit Checks of Applicants

When evaluating an applicant for employment, an employer may obtain a "consumer report," including a report of credit standing or creditworthiness. Many states, however, have requirements that an employer inform the applicant in writing that a consumer report is being requested and the results of that consumer report.

Sometimes an employer may wish to obtain an "investigative con-sumer report." Such reports include information on a person's general character, reputation, living conditions, or other personal matters obtained through interviews with friends, neighbors, or associates. Many states require that prior written authorization be obtained from the applicant before the employer requests a consumer report. Provided advance authori-zation is requested from the applicant, the employer is permitted to make an adverse employment decision on the basis of a refusal to grant permission for an administrative consumer report.

In addition to various state requirements, the Federal Fair Credit Reporting Act requires employers to inform the applicant if an application is denied, even in part, based on information obtained from a consumer report and to disclose the name and address of the reporting agency.

3.0 EMPLOYMENT CONTRACTS

Today, the employment relationship is generally regarded as a contractual one, conditioned on the traditional requirements of offer and acceptance. The common law statute of frauds doctrine requires a contract to be in writing if "by its terms" it cannot be performed within one year. It has been established by case law precedent that the statute of frauds applies to employment contracts. Therefore, oral employment contracts that have no possibility of performance within one year will be deemed unenforceable by operation of the statute of frauds. An oral employment agreement that does not have as one of its terms the duration of employment is valid and is not barred by the statute of frauds.

3.1 The Employment-at-Will Doctrine

The common law employment-at-will rule provides that an employee who is not hired for a specific duration of employment may be terminated by the employer at any time, for any reason. Under the common law rule, an employee who is hired for an indefinite term and who is discharged has no legal right to challenge the termination decision regardless of how unfair it may have been. However, courts recognized that a person who is hired for a specific term has a reasonable expectation that employment will last for the stated period unless there is a just or good reason for the termination of that employment. Therefore, if an employee hired for a definite term is discharged without good cause, under the common law, the employer would be liable for breach of the employment contract.

Some states have modified the common law rule by creating exceptions to the employment-at-will doctrine. The two most common exceptions are (1) an implied covenant of good faith and (2) considerations of public policy. The implied covenant of good faith exception is basically an implied promise, presumed to be part of the employment relationship, that the employer will not terminate the employee arbitrarily or without cause. The public policy exception prohibits an employer from terminating an employee because the employee exercised a statutory right, refused to violate the law, or otherwise acted to further the public interest.

3.2 Employee Handbooks and Personnel Manuals

Until recently, employers tended to view employee handbooks and manuals merely as general policy statements or guidelines that did not impose binding contractual obligations upon the employer. Recent court decisions, however, have held that an employer may, in certain circumstances, become contractually bound by representations made in company manuals and relied on by employees. In some cases, courts have held that a terminated employee could maintain a breach of contract action against his employer, even though he had been hired as an employee-at-will for an indefinite period of time. In doing so, it has been acknowledged that an employer's otherwise unfettered right to terminate an at-will employee might be limited by the inclusion of a "just cause" provision in the employer's handbook on personnel policies. Stated another way, the company handbook on personnel policies might become part of the employee's contract of employment.

Restrictions on the employer's right to terminate an employee, contained in an employee handbook or manual, will not be enforced as part of the employment contract unless the purported restrictions are explicit, specific, and unequivocal. General policy statements or supervisory guidelines providing, for example, that "employees should have job security" or that "employees are assured of steady employment as long as you are performing well" are not enough. In addition to requiring explicit and unequivocal limitations on an employer's right to terminate, courts have also made it clear that an employer will generally not be contractually bound by statements contained in an employee manual unless the employee can prove that he knew of the provisions in the manual at the time of hire and that he relied upon them in accepting employment. An employee's mere continuation of employment after receiving the handbook, or the rejection of other employment opportunities and reliance on the provision of an employee manual given out after the employee was hired, are generally not enough to maintain an action for breach of contract.

3.3 Intentional Interference with Contractual Relations

Certain actions of individuals not party to an employment contract that intrude into the employment relationship may give rise to claims of unlawful interference with contractual relations. That is, claims may arise that the third party unlawfully induced either the employer or the employee to breach the employment contract.

3.3.1 Enticement of Employee Under an Employment Contract   Claims by employers alleging unlawful interference with contractual relations often involve the following fact pattern: a former employee (or a competitor) communicates with a current employee to induce him to breach his definite-term employment contract by leaving his present employment and commencing employment with the inducing party. To establish a claim for unlawful interference with contractual relations, an employer must show (1) the existence of a valid employment contract, (2) knowledge of that contract by the inducing party, (3) intentional solicitation to induce the breach of contract, and (4) damages caused by the interference. Intentional solicitation can be inferred by a third party's offer to an employee of a higher salary or more favorable terms when the offer is made with knowledge of the employee's existing contract. However, it is not necessary for the employee to actually accept the offer. Intentional solicitation can be found even when the acts of the third party do not, or are not even designed to, culminate in a competing contract.

The foregoing discussion of unlawful interference contemplates a definite-term employment agreement binding the employee. A different rule governs when the employment is at-will, where the employee is entitled to terminate the employment at any time, for any reason. The test for unlawful interference of an at-will contractual relation provides that the mere inducement of an at-will employee to move to a competitor will not give rise to liability unless the purpose was solely to produce damages or unless the means employed were dishonest or unfair.

3.3.2 Procuring the Discharge of an Employee   If an employee is discharged due to the influence of a third party, that third party may be liable to the former employee for unlawful interference with contractual relations.

This situation typically arises when an employee is discharged upon the recommendation of a supervisor or company official. In most instances, a corporate employer cannot interfere with its own contract. Therefore, unless the supervisor, officer, or director acts outside the scope of their employment, there is no legal remedy.

4.0 INDIVIDUAL EMPLOYEE RIGHTS

With increasing frequency, federal legislation has been enacted to protect individual employee rights in the employment relationship. The primary emphasis has been on federal legislation enacted by Congress. However, in many instances, individual states have passed similar or supplemental legislation.

4.1 Employment Discrimination Protections

During the past 30 years, there has been a virtual explosion of federal and state laws modifying the at-will nature of employment by prohibiting employers from terminating employees or making employment decisions based on certain protected statuses. Following the enactment of these various employment discrimination laws, a tremendous amount of litigation resulted involving the interpretation and application of these laws. Unless employment discrimination laws are carefully evaluated by employers prior to making employment decisions, serious risks and liabilities are presented.

4.1.1 Title VII of the Civil Rights Act of 1964   Title VII of the Civil Rights Act of 1964 (Title VII) is the primary federal anti-discrimination statute. Title VII applies to employers that employ 15 or more people. Title VII makes it unlawful for an employer to discriminate against an individual in employment based on (1) race, (2) color, (3) religion, (4) sex, and (5) national origin. Specifically, Title VII provides that it is unlawful to fail to refuse to hire, or to discharge an individual, or to otherwise discriminate against any individual with respect to compensation, terms, conditions, or privileges of employment based on the foregoing protected classifications.

This federal statute also makes it unlawful for an employer to limit, segregate, or classify its employees or applicants for employment in any way which would deprive any individual of employment opportunities or otherwise adversely affect employment status. Additionally, Title VII makes it an unlawful employment practice to discriminate against an individual because he or she has exercised rights under the statute.

In 1978, Title VII was amended by the Pregnancy Discrimination Act. As a result of this amendment, Title VII now prohibits discrimination in employment against women affected by pregnancy or related conditions.

4.1.2 Age Discrimination in Employment Act   The Age Discrimination in Employment Act (ADEA) applies to employers with more than 20 employees and prohibits age discrimination against employees who are 40 years of age or older. The ADEA originally prohibited discrimination against individuals at least 40 years of age but less than 60. In 1978, the upper limit was raised to 70, and the ADEA was amended effective January 1, 1987, to eliminate the upper age limit.

As under Title VII, "discrimination" is broadly defined to include failure to hire or to discharge, denial of employment, and any other act adversely affecting the terms and conditions of employment because of an individual's age.

4.1.3 Equal Pay Act   The Equal Pay Act makes it unlawful for an employer to discriminate on the basis of sex and the wage rates of employees doing jobs requiring equal skill, effort, and responsibility that are performed under similar working conditions, unless the wage differential is paid pursuant to (1) a seniority system, (2) a merit system, (3) a system that measures earnings by the quantity or quality of production, or (4) a differential based on any factor other than sex.

4.2 Polygraph Testing

The Employee Polygraph Protection Act of 1988 (EPPA) prohibits most employers from using any type of "lie detector" test either for pre-employment screening or during employment. Although the EPPA contains some narrow exceptions to the general prohibition, virtually all use of lie detectors by employers is either prohibited or so restricted as to make such use impractical. State and local governments are excluded from the coverage of the EPPA.

The EPPA prohibits covered employers from requiring, requesting, suggesting, or causing any employee or prospective employee to take or submit to any type of "lie detector" test. The statute also prohibits any covered employer from inquiring into or using the results of a lie detector test or taking any employment action against an employee or prospective employee on the basis of such tests.

There are only a few narrow exceptions to the EPPA's general prohibition on the use of lie detector tests. Testing by polygraph is permitted if (1) the test is administered in connection with any ongoing investigation involving economic loss or injury to the employer's business or (2) the test is administered to a prospective employee who would have direct access to the manufacture, storage, distribution, or sale of any controlled substance, or involves the investigation of any employee involving possible loss or injury connected with the manufacture, distribution, or dispensing of controlled substances.

Before an employer may take any action on the basis of the results of a polygraph test, the employer must review the test results with the examinee and provide the examinee with a written copy of the opinion or conclusion rendered by the examiner and a copy of the questions asked during the exam, along with the responses. Finally, an employer is prohibited from disciplining, discharging, or discriminating against employees or applicants solely on the basis of polygraph test results, without other supporting evidence of the employee's misconduct.

4.3 Drug Testing

As has been discussed, the ADA prohibits employers from discriminating against "qualified individuals with disabilities" in regard to employment. A definition of "disability" under the ADA includes a physical or mental impairment that substantially limits one or more major life activities. Only qualified individuals with disabilities are protected. A "qualified individual with a disability" means an individual with a disability who, with reasonable accommodation, can perform the essential functions of the job at issue. Individuals, including job applicants, who (1) have successfully completed a drug rehabilitation program and are no longer using illicit drugs, or (2) are participating in a rehabilitation program and no longer using drugs, are protected under the ADA as "qualified individuals with disabilities." The ADA expressly provides, however, that the term "qualified individual with disability" does not include any employee or applicant who is currently engaged in the illegal use of drugs.

The ADA does not expressly prohibit or authorize drug testing for applicants or employees. The ADA does state that an employer does not violate the act by adopting or administering reasonable policies or procedures, including drug testing, designed to ensure that rehabilitated or rehabilitating drug users or addicts are not currently engaging in illicit drug use.

4.4 Medical Examinations

The ADA, as well as laws enacted in many states, restricts tests, inquiries, and medical examinations relating to an applicant's or an employee's disabilities. Job applicants may not be questioned about the existence, nature, or severity of a disability, but may be asked whether they are physically or mentally able to perform the functions of the position for which they are applying. Applicants may not be required to undergo a medical examination prior to receiving a job offer. In addition, a job offer may be conditioned upon successful completion of a medical examination only if (1) all new employees are subjected to the same examination regardless of disability, (2) the information concerning the examination is kept confidential and in separate files, and (3) the results are not used for discriminatory purposes.

Current employees may not be required to take medical examinations and may not be questioned as to whether they have a disability. The only exceptions to this general rule are voluntary medical examinations that are part of an employee health program and examinations or inquiries shown to be job related and consistent with business necessity.

When an employer seeks to disqualify an employee or reject an applicant for employment on the basis that a disability impairs the employee's ability to perform the job, a medical examination may be required to verify the employer's opinion. In many cases, employees who have been disabled are later capable of returning to work and cannot be discriminated against on the basis of their past disability unless a current examination confirms their inability to perform the job without unduly burdensome accommodation.

Many states have enacted legislation prohibiting testing for acquired immune deficiency syndrome (AIDS) without an individual's informed consent and place strict limitations on the disclosure of confidential information obtained from AIDS tests.

4.5 Sexual Harassment in the Workplace

Sexual harassment is a form of sex discrimination prohibited both by Title VII of the Civil Rights Act of 1964 and various state laws. There are two recognized types of sexual harassment: (1) quid pro quo harassment and (2) hostile work environment harassment.

Quid pro quo harassment is typified by the situation where employment advancement or benefits are conditioned upon submitting to unwelcome sexual advances. Complaints of quid pro quo harassment may be brought not only by employees who are propositioned, but also by employees who are denied advancement or an employment benefit because a promotion or benefit was awarded to another employee who acquiesced in the supervisor's advances.

Sexual harassment has also been held to include a second category of conduct where the harassment creates an offensive or "hostile" work environment. A "hostile" work environment has been defined as unwelcome sexual advances, request for sexual favors, or other verbal or physical conduct of a sexual nature where such conduct has the purpose or effect of unreasonably interfering with the individual's work performance. For this type of sexual harassment to be found, the conduct must be sufficiently severe or pervasive to alter a term or condition of the victim's employment and create an abusive working environment.

Merely uttering epithets that cause an employee to feel offended does not create a hostile work environment. If conduct is not severe or pervasive enough to create an environment that a reasonable person would find hostile or abusive, then an employee does not have a legal claim. Likewise, if the employee does not subjectively perceive the environment to be abusive, there is no claim for harassment. To determine whether an environment is hostile or abusive, a court will typically look at the totality of circumstances. Such circumstances may include the frequency of the discriminatory conduct, its severity, whether it is physically threatening or humiliating, or a mere offensive utterance, and whether it unreasonably interferes with an employee's work performance.

There is no clear line between a hostile work environment on one hand and flirtation or rudeness on the other. The nature of the business may be critical; conduct that is acceptable on a construction project may not be acceptable in a business office. Additionally, harassment need not be of a sexual nature to constitute sexual discrimination. Rather, it is enough if the harassment is based upon the gender of the employee.

A key factor in determining whether conduct constitutes sexual harassment is whether the conduct in question is "unwelcome," in the sense that the employee did not solicit or incite it, and regarded it as offensive or undesirable. Evidence of a contemporaneous complaint or protest is not a necessary element of a harassment claim, but may strengthen it. Past conduct of the victim that is offered to show "welcomeness" must relate to the alleged harasser.

The victim's employer and the harasser may be liable to a victim of sexual harassment. Employers are typically liable for any acts of their supervisors. This may be true even if the specific acts of harassment were not authorized or forbidden by the employer. Lack of knowledge of the occurrence may not be a defense. An employer will also be liable for the harassing acts of a victim's co-workers, if the employer knew or should have known of the conduct and failed to take immediate and appropriate corrective action. An employer may also be liable for the acts of nonemployees (e.g., customers or vendors) if the employer knew or should have known of harassing conduct toward an employee and failed to take immediate and appropriate corrective action.

5.0 CONFIDENTIALITY AND THE EMPLOYMENT RELATIONSHIP

An employment issue being litigated with increasing frequency involves employees who obtain access to employer's trade secrets, but subsequently leave to join another company and form their own company. Particularly in the technology industries, job mobility is high, and start-up companies comprised of former employees proliferate. Trade secrecy problems are a consequence of rapid growth, entrepreneurial interests, and competitive commercial environments. The law in this context involves close balancing of strong and competing interests, both of which are socially recognized as vital concerns. On the one hand, use of employees to develop and exploit secret industrial information is essential to the development and expansion of commercial technology. The employer's interest in retaining and enforcing its secrets is an essential element of technology growth, since it provides a financial incentive for development. In contrast, there are significant reasons to avoid constraints on the individual employee who seeks new employment or establishes his own business. In part, these relate to concepts of individual liberty and mobility. To the extent that trade secret barriers prevent an employee's use of information, the employee's free selection of jobs and ability to translate personal knowledge into financial gain are restricted.

The employment relationship is regarded as presumptively confidential with regard to trade secret information. While confidentiality is implicit in most employment relationships, the enforceability of specific restraints is linked to the underlying question of whether a trade secret exists and was maintained by the former employer. To establish any trade secret claim, there must be a reasonable effort at internal and external secrecy. Simply maintaining physical security against external intrusion is inadequate as to restraints on employees. Internal, enforced limitations on access to specific information, as well as notices pertaining to the proprietary nature of specific documents or procedures, are critical.

5.1 General Knowledge Versus Trade Secrets

A central issue in the employment relationship typically involves the extent to which protection of a claimed trade secret affects an employee's ability to use his general skill and knowledge in subsequent employment. While an employer has a right to protect commercially valuable secrets, this right is not extended to preventing a former employee from engaging in his own profession by employing his own general knowledge and skill. Drawing a distinction between general knowledge and a particular trade secret is a balancing process.

Trade secret enforcement against a former employee also varies depending on the employee's general level of skill and role in developing the particular secret. Generally, an employee's general knowledge and ability cannot be preempted in the absence of an express contract. The enforceability of a secret is counterbalanced by the desire to avoid the employer's controlling skills that it did not contribute to developing. In contrast, where the employee acquires substantial additional skill on the job, he does so in part as a result of the employer's support. Arguably, this justifies some restraint based on the employer's interest even at the expense of the employee's general mobility. An important factor is the extent to which the employee participates in developing the secret process, design, or information. Employer protection for a trade secret is diminished if the employee is involved with, or responsible for, acquisition of the secret. As discussed in the paragraphs that follow, a developmental role may give the employee ownership of the secret. However, even if ownership vests in the employer, the developer-employee has a greater interest in retaining a right to use the product of his own skills or at least the experience and ability directly gained in its development. This claim is enhanced if the employer did not actively assert its proprietary rights. In contrast, the employer's position is enhanced if it supported development, asserted rights to it, and invested with intent to exploit it.

5.2 Confidentiality Agreements

A common provision in employment contracts is one that expressly binds the employee to the confidentiality of secret information obtained during the employee's work. Confidentiality agreements have an important role in an employer's internal security program. Confidentiality clauses serve to establish that the alleged secret holder has undertaken reasonable steps to insure that secrecy in fact exists. Failure to obtain confidentiality agreements from at least those employees directly involved in the secret processes may forfeit any claim to trade secret status.

Employers, at times, have had difficulty in enforcing confidentiality agreements. The major difficulty for employers lies in the context in which such agreements are negotiated. The general perception among courts is that employment contracts that contain confidentiality agreements are not a product of bargaining, but are imposed as a condition of employment on individuals. This perception may lead to a reluctance to enforce confidentiality agreements according to their expressed terms.

Consequently, many courts view the enforcement of confidentiality agreements as essentially dependent on basic trade secret law. Thus, despite a contract restricting disclosure of confidential or secret information, it may be necessary to establish that a trade secret was in fact involved and to distinguish protected secrets from the general knowledge and experience of the employee. Generally, a confidentiality contract cannot elevate non-secret, nonconfidential material to a protected status or substantially preempt an employee's right to use general knowledge and skill.

These comments apply to general confidentiality agreements that refer broadly to confidential, proprietary, or secret information. If the confidentiality clause is specific, it may substantially enhance enforcement. For example, where a confidentiality agreement makes specific reference to a particular product or work system, employer protection will generally be afforded. In these cases, courts have held that a specific confidentiality agreement places the employee on clear notice as to the employer's claim and facilitates protection, without broadly restricting the employee's use of general skills.

5.3 Noncompetition Agreements

Another form of employment agreement used to protect trade secrets is a noncompetition agreement, which bars the employee from engaging in professional activities in competition with his former employer.

A noncompetition clause conflicts with policies supporting an employee's right to use general skills and experience in employment. The clause creates a form of economic monopoly over the employee, forcing him to stay with a particular employer or change commercial fields. Consequently, there is substantial controversy over the enforceability of noncompetition clauses in employment agreements. In some states noncompetition clauses are barred by statute. In other states, statutory limits restrict the scope of the clauses to instances involving express protection of trade secrets.

If not prohibited, noncompetition clauses are generally enforceable if they contain substantially reasonable restrictions. That is, a question that will be examined with respect to the enforceability of such clauses is whether the protection sought by the employer is reasonable when compared with the restrictions that it might place upon the employee's ability to earn a livelihood. More specifically, reasonableness focuses attention on the geographic scope, duration, and type of activity precluded. Another relevant consideration concerns the extent to which the noncompetition clause is designed or needed to protect valuable secrets or confidential material. At a minimum, a showing of access to confidential material is essential. The critical issue involves the extent to which the activities proposed by the agreement match the employer's interest without unnecessarily restricting the employee. The enforceability of a noncompetition clause increases if it is narrowly drawn and the boundaries of the restraint clearly reflect the employer's particularized concerns. Regardless of substantive scope, a covenant not to compete may be invalid if it fails to sufficiently narrow geographic terms and conditions. Whether geographic, duration, or activity elements are at issue, a critical question involves whether the agreement is drafted in a manner that clearly reflects protectable employer interests. Given a close and identifiable relationship to a specific employer interest, both the interests of the former employer and the employee can be protected. In its absence, the employee's right to economic mobility is predominant.

Depending on the state involved, a judicial determination that part of a noncompetition clause is unreasonable leads to differing results. In some states, an unreasonable covenant is void and unenforceable. However, most states offer a more flexible approach under which some terms of the covenant may be enforceable if the agreement is divisible or otherwise subject to interpretation. Some courts have narrowed the terms of the covenant or applied the so-called blue pencil approach, in which offending terms of the contract are deleted if the remainder of the contract is enforced.

Enforcement of a noncompetition agreement typically means that injunctive relief is issued against the former employee precluding that employee from violating the agreement. In some instances, damages may be assessed against the former employee for violating the terms of the noncompetition agreement.

6.0 EMPLOYEE OWNERSHIP OF WORK PRODUCT

The employee-employer relationship is a common source of joint development and productivity. Disputes over ownership of work product between employers and employees typically involve distinct policy issues and valid competing claims to property. The employer's claim is based on financial and resource contributions. While the claim that an employer is the developer and inventor of a work product is often a fiction, it is essential that an employer receive the right to control in at least some circumstances. This control is a primary incentive for providing the resources for development. A product of creative employees is often the primary, most marketable asset of the employer.

The competing view is that work product property rights should reward the individual inventor or author. This view acknowledges the special attributes of the individual and the fact that individual creativity is essential to technological growth. Unless an individual receives some financial benefit, the personal incentive for creative work is reduced, and all potential development suffers.

These conflicting interests arise only where the employee has made a substantial, creative contribution to development of a product. In many cases, employees are hired merely to execute mechanical construction of an invention or to operate experiments under direct supervision. In such cases, no ownership claim by the employee arises. The typical ownership issue arises as a result of an employee's creative impetus and an employer's financial resources.

Generally, developments made by an employee within the boundaries of the employee's work assignment are the property of the employer. The employer invests substantial resources in the expectation of obtaining a marketable or useful product. Since both the employer and the employee are aware of this, the employee implicitly conveys his rights in the property developed. However, the presumption generally applied is that work produced by an employee is the property of the employee. An employer's claim to the employee's work product turns on the degree of active support and direction that the employer provides. Under patent and copyright law, developments outside of the general reach of a research position are not allocated to the employer in the absence of an express contract. In many cases, it is difficult to define a relationship between the creative product and the employee's work assignment. The most difficult circumstances involve an employee hired for general research work who undertakes personal research leading to a valuable development. In the absence of a contractual assignment of rights, ownership depends on the circumstances of the development and the employee's work assignment. Work related to the employer's main interest should be given to the employer. This is most likely if the employer's resources were integral to the employee's work. The expectations of the parties, implicit in the context or explicit in their behavior, are also relevant. If the employee is discouraged from and not supported in his research and development, it is inappropriate to grant ownership to the employer.

In the absence of an express contractual agreement, the employee is entitled to use his general skill and expertise, even in competitive employment. Where the employee is the developer, the level of attributable general ability is often high and includes at least some ideas, information, or skills integral to the secret itself. This context requires explicit proof that isolates a secret and demonstrates that the employee remains free to use his own expertise and skill. Thus, an employee who develops a particular data processing program for one employer is not barred from program development for another. The difficulty of distinguishing general secrets from general skills provides a rationale for an explicit provision in employment contracts. In fact, some cases have suggested that in the absence of contractual restrictions, the employee has an equal right to utilize his own work product.

7.0 REFERENCES

Harden, Patrick. *The Developing Labor Law.* Washington, DC: Bureau of National Affairs, 1992.

Merritt, Raymond W., and Clifford R. Merritt. *Corporate Counseling.* Albany: New York State Bar Association, 1988.

Nimmer, Raymond T. *Law of Computer Technology.* Warren, Gorham & Lamonte, Boston, MA: 1995

Rabin, Robert J., Eileen Silverstein, and George Schatzki. *Labor and Employment Law.* Minneapolis: West, 1988.

Toldt, E. C., ed. *Law and Business of Computer Software.* Deerfield, IL: Clark, Boardman & Callaghan, 1995.

PART 3   ENGINEERING PROFESSIONALISM

9

Engineering Ethics

Deborah G. Johnson

1.0 INTRODUCTION[*]

1.1 Overview

The codes of several engineering societies suggest that engineers have responsibilities to (1) employers, (2) clients, (3) co-professionals (or the profession as a whole), and (4) society (or the public). After a brief discussion of what it means to be a professional, this chapter will examine each of these sets of responsibilities and the problems that arise when they come into conflict.

Responsibilities to employers arise out of an employment contract which involves a delicate balance between doing what one is told and at the same time adhering to professional standards. Under this responsibility come such issues as what is entailed by loyalty to employer, how far the application to keep trade secrets goes, and whistleblowing.

Engineers have responsibilities to clients when they are employed in

---

[*]Many of the ideas in this chapter originally appeared in the chapter introductions of Deborah G. Johnson, ed., *Ethical Issues in Engineering* (Englewood Cliffs, NJ: Prentice Hall, 1991).

large firms, and even more directly when they are in private practice. Responsibilities to clients raise issues about what the proper role of the engineer should be in relation to a client, given that they have knowledge which their clients do not possess. Should engineers act as agents of clients? Should they act paternalistically on behalf of clients? Or should they find some middle ground allowing the client to be part of the decision making process? When it comes to clients, the matter of conflicts of interests is also important.

It is somewhat difficult to separate responsibilities to co-professionals or to the profession as a whole from social responsibilities in that many of the obligations that engineers see themselves as having to one another arise from the need to develop relationships which promote public trust. Practices such as giving credit for work done and not publicly criticizing one another do this.

Responsibilities to society are probably the most important ethically as well as in terms of earning public trust, for these have to do with protecting the safety and welfare of society. One of the major issues under this category arises when the responsibility to protect the public comes in conflict with loyalty to an employer or client. Such conflicts are apparent in whistleblowing, which has become an important topic in engineering ethics.

In discussing each of these sets of responsibilities, brief case descriptions of engineers facing difficult situations will be presented. The responsibilities that are at issue will be identified and where possible, arguments for what the engineer ought to do will be given.

1.2 Roles and Responsibilities

The starting place for engineering ethics is recognition that the endeavors of engineers (individually or as members of groups) have a powerful impact on the world. While the twentieth century is often characterized as an era of rapid technological growth, societies have always been shaped by the technologies they have used. Most analyses of technology and its impact on society focus on economic, cultural, and political factors. Yet engineers and engineering play a critical part in what technologies are developed, how they are used, and what impact they have.

The impacts of technology have not always been without drawbacks, nor without unforeseen, negative consequences. Technology has, indeed, been called into question in recent decades, and this critical perspective has raised serious questions about the role of engineers in our society.

Occupational roles are socially shaped; that is, they are shaped by the social institutions of which they are a part. The role of the engineer is the result of historical evolution and is influenced by evolving social practices such as engineering education, professional societies, regulatory policies, the culture of corporations, state licensing procedures, and so on. When exploring issues of professional ethics, occupational roles can be understood to be clusters of rights and responsibilities. Being a police officer, for example, entails having the right to use force and inflict harm in certain situations where such behavior would be forbidden to others. As well, it involves responsibilities, such as intervening when an individual's security is threatened, and pursuing criminal suspects, when others might simply be expected to get out of the way. Similarly, the role of engineer involves rights and responsibilities. Perhaps the most important right of engineers is the power that is exercised when a licensed engineer signs off on plans, attesting to the safety of the design. In this chapter, the focus will be more on the *responsibilities* of engineers.

The role of the engineer involves responsibilities to four different parties: society (or the public), employers, clients, and the profession (or to members of the profession). These responsibilities are generally stated in professional codes of conduct. Professional codes of conduct serve as a starting place for engineering ethics since they are representative of what engineers believe to be their ethical and professional responsibilities. Codes tell us what members of the profession think is their proper role in society. Changes that have been made in codes over time reflect changes in the way engineers have perceived their responsibilities.

Of course, professional codes of ethics have to be understood to have a multiplicity of purposes. Codes may be seen as statements to the public of a commitment to behave in ways that promote social goods and do not harm individuals or society. They may be aimed at providing guidance to members of the profession or as a sensitizing or socializing device. As well, they may be a mechanism for protecting engineers against employers; that is, an engineer might point to a professional code to support his or her refusal to do something an employer has requested. In any case, a review of the codes of professional conduct suggest that engineers have responsibilities to society, employers, clients, and their profession.

2.0 RESPONSIBILITY TO SOCIETY

The "Code of Ethics for Engineers" of the National Society of Professional Engineers (NSPE) specifies that engineers should hold the safety, health, and welfare of society *paramount*. It is not far-fetched to say that the bottom line in engineering ethics is the idea that the engineering enterprise ought to be aimed at the good of humanity and that individual engineers ought to be using their skills to improve the lot of humanity. This is an idea which has not been given prominence in recent years, but is in the historical roots of the profession. At the end of the last century and early in this century, engineers believed that their work would solve social problems and make life better.[1]

The distinction between *engineers* and *engineering* is important because too often engineering ethics is thought to be concerned only with individual behavior. The importance of collective action and of the organization of engineering is ignored. Studies of engineering ethics should focus both on *how* individual engineers ought to behave as well as on *how* the profession ought to be organized and how it ought to manage its responsibilities to society.

Claiming that engineers have responsibility to protect the safety and welfare of society is, however, the easy part. Few will deny this. The hard part comes in trying to specify what this responsibility entails. Engineers often find themselves in complex situations in which their responsibility to the public is in tension with other responsibilities. This has become particularly apparent in cases in which engineers have blown the whistle (or failed to blow the whistle) on their employers—be the employer a corporation or government agency.[2]

One way to try to understand what an engineer's social responsibility entails is to explore the grounds for attributing this responsibility to engineers. A variety of accounts have been offered in the literature on engineering ethics and professional ethics in general. Engineers master and make use of specialized bodies of knowledge, and an intuitively powerful idea is the claim that "special knowledge carries with it special responsibility." Many people seem to believe this, though when pressed, it is hard to explain why this correlation exists. One may want it to be so, but what makes it so? In a sense, the correlation is filled in by another account that has a sociological flavor. A number of scholars of professional ethics have suggested that one should think of professions as having a social contract with society.[3] Society grants professions special powers or privileges and the right to practice the profession. It supports professions with access to educational institutions, recognition of their professional organizations, legal protection, and so on. In exchange for this, professions promise to regulate themselves in ways that protect society and promote social goods. Professions must ensure that members will not abuse their special powers and privileges. On this account, then, engineers have social responsibilities because their social contract with society calls for this. Society would never support the practice of engineering unless there was the promise that it would promote social goods or, at least, that it would not be harmful to society.

This account does not tell very much about what an engineer is obligated to do in order to fulfill this responsibility. Does this responsibility require that engineers blow the whistle whenever they see something of concern? Should they refuse to work on risky projects? Should they make public statements promoting public policies for technologies? Richard De George makes headway on this in an article that has become a classic in engineering ethics.[4] Focusing on the *Pinto* case, De George argues that the engineers in the *Pinto* case did the right thing. They saw the problem with the placement of the gas tank, and they informed management about the risks that were involved. They even suggested adding a part that would remedy the problem. Management considered what the engineers reported, but decided against doing anything. At that point, the engineers did no more.

De George defends the engineers by pointing out that engineers have expertise when it comes to identifying and calculating risk and knowing how to reduce it, but they do not have expertise when it comes to determining how much risk is acceptable. It is up to management and the public to determine this. Presumably, the public expresses its sense of what is an acceptable risk through the marketplace and through government regulation. So De George builds on the correlation between special knowledge and special responsibility and sees engineers' special knowledge as limited to only a part of what is at issue when it comes to safety. Their responsibility cannot extend beyond their expertise.

Kenneth D. Alpern takes issue with De George.[5] He argues that De George lets engineers off the hook much too easily. Alpern argues that engineers must be willing to make greater sacrifices than others, and he bases his claims on a different sort of account of the origins of engineers' social responsibilities. Alpern proposes that these responsibilities come from a fundamental principle of ordinary morality, that one must "do no harm." He supplements this principle with a corollary of proportionate care: "When one is in a position to contribute to greater harm or when one is in a position to play a more critical part in producing harm than is another person, one must exercise greater care to avoid so doing." Since engineers are in a position to do greater harm, they have a greater responsibility. Alpern seems to suggest that engineers who work on a project are causally connected to negative effects that those projects or products might have even if they have only worked on a small piece of the project. They ought not to contribute to projects that they believe are too risky or harmful. Alpern believes that engineers should be told that they may have to make sacrifices when they enter the profession of engineering. By sacrifice he seems to mean that engineers may have to refuse to work on projects to which they are assigned or they may have to blow the whistle on their employers and may suffer as a result; they may be fired from a job, may be demoted, may be labeled "a trouble maker," and so on. These are consequences they should endure because their actions produce the risks and harms. Individuals should not enter the profession unless they are willing to make such sacrifices for social good.

In their work on engineering ethics, Michael W. Martin and Roland Schinzinger propose a new way of thinking about engineering which they believe brings the social responsibilities of engineers into the fore.[6] They argue that engineering, by its very nature, is experimental. It is experimental because engineers learn by trying things and seeing if they work or fail. There is always some risk involved in developing a new technology or using an old engineering principle in a new context. Given this understanding of engineering, Martin and Schinzinger argue that we should think of the responsibilities of engineers on the model of the responsibilities of those who do experiments on humans. The principle that is now accepted in medical and social scientific experimentation is that the experimenter must inform subjects about the risk involved in participation and must obtain the subject's consent before using the subject in an experiment.

Martin and Schinzinger carry this principle over to engineering. Engineers should inform those who will be put at risk by their projects and seek their consent. This means that engineers should not, themselves, decide what is acceptable risk, but they must ensure that those affected have a chance to make the decision. In other words, the social responsibility of engineers is to keep the public informed about technologies and their risks and benefits. The Martin and Schinzinger account leads to a conclusion that is similar to De George's. Engineers should bring forward their understanding and analysis, but others should have the say as to whether a project should be undertaken.

Although there are still many unanswered questions, this analysis clarifies the social responsibilities of engineers. There seems no doubt that society will be better off if engineers take responsibility for the projects on which they work. Ordinary citizens do not have the expertise to evaluate the risks of technologies and anticipate their effects. While one has some protection through the market, government regulation, and public policy, these mechanisms lag behind the knowledge of engineers.

3.0 RESPONSIBILITIES TO EMPLOYER

One of the most discussed topics in engineering ethics, at least in the 1980s, has been whistleblowing. As already mentioned, whistleblowing arises when engineers have a conflict between their responsibility to the public and their responsibility to their employer. The issue arises in engineering more so than in some other professions, such as law and medicine, because the majority of engineers do not work in private practice. They work primarily in corporations and government agencies, and in these contexts, they do not have as much autonomy as those in private practice. Engineers work in teams and generally on a piece of a large project. They work as employees.

The employee status is in tension with the necessities of professionalism and social responsibility. If engineers are to use their expertise on behalf of society, then they need the autonomy to do so. Typically, however, they work in contexts in which their employers expect loyalty. This expectation is particularly powerful given that the career path of many engineers is into the ranks of management.[7] Indeed, this tension can be understood in several ways. It is a tension between having the status of professional versus the status of employee; a tension between social responsibility and loyalty to employer; and, a tension between being evaluated by the criteria of science and being evaluated by the criteria of business.[8]

The expectation of employers that engineers (and other employees) must be loyal seems a reality that cannot be denied. While some have argued that loyalty is not appropriate to the employment context and is only a myth perpetuated by employers to get employees to behave in certain ways,[9] the best approach seems to be to recognize some legitimacy to an obligation of loyalty to employers, but at the same time recognize that there are limits to what employers should expect in the name of loyalty. For example, in situations in which an engineer is worried about the safety of a product about to be released, and is told to keep quiet about his or her other concerns because the project is already over budget and late, loyalty might call upon the engineer to pursue internal mechanisms to get the problem addressed before going public. The obligation of loyalty cannot require that engineers blindly obey every directive given to them by employers, and it cannot mean that engineers should never blow the whistle on their employers.

Another area that points to limitations on the obligation of loyalty to employer is trade secrecy. Employers have a legitimate need to protect the ideas they are developing for the marketplace. If their ideas are stolen, the time, effort, and money they have invested in developing a new product will be lost. But how far can employers go to protect their new ideas? Can they go so far as to claim that they have the right to restrict the future employment of their employees—because, in effect, they own knowledge that the engineer acquired while in their employ? Should employers have the legal right to constrain engineers from working for their competitors? Here again the limits of loyalty are pressed, for one may recognize the legitimate claims of employers to trade secrets, recognize an employee's obligation to keep those secrets, yet still claim that it is wrong for an employer to prevent an engineer from going to work at another firm on grounds that the engineer might inadvertently reveal a trade secret. The issue calls for a delicate balancing of employer rights and employee rights. Typically, it involves drawing a line between general knowledge in a field and a fairly specific trade secret, a line that is not always so easy to draw.

4.0 RESPONSIBILITIES TO CLIENTS

When engineers are not employed in corporations or government bureaucracies, they are often self-employed and work as consultants for clients. They may also work as employees of engineering firms that supply engineering services to clients. Most of what has been written about obligations to clients, even the statements in the professional codes of conduct, seems to have been written for engineers who are self-employed or employed by other engineers (in consulting firms). This is unfortunate since obligations to clients are extremely complex when the engineer is serving clients as part of his or her job as an employee of a company. Which should have the primary priority, the good of the client or the good of the corporation? In most cases these interests will not conflict, but now and then they do. For example, suppose an engineer who works for a company that sells computer products is assigned to a client company to help the client company make decisions about how to automate their various units. After working with people in one of the units, the engineer realizes that the very best way to automate the unit's operations (allowing them to do what they want to do with ease and less expense) would be to use a product that is sold not by the employee's company, but by the company's competitor. Making this recommendation will be serving the client well, but it will not be furthering the interests of the engineer's employer.

Conflicts aside, it is important to be clear on the proper role of a professional in a client-professional relationship. In his book *Professional Ethics* (1989), Michael Bayles identifies several models of the client-professional relationship.[10] At the extremes, we have the agency model and the paternalistic model. He rejects each of these. The agency model sees a professional's proper role as that of an order-taker. The professional has special knowledge that is used to do what the client wants. The professional acts as "an agent" of the client. Bayles rejects this model because it does not do justice to the special knowledge that professionals have. The professional's knowledge is often helpful to a client in figuring out what they want. For example, a patient does not go to a doctor and tell the doctor what is to be done. The patient explains or describes a problem and the doctor figures out the cause and recommends treatment. Even in engineering the client does not specify exactly what is wanted, but rather describes something the client wants to be built or designed and the engineer helps to figure out what the best solution would be. The agency model conceives expertise too narrowly. At the other extreme, the paternalistic model fully recognizes the expertise of the professional so much so that it supposes that a client must turn over decision-making power entirely to the professional. It supposes that when a client goes to a professional, the client tells the professional what the problem is and then, the professional, using his or her specialized knowledge, determines the optimum solution to the problem and acts in the best interests of the client. Bayles also rejects this model as it gives the professional too much power, failing to recognize that many aspects of decision making involve more than the application of the professional's expertise. Even in the case of the doctor-patient relationship, doctors are not expected to make decisions for their clients. They are expected to lay out the options and the risks and promises of each. Patients must evaluate what is best for them.

Rejecting both of these, Bayles argues for what he calls the fiduciary model. In this model, the professional's superior knowledge is recognized, but the client retains a significant authority and responsibility in decision making. The professional has a responsibility to provide information to the client, but must not take decision making out of the client's hands. With this understanding of the client-professional relationship, the importance of trust in client-professional relationships comes into the fore. Since the client does not have the knowledge that the professional has, the client must trust the professional to lay out the problem and involve the client at crucial points. The importance of trust leads, in turn, to the importance of honesty, candor, competence, diligence, loyalty, and discretion.[11] These obligations are repeatedly mentioned in the codes of conduct of engineering professional organizations.

One issue that seems to come up frequently in engineering, both in relationships between consulting engineers and clients and between employed engineers and clients, is conflicts of interest. In the client-professional relationship, the professional is expected to act in the interests of the client. At first glance, this may appear to imply that professionals are not to have interests of their own or, perhaps, that the interests of the client and the professional are always in harmony. One might argue that they are in harmony in the following way. A professional has an interest in serving a client well so that the professional will get the client's future business and will develop a good reputation (which assists him or her in getting other clients). The client has an interest in getting something done and so is willing to hire the professional, paying what is necessary so as to get the expertise and labor of the professional. In theory all of this is true, but in reality things are a bit more complicated. People have many short-term as well as long-term interests, not to mention that their interests are multifaceted. The professional's interest in making money, for example, is in tension with the client's interest in having to pay as little as possible. Hence, working out client-professional relationships which serve the interests of all is not a simple matter.

A good definition of conflict of interest is as follows: A person has a conflict of interest if (1) he or she is in a relationship with another requiring the exercise of judgment in that other's service and (2) he or she has an interest tending to interfere with the proper exercise of judgment in that relationship.[12] In the codes of ethics of some professions, one is required to remove oneself from situations in which there is even the appearance of a conflict of interest. Conflicts of interest situations arise in engineering in a variety of ways. The NSPE has analyzed many conflict of interest situations in its *Opinions of the Board of Ethical Review*.[13] Typically, they involve engineers acting in decision-making roles where they have personal or financial relationships that might affect their judgment. For example, an engineer serving as city engineer for a municipality reviews and approves plans for a development project to be undertaken by a private development corporation. He does not mention that his wife is a major investor in the development corporation.[14] In another case, an engineer specifies parts to be used in a project which his firm is doing and does not mention that he is a silent partner in the firm that makes the specified parts.[15] In both these cases, the engineer has an interest that could, even though it might not, interfere with his or her judgment on behalf of a client. If engineers routinely acted in conflict of interest situations, trust and confidence in engineers would be eroded.

So, as in the case of social responsibilities and responsibilities to employers, engineers must be sensitive to their responsibilities to clients. Ethical behavior in these relationships is by no means a simple matter.

5.0 THE PROFESSION AND RULES
OF FAIR PLAY

There are several ways to approach responsibilities to the profession. Some accounts have made it the overarching responsibility. Davis, for example, argues that engineers make a commitment to one another to play by certain rules, and this is the basis for most of the responsibilities of engineers.[16] Others have seen this category more as a way of focusing on behaviors that might be thought of as working against the other responsibilities. For example, some engineers may believe they have a responsibility to keep quiet about the incompetence of fellow engineers. In other words, there is some sense that engineers owe something to one another and, hence, must behave in ways that do not denigrate or threaten one another.

Yet another approach—the one taken here—is to focus on some of the rules that constitute engineering practice. Earlier I cautioned that engineering ethics should not just focus on individual engineers but also on the way in which the profession is organized. A number of rules or practices impact engineering as well as the public perception of engineering. They promote public trust and confidence and, appearances aside, promote positive outcomes from engineering endeavors.

The prohibition of bribery can be understood in this context. Some may think it unnecessary to discuss bribery in the context of engineering ethics since it is illegal, and also because it is not unique to engineering. Nevertheless, engineers do often find themselves in situations in which they are offered bribes or are expected to give bribes, and both activities hurt the enterprise as a whole.

While it is often taken for granted that engineers practice engineering in the context of business (which means a capitalist system for many engineers), it is too often forgotten that capitalism itself needs to be justified. The standard justification of capitalism is that it produces positive results. The idea is that in open competition, the best products—highest quality for lowest price—will survive, and this will benefit all concerned. Bribery undermines this goal. It undermines open competition by encouraging those who make choices—about what products are purchased, what companies are allowed to sell their products in a country, what company receives a contract—to choose not on the basis of the best product or service, but on the basis of their personal benefit. This is extraneous to the product or service. When bribery is involved in an activity, there is no guarantee that the best products will survive.

One form of bribery that has received a fair amount of public attention is bribery in international business. In some countries, bribery of officials is common practice. Engineers may have to deal with such officials and may be expected to give bribes or receive bribes. The U.S. government, however, has passed legislation that prohibits such practices, the Foreign Corrupt Practices Act (1977).

The bribery issue leads inevitably to questions about gift-giving in doing business. When does a gift, say, dinner or a turkey given at Christmas time, become a bribe? While the line may be drawn at some dollar amount, such a line is always somewhat arbitrary. Gifts seem inappropriate in the context of doing business since they are always aimed at pleasing someone, someone who is supposed to be making a business decision.

A second important issue having to do with fair play in engineering is competitive bidding. For many years, competitive bidding was not practiced, and several professional codes specifically prohibited consulting engineers from competing for jobs on the basis of proposed fees (e.g., in the American Society of Civil Engineers). That changed in 1978 when the Supreme Court ruled that professional societies were unfairly restraining free trade by banning competitive bidding. During the 1970s several highly publicized scandals came to light, suggesting that government officials were receiving personal "gifts" for selecting certain firms to receive government contracts. This added to the public suspicion that the lack of open, competitive bidding was leading to corruption.

On the other hand, engineers have argued that competitive bidding will lead to the selection of inferior engineering services. Those who make the selection may not be engineers (i.e., not in a good position to determine the qualifications of various engineering firms). If clients opt for the least expensive bid, this may encourage engineers to cut safety and quality. It may also mean less innovation in engineering because doing things the old way usually costs less than trying to develop something new. Nevertheless, there is still the problem that when there is no competition, it is much easier for engineering firms to take advantage of clients. In open competition the pressure is on engineering firms to charge as little as possible for the services they provide. This favors the client's interests.

These two issues—bribery and competitive bidding—raise broad questions not so much about the behavior of individual engineers, but rather about the rules that are or should be operative in the system in which engineers practice. The rules should be such that engineering serves society. If they are, then engineers will have a reason for following them even if they go against the individual engineer's immediate self-interest. All engineers indirectly benefit from a system of engineering that serves humanity and commands the respect of the public.

6.0 CONCLUSION: CHANGING ENGINEERS AND ENGINEERING

Engineers face many ethical issues in their professional practice. Their responsibilities to society, employers, clients, and the profession are complex and often in conflict. In recent years, a number of proposals have been made for changes in engineering that would improve the role of engineer and promote responsible behavior. These proposals are quite wide ranging in targeting different aspects of engineering. They include the following: changing the licensing process, changing the education of engineers, strengthening the role of professional societies, changing corporate culture, creating ombudspersons to whom engineers can report their concerns so as to avoid the need for whistleblowing, and creating awards and other forms of support for engineers who behave in admirable ways.

It is important to remember that change does not have to be an either-or matter; that is, one does not have to pick just one of these levers for change. While it is important to consider which approaches are most likely to make the most or best improvement in engineering, a many-pronged approach to change is plausible.

ENDNOTES

1. Edwin T. Layton, *The Revolt of the Engineers: Social Responsibility and the American Engineering Profession* (Baltimore: Johns Hopkins University, 1986).

2. See, for example, Alan F. Westin, *Whistle-Blowing! Loyalty and Dissent in the Corporation* (New York: McGraw-Hill Book Company, 1981); Robert M. Anderson et al., *Divided Loyalties: Whistle-Blowing at BART* (West Lafayette, IN: Purdue University, 1980); and Roger M. Boisjoly, "The Challenger Disaster: Moral Responsibility and the

Working Engineer," in D. G. Johnson, ed., *Ethical Issues in Engineering* (Englewood Cliffs, NJ: Prentice Hall, 1991).

3. Lisa Newton, "The Origins of Professionalism: Sociological Conclusions and Ethical Implications," *Business & Professional Ethics Journal,* Vol. 1, no. 4 (1982), pp. 33-43, and Robert F. Ladenson, "The Social Responsibilities of Engineers and Scientists: A Philosophical Approach," in Albert Flores, ed., *Ethical Problems in Engineering,* Volume 1, 2nd ed. Rensselaer Polytechnic Institute, Troy, NY (1980), pp. 238-245.

4. Richard T. De George, "Ethical Responsibilities of Engineers in Large Organizations: The Pinto Case," *Business & Professional Ethics Journal,* Vol. 1, no. 1 (1981), pp. 1-14.

5. Kenneth D. Alpern, "Moral Responsibility for Engineers," *Business & Professional Ethics Journal,* Vol. 2, no. 2 (1983), pp. 39-48.

6. Michael W. Martin and Roland Schinzinger, *Ethics in Engineering,* 2nd ed. (New York: McGraw-Hill, 1989).

7. Layton, *The Revolt of the Engineers.*

8. Ibid.

9. Ronald Duska, "Whistle-Blowing and Employee Loyalty," in D. G. Johnson, ed., *Ethical Issues in Engineering,* pp. 241-247.

10. Michael D. Bayles, *Professional Ethics,* 2nd ed. (Belmont, CA: Wadsworth, 1989).

11. Ibid.

12. Michael Davis, "Conflict of Interest," *Business & Professional Ethics Journal,* Vol. 1, no. 4 (1982), pp. 17-27.

13. National Society of Professional Engineers, *Opinions of the Board of Ethical Review,* Volume II, 1967, and Volume III, 1971. NSPE 2029 K St. N.W., Washington, DC, 20006.

14. Ibid., Case No. 66-5 (1967).

15. Ibid., Case No. 69-8 (1971).

16. Michael Davis, "Thinking Like an Engineer: The Place of a Code of Ethics in the Practice of a Profession," *Philosophy & Public Affairs,* Vol. 20, no. 2 (1991), pp. 150-167.

10

The Role of a Technical Professional Society in an Engineering Career

John J. Guarrera and Charles C. Olsefsky

1.0 INTRODUCTION

Sometime early in a career in engineering an individual might be encouraged to join a technical professional society. This could have taken place sometime during the junior or senior years of college. It could have been encouragement from a faculty member or another student who was already a student member of a society. Perhaps it was while pursuing a masters degree or at the suggestion of an immediate supervisor, a mentor on the job, or a fellow engineer. They all suggested that joining could be job enhancing. Although a very positive incentive, which of the myriad societies should be joined? There are many excellent technical societies, but the decision should be based on the particular field of expertise and personal interest of the prospective member. Depending on the technical areas of interest, joining more than one society may be the thing to do.

2.0 FOUNDING SOCIETIES

In the beginning of this century, as technical developments began to emerge and become more complex, many of the practitioners felt the need to organize into technical professional societies.[1] They would exchange ideas, writing and presenting technical papers. There was also an emerging technical industry, and the desire of engineers to keep abreast of new developments resulted in exhibitions sponsored by these societies. Society committees established standards in terminology definitions and equipment which were used by the manufacturing industry, design engineers, various government agencies, and others involved in the technology.

The first group to organize was the American Society of Civil Engineers (ASCE) in 1852; its membership today is about 90,000. The second society to organize was the American Institute of Mining Engineers (AIME) in 1871; its membership today is about 10,000. The third to organize was the American Society of Mechanical Engineers (ASME) in 1880; its membership today is about 120,000. The fourth group to organize was the American Institute of Electrical Engineers (AIEE) in 1884. The next society to organize was the American Institute of Chemical Engineers (AIChE) in 1908; its membership today is about 50,000. These five societies are known as the founding societies. All exist with the exception of the AIEE. In 1962 the members of the AIEE and the Institute of Radio Engineers (IRE), founded in 1912 by those members of the AIEE interested in the newly developing radio communications technology, voted to merge the two organizations. This resulted in the world's largest technical professional society, the Institute of Electrical and Electronics Engineers (IEEE), with a membership today of about 320,000 world-wide.

3.0 ACTIVITIES

3.1 Technology

3.1.1 Technical Information Source   Most of the engineering societies make themselves available to federal and state governments to answer technical questions in their respective areas of expertise. One of the important lessons learned, however, was that just being available was not enough. There are active groups with vested interests available to give advice and information to pursue a particular cause which may not be in the public interest. Rather than a passive role, waiting to be asked, the engineering societies discovered that a pro-active role was necessary for their technical know-how to be of value.

The National Society of Professional Engineers has been very active on the Washington scene for many years with its affiliated state societies active at the state government level. In view of the importance of pro-active involvement, most of the larger societies have developed a significant presence in Washington, DC. The societies' role in Washington has expanded to include the interests of their engineer members in areas of pension and health care reform.

Many of the complex public policy issues facing the world today need to be addressed by people with strong technical backgrounds and education. Most members of Congress who represent the public interest do not have technical expertise and are not technically trained. This is where members of technical societies are able to volunteer their services either informally or as volunteer staff members to congressmen or to the executive branch of government. Many societies have Fellow-type programs. This type of program links engineers with the government and provides a much needed private sector perspective on complex public policy issues involving technology. George F. Swetman, Jr., an IEEE congressional Fellow, has described his experiences as a legislative assistant to a U.S. senator in the July 1994 issue of the IEEE *Spectrum* magazine.[2]

Many societies provide frequent testimony to the legislative and executive branches in support of increased research and development, commercialization of technology, alternative energy sources, the information highway, health care engineering, and technology literacy. With this type of experience, members can now educate their Fellow members about the legislative process. Another program called the Executive Fellow Program was developed to assist the Commerce Department's new Technology Administration, which is involved in advancing U.S. competitiveness in electronics, manufacturing, and technology. The activities of Fellows are voluntary and they or their employers are responsible for salaries, benefits, and all other expenses.

3.1.2 Continuing Education   For a lifetime career in engineering, which is not assured with an engineering degree, engineers must maintain current and up-to-date knowledge in their area of interest. In addition, they must stay current in related and other fields to be mobile when the economy requires a change in technical needs. Frequently, engineers become narrow in technical expertise because of their work, which makes them very valuable to the company. However, when the need for their expertise is no longer needed, the company cannot continue to employ them, at their current compensation, while they learn new skills.

Continuing education is the responsibility of the engineer. Technical societies and universities are the main source of new and cutting-edge technology in their publications, meetings, conferences, courses, and short courses. It is each engineer's responsibility to take advantage of all the resources available to maintain their expertise and broaden their knowledge base into new areas.

3.1.3 Networking   Networking is meeting other engineers and company executives active in the same or related field of business. Engineering societies provide many opportunities to meet other engineers, and at some major conferences, chief executives of companies in related fields. It is extremely important to "rub shoulders" with peers in the same and related fields of work. Good employment opportunities are seldom found in the help wanted columns of the newspaper, but are frequently discussed at conferences and meetings. Technical discussions at meetings can frequently help solve sticky problems by just talking.

3.1.4 Training and Growth of Members   Many of the larger technical professional societies support student branches at the colleges and universities that have compatible technical programs in their curriculum. This then becomes the beginning of leadership training for the members of the societies.

The student branches are formally organized with officers and committees to carry out programs of interest to the students. This gives the students an opportunity to take on leadership responsibilities, which experience they can take with them to their professional careers.

In a similar way the local subunits of the societies are also organized, giving the local officers an opportunity for leadership experience which then can continue into regional, national, and international assignments. As active members move up in the ranks of the offices of their society, the leadership experience they obtain becomes ever more important in their professional growth.

3.1.5 Publishing   All societies publish material of interest to their members. In some cases this is a simple newsletter that publishes only meeting notices. In most cases there are comprehensive refereed proceedings where members publish original research work, new product development, and technical articles. Larger societies may be divided into regional sections or technical groups. Further, many societies have professional societies devoted to a particular technology sector. All publish journals, proceedings, or magazines catering to their field of interest. For example, the IEEE is known worldwide as being the largest publisher of technical literature in the field of electrotechnology.

3.1.6 Standards   Most professional technical societies are involved in developing standards. Usually a committee is formed with experts in a particular field representing manufacturers, users, government, and academe who volunteer their time and effort to develop a particular standard. These standards are then adopted first by the society and later by other entities such as a manufacturing firm, a government agency, or a foreign country. Standards usually cover materials, definitions of units, industrial methods, and testing methods. Standards enable a product manufactured by one manufacturer in any country of the world to work with or replace a product manufactured elsewhere.

Standards are very important for the practice of engineering, and it is a very serious responsibility for the societies that take the lead in their development. Although the volunteers do the work, the institutions involved have the obligation to police the use and application of standards under their control, as the ASME discovered the hard way in the famous *Hydrofoil* case. Although the harm was done by two volunteers with vested interests, the society was held responsible for not recognizing their conflict of interest. The result was financially devastating to the ASME, which was held responsible and liable for the damages to a company that was in competition with the company where the two volunteers were employed. The ASME appealed the case to the Supreme Court with supporting briefs backing their position from most of the organizations in the standards business. They lost the appeal, and those societies in the standards business have had to change their way of appointing committees and monitoring their work.

3.2 Professionalism

3.2.1 Member Development   The advantages of membership in a technical professional society are many. First and foremost is professional growth. This is accomplished by attending local, national, and international meetings and symposiums. Meeting face to face with one's peers is very broadening. The opportunity to listen to technical papers being presented and then to discuss or debate the issues with the author are self-educational. Writing and presenting papers at the various meetings and exhibitions places one as a technological leader. The availability of one's professional society publications keeps an engineer well informed in the developments of his profession. Another advantage is that of networking. Being aware of potential advancements in position or status increases one's economic status. It is important, especially for students who are just beginning the engineering journey, to avail themselves of all sources of information both technical and economic.

3.2.2 Ethics   Most engineering societies have adopted a code of ethics. Unfortunately, they could not agree on a single code for all engineers although they are all similar and cover the same basic principles. Most states have a code of ethics that all professional engineering registrants are obligated to follow as part of the licensing procedure. Following is the "model code" recommended by the National Council of Engineering Examiners (NCEE):

Preamble

In the pursuit of their professions, engineers and scientists should use their skills and knowledge to enhance the quality of life for all and should conduct themselves in an honorable and ethical manner so as to merit confidence and respect. This code is a guide to the balanced discharge of their responsibilities to society, to their employers and clients, to their co-workers and subordinates, to their professional colleagues, and to themselves.

Article 1. Engineers shall regard their responsibility to society as paramount and shall:

1.1 Inform themselves and others, as appropriate, of the consequences, direct and indirect, immediate and remote, of projects they are involved in

1.2 Endeavor to direct their professional skills toward conscientiously chosen ends they deem, on balance, to be of positive value to humanity; declining to use those skills for purposes they consider, on balance, to conflict with their moral value

1.3 Hold paramount the safety, health, and welfare of the public, speaking out against abuses of the public interest that they may encounter in the course of professional activities in whatever manner is best calculated to lead to a remedy

1.4 Help inform the public about technological developments, the alternatives they make feasible, and possible associated problems

1.5 Contribute professional services to worthy causes as appropriate

Article 2. Engineers shall practice their profession in a responsible manner, associating themselves only with honorable enterprises and shall:

2.1 Keep their professional skills up to date and be aware of current events and societal issues pertinent to their work

2.2 Be honest and realistic in making claims and estimates, never falsifying data

2.3 Accurately describe their qualifications for proposed engineering assignments

Article 3. Engineers shall, in relations with employers and clients:

3.1 Act as faithful agents or trustees in business or professional matters, provided such actions conform with other parts of this code

3.2 Keep information on the business affairs or technical processes of an employer or client in confidence while employed and later, until such information is properly released, provided such confidentiality conforms with other parts of this code

3.3 Disclose any circumstance that could lead to a conflict of interest

3.4 Neither offer nor accept bribes

Article 4. Engineers shall, in relations with colleagues, co-workers, and subordinates:

4.1 Seek, accept, and offer honest professional criticism, properly credit others for their contributions, never claiming credit for work not done

4.2 Treat them fairly in all respects, regardless of such factors as race, religion, sex, age, ethnic background, or disabilities, and respect their privacy

4.3 Help promote their professional growth

4.4 Report, publish, and disseminate information freely, subject to legal and reasonable proprietary or privacy restraints, provided such actions conform to other parts of this code

4.5 Promote health and safety in work situations

4.6 Encourage and support adherence to this code, never giving directions that could encourage others to compromise their professional responsibilities

A thorough discussion of each element of the model code is given in Stephen Unger's book, Controlling Technology, along with a discussion of other societies' codes of ethics.[3] His book also has a thorough discussion of several case histories, including the BART case, which involved the active participation of the IEEE and the California Society of Professional Engineers (CSPE), and the Virginia Edgerton case, which involved the IEEE.

The *BART* case resulted in a brief submitted by IEEE to the court establishing the obligation for an engineer to abide by a code of ethics in the workplace and accentuated the responsibility for public safety superseding all other obligations. The *Virginia Edgerton* case demonstrated the role of the engineering society to hold hearings and investigations into situations where a member, by following the requirements of the code of ethics, is harmed by an employer.

Unger's book contains a complete transcript of the IEEE brief; the conclusion is quoted here to demonstrate the implied obligation for the engineer to protect the public safety.

IEEE BART Case Brief
Conclusion:
. . . we urge this court to acknowledge that an engineer has an overriding obligation to protect the public.
Specifically, we urge this court:
(1) To rule that evidence of professional ethics is relevant, material and admissible in this case; and
(2) To rule, as to any motions for judgment or any jury instructions, that an engineer is obligated to protect the public safety, that an engineer's contract of employment includes as a matter of law, an implied term that such engineer will protect the public safety, and that a discharge of an engineer solely or in substantial part because he acted to protect the public safety constitutes a breach of such implied term.

The *BART* case was settled out of court and therefore no court precedence was established in connection with the IEEE brief.

3.2.3 Member Conduct   Some of the societies have established a Member Conduct Committee for the purpose of hearing a complaint against a member or of hearing a complaint by a member who has been harmed by following the code of ethics. The Virginia Edgerton case was the first case to be reviewed by the IEEE Member Conduct Committee after its formation in February 1978. A complete treatment of this case is in Unger's book.[4] To demonstrate the role of a society in matters of member conduct hearings, the conclusion of the Member Conduct Committee (MCC) follows:

Conclusion
The MCC concludes that Ms. Edgerton has adhered to the IEEE Code of Ethics. It is our opinion (1) that her professional training and experience qualified her to discern the potential for degradation of the police emergency dispatch system, (2) that she undertook reasonably to inform the project director of her concern, and (3) that her communication of this same concern to the Criminal Justice Steering Committee represented a good faith attempt to protect the community interests served by the computer applications about which she was informed. We believe the attempts were appropriately directed to those persons which were in part or whole responsible for the ultimate compatibility of the systems involved. Ms. Edgerton's adherence to the Code has jeopardized her livelihood. Moreover, it is our opinion that the action by those responsible for her employment termination compromised the discharge by her of her professional responsibilities.

This conclusion of the IEEE MCC did not rescind the termination, but it did clear her reputation, and that appears to have helped her in her ongoing career objectives.

3.2.4 Support for Discriminated Members   Since the passage of the Age Discrimination in Employment Act (ADEA) by Congress, many professional societies formed age discrimination committees. The purpose of these committees was to aid members who felt that they had been discriminated against. The discrimination may have been denial of a promotion, denial of a job opportunity, or the denial of any benefit solely on the basis of age. The Age Discrimination Committee (ADC) provided information as to the legal definition, the kind of supporting information needed to prove discrimination, moral support, and in some societies reference to attorneys who practiced age discrimination cases. The IEEE has such a committee and has aided members who felt that they had been discriminated against. One case that involved the IEEE was that of aiding a member of a large corporation who had been a line manager and had been schooled in the techniques of laying off engineers, especially those in the 40 to 50 age group. Eventually, he was terminated. He tried to sue the company for age discrimination but could not find any lawyers who were willing to represent him. It turned out that when he did find a sympathetic lawyer, the large company (which happened to be in a relatively small, one-company city) immediately put his firm on retainer so that he then could not represent the individual. With the help of the IEEE Age Discrimination Committee, a lawyer was found, and the case was settled out of court. This out-of-court settlement prevented others, suing for age discrimination, from using that particular case as a legal precedent.

Another case involving the IEEE Age Discrimination Committee was that of a large electronic company that terminated several senior (in age) engineers and replaced them with recent graduates doing exactly the same tasks as the senior engineers. This company even gave them the same titles but at substantially reduced compensation. These senior engineers appealed to the IEEE Age Discrimination Committee, which supported them with information learned from the previous case. They sued and eventually were reinstated in their old positions. Again, this case was settled out of court and cannot be used as legal precedence.

3.2.5 International Mobility   There are many technical professional societies worldwide covering all the technologies. Most of the societies are national in nature, and many of the U.S. societies have American in their name. The IEEE, which is the result of the merger between the American Society of Electrical Engineers and the Institute of Radio Engineers has developed a very large international membership. There are IEEE Sections and Groups in most countries throughout the world, giving its members access to fellow members everywhere. The IEEE, along with most other engineering societies, sponsors meetings and conferences in many countries.

The IEEE transnational membership is unusual and, because of the large non-U.S. membership, decided to create the United States Activities Committee to look after the national interests of its members in Regions 1-6. This later became the United States Activities Board and is now also known as IEEE-USA.

3.2.6 University Accreditation   The purpose of accreditation is to identify to the public, prospective students, educational institutions, professional societies, potential employers, governmental agencies, and state boards of registration, the institutions and specific programs that meet minimum criteria for accreditation. The organization, in the case of engineering, that does this is the Accreditation Board for Engineering and Technology (ABET). ABET organizes and carries out a comprehensive program of accreditation of pertinent curricula leading to degrees, and assists academic institutions in planning their educational programs. ABET is recognized by the U.S. Department of Education and the Council on Post Secondary Accreditation (COPA) as the sole agency responsible for accreditation of educational programs leading to degrees in engineering. All professional technical societies provide volunteer members to serve on ABET committees and give guidance to ABET.

3.3 Government

3.3.1 Legislation   Most technical professional societies are now proactive on legislative activities in Washington. The National Society of Professional Engineers has been active the longest in recent years. Early in the history of the founder societies, the need for political muscle was the stimulus for their formation. However, until the engineering recession of the early 1970s, most societies concerned themselves with the dissemination of technical information through meetings, publications, conferences, short courses, and the publication of standards.

Many of the societies were forced by member demands to get involved in state and federal politics, especially where the well-being of the engineering community was concerned.

With IEEE leadership, many sister societies joined in the legislative arena of pension reform. The trigger for this was due to the concern of members who were laid off only to discover that the pension plan they expected to benefit from did not materialize. This was an easy and comfortable activity for joint support of the societies, and the Engineer's and Scientist's Joint Committee on Pensions (ESJCP) was formed. Support of many reforms were successful, including the Universal IRA, shorter vesting, improved reporting to employees, and many activities still ongoing. Although there is reasonable harmony in the pension arena, there are still some issues in which the societies must go their separate ways, which dilutes the power of the engineering societies in the politics of Washington.

An example of one society standing alone but with the enthusiastic support of its members and board of directors was the action taken by the IEEE to amend the Service Contract Act of 1965. This act protected the continuing rights of all employees on a service contract with the government on re-employment by a new contractor, except for engineers, doctors, and lawyers. This resulted in an untenable situation at government facilities such as Cape Canaveral where cutbacks occured and new contractors took over with low bids and the only salary reductions possible were the engineers. On taking over control, the contractors immediately fired all the engineers and advertised the engineering positions at less than half of the prior prevailing wage.

Having the largest number of involved members, the IEEE stepped up to the plate to try to help. It was successful in getting an amendment to the Service Contract Act approved by the cognizant subcommittee and then by the full Labor Committee of the House of Representatives. A companion bill was introduced in the Senate by then Senator Childs of Florida. While this was going on the IEEE met on a regular basis with the concerned industry groups who were strongly opposed to the legislation. These meetings led to the development of a joint recommendation to the Office of Management and Budget (OMB) for a prevailing wage requirement in all government contracts.

The prevailing wage requirement was agreed to by OMB and is still a requirement in all government contracts. The proposed amendment to the Service Contract Act of 1965 never became the law of the land, but there is no doubt that the pressure of the IEEE legislative efforts on the industry groups led to the OMB compromise.

3.3.2 Technical Position and Policy Statements The societies acting together have developed technical position statements on issues of common concern. There are many issues that the societies cannot seem to reach a compromise in order to present a unified position. This results in each society promulgating its own version on similar issues. The societies have been criticized by congressional staff, members of Congress, and the executive branch for their inability to present a unified position on most issues. The American Association of Engineering Societies (AAES) is trying to address this problem by speaking out for all the societies it represents. This seems to make sense; however, when the AAES positions and statement, get back to the individual societies, they frequently disagree with them even though their representatives were involved in the AAES approvals. Future engineers need to pay serious attention to this lack of unity in the profession in order for the engineering community to be recognized as an important body in the political arena.

ENDNOTES

1. A. Michal McMahon, *The Making of a Profession: A Century of Electrical Engineering in America* (Piscataway, NJ: IEEE Press, 1984).

2. George F. Swetman, Jr., "A Capital Experience, *IEEE Spectrum* (July 1994),Vol 37; Number 7; page 40

3. Stephen H. Unger, *Controlling Technology—Ethics and the Responsible Engineer,* 2nd ed. (New York: John Wiley, 1994).

4. Ibid.

5. American Associations of Engineering Societies, *Directory of Engineering Societies and Related Organizations* (Washington, DC: AAES, 1994).

PART 4   ENGINEERS AND GOVERNMENT

11

Engineers and the Federal Government

Chris J. Brantley

1.0 INTRODUCTION

Technology affects nearly all aspects of life in modern society. Consider, for example, how extensively technology is employed in communications, transportation, education, health care, national defense, and entertainment. In this age of information, communication is available across continents electronically with the click of a mouse. The remotest corners of the globe can be reached with satellite communications and global positioning technologies. Bioengineers are creating and patenting new forms of life. New medical technologies are extending life expectancies and forcing reconsideration of ethical and moral notions of life and death. The computer chip has made military weapons systems "smart." At the same time, mastery of the atom has rendered world war unthinkably dumb.

In each of these examples, technology has and continues to dramatically change the ways in which people live and work. In this high-tech age, national competitiveness and the ability of industry to create high-value jobs depend increasingly on success in developing and commercializing emerging technologies as new products and services that can be sold in a highly competitive global marketplace. All these issues, and many more, are the subjects of government programs and regulations at the national, state, and local levels.

Engineers enjoy a special place in our modern society. They have an ethical obligation as members of the engineering profession to use their unique knowledge and skills for the benefit of society. Engineers' unique knowledge and experience enables them to contribute as citizens to the development of sound public policies and laws on the myriad issues that shape our increasingly complex, technologically based society. The thousands of engineers who work in government apply their skills to help develop and effectively implement these policies, laws, and the resulting programs.

Yet, only a very few scientists and engineers sit in the halls of power and participate directly in the public decision-making process. On the whole, scientists and engineers are not taking full advantage of the opportunities available to affect public policy on the issues that concern them. Corbin McNeill notes that "engineers have overcome tremendous technological challenges throughout U.S. history . . . but in recent years, engineers' inability to confront political issues has often stymied needed projects."[1] In this same vein, engineer Richard Weingardt has observed that "in the main, we are thought of as capable, if not brilliant, in problem-solving skills. However, we are not often asked—nor do we volunteer—to be involved in the 'idea' stage where the agenda for development is set."[2] This is not only contrary to the personal interests of scientists and engineers, but potentially harmful to our society. To understand how and where engineers can make contributions to sound governmental policy, it is important to understand the systems and processes by which these policies and laws are developed. In this chapter, the focus is on the federal government and its systems. The following sections examine the principle characteristics of the federal system in the United States, along with the processes of each of its component parts: the executive branch, Congress, and the judiciary. The chapter concludes with some further observations on the role of engineers in society.

2.0 THE FEDERAL GOVERNMENT

As created by the U.S. Constitution, the federal government is organized into three branches, each with its own distinct powers and responsibilities. A Congress possessing all "legislative" powers was created to pass laws providing for the national defense and public welfare. An executive branch headed by a popularly elected president was established to implement those laws and wield all "executive" powers. A Supreme Court and judicial branch were formed to exercise "judicial" powers to resolve any legal disputes arising under the Constitution, laws, and treaties of the United States.

This organization and the division of powers enumerated in the Constitution reflects several fundamental characteristics installed by the Founding Fathers in our government to provide safeguards against the potential for dictatorship and tyranny.

First, the government created by the U.S. Constitution is a republic. The republican or "representative" form of government contrasts in theory with true democracies in which citizens exercise sovereignty directly through majority vote and personal action. A republic is governed by popularly elected representatives, who wield governmental powers on behalf of the citizens whom they are elected to represent. Although conceived as a national form of government whose authority is derived directly from "We the People," the U.S. government is also federal in nature, being a federation or union of 50 states. The federal government is designed on the concept of "limited government," or the notion that government should be granted only those powers necessary to perform the tasks it is charged to undertake. One aspect of our "limited" federal government is the doctrine of reserved powers, which holds that any powers not explicitly granted to the national government by the Constitution are reserved to the states.

In addition to reserved powers, the Founding Fathers carefully divided governmental powers between the three coordinate branches of the federal government so as to establish "checks and balances," which ensure that no branch can achieve ascendancy over another. For example, Congress has the power to pass legislation, but the president can exercise the veto to prevent it from becoming law. Congress can override a veto by a two-thirds vote. The president serves as Commander-in-Chief of the armies, but only Congress can declare war and raise armies. The president can propose budgets, but only Congress can fix taxes and appropriate monies. Yet, even with these limits and checks and balances, adoption of our Constitution was not assured until the signers agreed to append the Bill of Rights, a series of 10 amendments to the Constitution guaranteeing basic rights such as freedom of speech, religion, and assembly.

One result of this separation of powers and the system of checks and balances is a time-consuming and often inefficient government process frequently characterized by conflict and stalemate between the respective branches. Decisive action is possible only when there is broad consensus on how best to proceed. It is this "inefficiency," however, which prevents the consolidation and abuse of power and affords considerable protection to personal freedoms.

3.0　THE CONGRESS

Congress is the mechanism by which the collective national, regional, and individual interests of Americans can be heard and acted upon. It is a forum for public debate and political compromise. It also serves as an important check on the "imperial" power of the presidency. The following section outlines the constitutional powers of Congress and examines its organization during the 103rd Congress (1993-1994) and processes before focusing on its role and relationship to engineering and technology policy.

3.1　Constitutional Powers

Article I of the U.S. Constitution provides that "all legislative Powers herein granted shall be vested in a Congress of the United States." Eighteen specific legislative powers are detailed in Section 8 of Article I, including the power to levy and collect taxes, to regulate commerce with foreign nations and between states, to coin money, to establish federal courts, to declare war and raise armies, and to promote "the Progress of Science and useful Arts" by providing protection for intellectual property. The eighteenth provision specified by the Constitution authorizes Congress "To make all Laws which shall be necessary and proper for carrying into Execution the foregoing Powers, and all other Powers vested by this Constitution in the government of the United States, or in any Department or Officer thereof."

Thus, Congress possesses broad powers to provide for the common defense and general welfare of the United States, including the power to approve treaties, regulate interstate and foreign commerce, raise or lower taxes, appropriate money for federal programs, confirm top executive branch and judicial appointments, and impeach federal officials, including the president and vice president.

3.2　The Organization of Congress

The basic organization of Congress is also outlined in Article I of the Constitution, which provides for a bicameral legislature composed of both a Senate and a House of Representatives.

The Senate is comprised of 100 members, with two senators selected from each of the 50 states to serve six-year terms. Terms are staggered at two-year intervals. The House of Representatives is currently comprised of 435 voting representatives (or "Congressmen" and "Congresswomen") who represent the 50 states and 5 delegates who represent the U.S. territories such as the District of Columbia and Puerto Rico. The representatives are apportioned among the states according to their respective populations as determined by the National Census. Each state is guaranteed at least one representative. When there is more than one per state, each representative is assigned to represent a specific congressional district within that state.

Although a permanent body, Congress actually only meets for a two-year term, beginning on January 3 of odd-numbered years. The two-year term of Congress is divided into two sessions, each of which is typically one year long. Any legislation introduced in Congress that fails to pass within its current two-year term automatically dies and must be reintroduced in the next Congress if it is to be further considered.

3.3 Congressional Leadership and the Party System

Very little is said by the Constitution regarding the leadership structure of Congress. Article I, Section 2, provides simply that the House of Representatives shall choose a Speaker and such other officers as are required. Article I, Section 3, provides that the vice president of the United States shall serve as president of the Senate, being able to vote only to break ties, and that a president pro tempore will be appointed to serve in the absence of the vice president. The powers of these congressional leaders have evolved over time in response to personalities, political pressures, and the needs of the institution. Perhaps the most significant defining factor has been the role of political parties in the governing process. The Founding Fathers did not conceive of the two-party political system that has evolved in the United States, and so there are no provisions in the Constitution to define or limit the roles that the political parties have come to play. Today, as a result, congressional leaders are elected by the majority party in their respective chambers to champion the party's goals and policies.

The power of congressional leaders to control the rank and file members of Congress on any given issue is dependent on individual personalities and abilities, the strength and resources of the party, the mood of the public, and the leadership role played by the president. The political parties can provide additional leverage through campaign support and funding, although access to television and to political action committee (PAC) contributions has given congressional candidates a greater deal of independence.

In the House of Representatives, the Speaker of the House enjoys considerable prestige and influence as the chief officer of that body. The

Speaker stands second in line behind the vice president to the presidential succession. The Speaker's influence derives from his personal political skills as a consensus builder and coalition maker among his 434 counterparts in the House. The Speaker's influence is reinforced by control over various procedural rules including the power to schedule floor business and recognize members who wish to speak.

The House majority leader is chief deputy to the Speaker and serves as floor leader and chief legislative manager for the majority party. A counterpart, the minority leader, performs similar duties for the minority party.

The rank and file in the House of Representatives can check the power of their leaders through the two-party caucuses, the Democratic Caucus and the Republican Conference. Established in the early 1800s, party caucuses are forums for members of each political party to debate legislative strategy and set party rules. The respective party caucuses also elect the chairmen and ranking minority members to each of the House committees.

Although designated as the president of the Senate by the Constitution, the vice president of the United States does not typically preside over that body unless a tie vote is expected or there is a ceremonial purpose. The formal Senate leadership, therefore, devolves to the president pro tempore, who is third in line in the presidential succession after the vice president and the Speaker of the House.

Unlike the House, the highly egalitarian Senate has limited the leadership functions of the president pro tempore to those of a presiding officer. Accordingly, the president pro tempore enjoys the power to recognize members desiring to transact floor business, decide points of order, appoint members to conference and special committees, enforce decorum, and administer public oaths. Much of the real power is invested in the Senate majority leader, who supervises the party apparatus and who, like his House counterpart, acts as the floor leader and chief legislative strategist. The Senate minority leader serves a similar function for the minority party.

Power in the Senate is much more diffuse than in the House. The nature of the office—that is, two elected per state for a six-year term—puts all senators on equal footing and encourages individualism. The smaller size of the Senate also allows for more collegial decision making. The rules of the Senate are considerably more flexible than those imposed in the House. For example, time for debate in the Senate is generally unlimited, and there are fewer restrictions on the "germaneness" of debate or amendments.

3.4 The Committee System

Much of the work of Congress is done in committee. In the 103rd Congress there were a total of 48 committees and over 212 subcommittees, each with its own specific jurisdiction or area of legislative responsibility. When new legislation is introduced, the first step in the consideration process is its referral to each committee with jurisdiction over the subject matter of the bill. Committees jealously guard their jurisdictions. They also control their respective legislative agendas. The committee chair determines what subjects on which to hold committee hearings, what legislation will take priority, and when specific bills will be marked up and voted on by the committee. Thus, the committees effectively control the content and timing of legislation presented for floor action. Far fewer bills ever emerge from committee than are introduced and referred there.

There are several types of committees. Standing committees are permanent entities created by legislation or congressional rule to conduct the annual business of Congress. There are currently 17 standing committees in the Senate and 22 standing committees in the House. (See Figure 11.1.)

The workhorses of Congress, standing committees are responsible for

Senate Committes	House Committes
-Agriculture, Nutrition, and Forestry	-Agriculture
-Appropriations	-Appropriations
-Armed Services	-Armed Services
-Banking, Housing and Urban Affairs	-Banking, Finance and Urban Affairs
-Budget	-Budget
-Commerce, Science and Transportation	-Disctrict of Columbia
-Energy and Natural Resources	-Education and Labor
-Environment and Public Works	-Energy and Commerce
-Finance	-Foreign Affairs
-Foreign Relations	-Government Operations
-Government Affairs	-Administration
-Indian Affairs	-Judiciary
-Judiciary	-Merchant Marine and Fisheries
-Labor and Human Resources	-Natural Resources
-Rules and Administration	-Post Office and Civil Service
-Small Business	-Public Works and Transportation
-Veterans' Affairs	-Rules
	-Commerce, Space and Technology
	-Small Business
	-Standards of Official Conduct (Ethics)
	-Veterans' Affairs
	-Ways and Means

Fig. 11.1   Standing Committees in the 103rd Congress

budgeting, appropriations, authorizations, revenue and taxes, and administrative/procedural matters. Each standing committee typically has several subcommittees.

Select (or special) committees are formed by Congress to conduct investigations or study specific issues such as ethics, aging, or Indian affairs. One famous select committee, the Senate Select Committee on Campaign Activities, investigated the Watergate affair in 1972. A select committee's composition, jurisdiction, and term are set by the resolution that created it. At least one such committee, the Permanent Select Committee on Intelligence, functions like a standing committee and has the power to consider and report legislation. In addition to the House and Senate Select Intelligence Committees, there was also a Special Committee on Aging and a Select Committee on Ethics in the House of Representatives for the 103rd Congress.

Joint committees contain members from both the House and the Senate and are formed to promote administrative efficiency. There were five joint committees in the 103rd Congress: Economic, Taxation, Library, Printing, and Organization of Congress. Like select committees, joint committees are created by statute or resolution establishing the committee's jurisdiction, size, and powers. The chair of the committee rotates between House and Senate. Joint committees are not generally authorized to consider or report legislation, but can conduct hearings, provide oversight, and make recommendations. The most important of the joint committees is undoubtedly the Joint Economic Committee, which was created to study national economic issues and to review the execution of fiscal and budgetary programs.

Not all committees are equal in the eyes of members of Congress. Members generally seek to serve on those committees that are most powerful and whose business relates to their personal interests or affects the economic interests of their state or district. A member from an agrarian district is likely to pursue a position on the Agricultural Committee, whereas a member whose state hosts several military bases will typically seek a slot on the Armed Services Committee. Similarly, members who have science or technical backgrounds or who represent districts with high technology business or large research-intensive universities are likely to pursue membership on the Senate Commerce, Science, and Transportation Committee or the House Science, Space, and Technology Committee. All members would jump at the chance to serve on the powerful tax committees (i.e., House Ways and Means and Senate Finance Committees) or the Appropriations Committees. The chairs of the 12 subcommittees of the House and

Senate Appropriations Committees are often referred to as the "Cardinals of the Congress" because of their ability to effectively control the distribution of federal funding to the states and districts.

Committees are the engines of the legislative process. Individuals or organizations who hope to inspire action on an important issue or influence the outcome of key legislation must be aware of the committee jurisdictions and committee politics that are involved. Committee hearings present one of the best opportunities for substantive input to Congress, which can be given in the form of oral testimony or submission of statements for the hearing record.

3.5 How Laws Are Made

Each year, members of Congress propose thousands of new laws, but relatively few survive the complex process of review and approval that leads to presentation of a law for presidential signature and implementation. This process, described in the paragraphs that follow, is summarized visually in Figure 11.2.

The process of making laws begins with the introduction of proposed legislation (i.e., a bill or resolution). New bills may be introduced in either the House of Representatives or the Senate. The one exception, outlined in Article I, Section 7 of the Constitution, is that "all Bills for raising Revenue shall originate in the House of Representatives; but the Senate may propose or concur with Amendments as on other bills."

When a bill is introduced in either chamber of Congress, it is immediately referred to the committee or committees that have jurisdiction over the subject matter of the bill. Each committee will then typically pass the bill down to its responsible subcommittee(s) for consideration. Many bills die at this stage because the leadership of the committee or subcommittee decides to take no action on the bill. This may occur due to substantive disagreements with the bill's author over the policy goals or implementation mechanisms proposed in the bill, because committee leaders have given higher priority to another bill on the same subject matter, or because other issues before the committee are deemed more pressing.

If the committee or subcommittee decides to take action on a bill, congressional hearings are then usually held. Once the hearing process and the public record are complete, the bill is referred to the next level, the full committee or the floor of the House or Senate.

A bill reported by a House committee is generally referred to the House Rules Committee, which establishes a "rule" specifying the conditions for

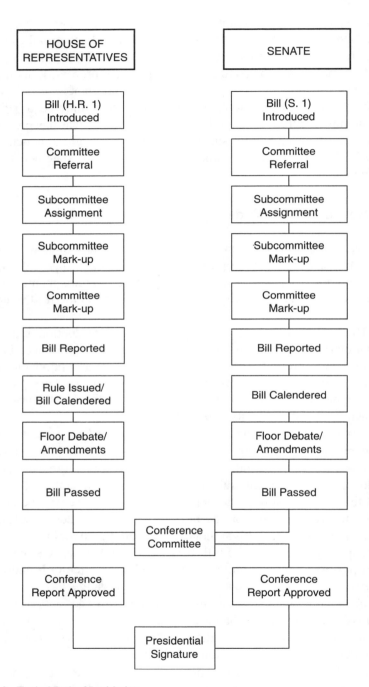

Fig. 11.2   Typical Path of Legislation

debate and any limitations on the number and type of amendments that may be offered. When cleared for floor consideration, the bill is then placed on one of four calendars, which determine when debate and votes will be held. This highly structured process helps the House of Representatives deliberate in an efficient, orderly manner. The political leadership, however, can use their control of the process to influence both the content of legislation and its prospects for passage.

The Senate procedures are much less formal. There is no Rules Committee, although the leadership controls the schedule and can use its powers to influence the consideration of legislation. Unlike the House, which places strict limits on the time available for debate, the Senate allows extended debate. This can lead to a "filibuster," where opponents of a bill can use the floor debate and/or various procedural motions such as quorum calls to block action on a bill. The classic filibuster, where the bill opponent holds the floor until the bill's supporters essentially give up or time runs out, however, is now rare due to the adoption of provisions for cloture of debate by a vote of three-fifths of the Senate.

Once passed by either the House or Senate, legislation is referred to the other chamber for consideration. The bill then goes through the same process of committee referral, floor debate, and voting. In many cases, each chamber of Congress will introduce and consider legislation on similar subjects simultaneously to expedite the process. Then, when both chambers have passed related bills (or where the Senate has amended House appropriations bills), a conference committee with members appointed from each chamber is created to work out the differences. The resulting compromise bill is referred back to each chamber for final approval.

After approval by both Houses of Congress, final bills are referred to the president of the United States. The president may choose to sign the bill into law, allow it to become law without his signature, or veto the bill and return it to Congress. Congress can override a presidential veto by a two-thirds majority vote in both houses, causing the bill to become law over the president's objections.

3.6 The Staffing of Congress

Members of Congress rely greatly on the support of their staffs to keep up with their heavy workloads. Today, there are over 36,500 congressional staffers, including clerks, janitors, and carpenters as well as professional staff, supporting the 535 members of Congress. Members look to their professional staffs to serve as repositories of expertise, competent to assess the issues and give them sound advice. Staffers often take on the roles of policy activists, looking for issues on which their members can introduce legislation, as well as erecting roadblocks to competing legislative initiatives.[3]

Staff titles and functions vary widely, although there are some standard conventions on the personal staffs of members of Congress. An administrative assistant (AA) typically runs the personal office, acting as the chief of staff and political advisor to the member. Legislative directors and/or legislative counsels are senior advisors who help coordinate the office's legislative efforts. Legislative assistants (LAs) are assigned to specific issue areas and handle the day-to-day legislative functions such as drafting bills, writing speeches, preparing for hearings, or meeting with lobbyists. An appointments secretary or scheduler handles the representative's calendar. Press secretaries or aides work with the media and prepare speeches, press releases, and press briefings. Legislative correspondents assist with constituent requests for information and prepare responses to constituent letters. Finally, case workers are typically employed in the member's state or district offices to help constituents resolve problems with executive agencies and departments and to serve as the member's local eyes and ears.

Committee and subcommittee staffs are usually run by a staff director or chief counsel and composed of a number of professional staff members. Committee staffers are asked to undertake a wide variety of functions, including working with the chairman to plan the committee's agenda, organizing hearings, conducting actual oversight and investigations, drafting and marking up bills and amendments, preparing reports to accompany approved bills, supporting the chairman during floor action or conference committee work on legislation, and serving as a liaison with executive branch staff and point of contact for special interest lobbyists.

3.7 Science, Engineering, and Technology in Congress

Congress establishes and funds agencies and programs to support science and engineering research and development efforts. Congress controls science- and technology-related activities by creating regulations that effect a wide variety of areas such as nuclear power, environmental pollution, or use of human and animal subjects in research. Congress also uses scientific and technical information in various ways to help make policy decisions on most important national issues.

Responsibility for science, engineering, and technology issues is diffused throughout Congress and its committees and is tied closely to the budget process of authorizations and appropriations. Members act on science, engineering, and technology issues in accord with their understanding of the issues and the interests of their constituencies. In recent years, for example, tight caps on discretionary spending and concerns about U.S. competitiveness have led members of Congress to support more applied research at the expense of support for basic research and to demand that all research be more closely tied to serving national needs.

In instances where science and engineering activity translates into federal funding and facilities within a member's state or district, sound "scientific" decision making in the national interest may give way to "pork barrel" politics designed to promote the economic interests of a state or region. For its part, the executive branch is just as likely to spread the benefits (e.g., R&D funding, procurement contracts, and construction of facilities) of its large science and technology projects geographically to ensure a broad base of congressional support for continued funding.

Dozens of congressional committees and subcommittees have important science and technology issues areas within their respective jurisdictions. Committee jurisdictions, however, are not always so clearly drawn. Science and technology legislation introduced by members often touches on issues or involve federal programs that cross committee jurisdictions.

The principal civilian science, engineering, and technology budget authorizing committees are the House Science, Space, and Technology Committee and its counterpart, the Senate, Commerce, Science, and Transportation Committee. The House and Senate Armed Services Committees are responsible for authorizing defense research and development and addressing issues related to defense industry and technology. Similarly, the House Energy and Commerce and the Senate Energy and Natural Resources Committees authorize civilian-and defense-oriented energy research and development. The Energy and Commerce Committee is also responsible for telecommunications issues.

The authorizing committees vie with the House and Senate Appropriations Committees for influence. Whereas the authorizing committees consider legislation that defines the purposes and sets funding limits on federal science and technology programs, the Appropriations Committees decide which programs will be funded and how much they actually receive. Appropriators do not always follow the guidance laid down by the authorizers. Moreover, key appropriations decisions are made within the Appropriation Committee's 12 subcommittees, each of which are responsible for funding different federal agencies. This not only discourages overall coordination of research and development funding, but places that funding in direct competition with nonscience and technology programs such as housing, veterans' affairs, and prisons. Other committees also play important roles related to science, engineering, and technology. The House Government Operations Committee and the Senate Governmental Affairs Committee evaluate the effectiveness of federal agencies and their science and engineering programs as a part of their oversight and investigations mission. The House Finance and the Senate Ways and Means Committees are responsible for all tax and revenue measures that affect science and engineering activity, such as the Research and Experimentation Tax Credit.

Members of Congress and the congressional committees draw information on science and technology issues from a number of resources to aid their decision making. To help them digest, analyze, and disseminate this information, they can call upon the assistance of five congressional support agencies.

The Congressional Research Service (CRS), a division of the Library of Congress, includes a Science Policy Research Division, which performs policy research and analysis and prepares issue briefs on science and technology issues.

Performing essentially an oversight function, the General Accounting Office (GAO) investigates and reports on executive branch programs and operations in response to requests by individual members of Congress and committees. The GAO reports on science and technology programs such as the space station have played a large role in shaping congressional debate on these programs.

The Office of Technology Assessment (OTA) was created to provide Congress with an independent mechanism for securing "unbiased" information and assessments of the physical, biological, economic, social, and political effects of technology and its applications.

The Congressional Budget Office (CBO) provides economic and budgetary information to help guide the congressional budget process. CBO performs both general and program-specific budget analysis on science, engineering, and technology programs.

The Government Printing Office (GPO) is responsible for printing and publishing the *Congressional Record* and the *Federal Register* and various other government periodicals and reports. The GPO releases copies of bills pending in Congress, reports of committee hearings, and related legislative materials.

3.8 Engineers and Congress

There are relatively few members of Congress with scientific or engineering backgrounds. There are also relatively few scientists and engineers employed on the personal or committee staffs of Congress. Why is this so? James Katz observes that technical brilliance is often accompanied by a lack of social skills, which can be a professional or political handicap. He also notes:

> A second important problem derives from the fact that scientists, by virtue of their professional training, are not likely to be sensitive to the political aspects and implications of technical information and scientific advice. Scientists and engineers are taught to be rational and critical, not to heed tradition for its own sake. They find it difficult in many cases to bow to sentiment at the cost of efficiency. They tend to view favorably the advantages of progress for society without weighing the costs such changes might impose on particular groups within society. The idea that sometimes people have to support something bad or stupid in order to get something they want ... can be repugnant to scientists who pursue truth and accuracy regardless of personal costs. The socialization process of becoming a scientist and engineer makes it inherently difficult for professionals to "adulterate" their advice with information about seemingly irrelevant, irrational factors that are the sine qua non of the exercise of democratic political power.[4]

Where, then, does Congress get the advice it needs to develop sound public policies on technically complex issues? Much of the information provided to Congress on technical issues comes from the executive branch, which can call upon its engineers employed in the various departments and agencies. Special interest groups including technical trade and professional associations offer technical advice and policy recommendations. Congress can hold hearings to gather input from experts in the field. Congress can also look internally to analyses prepared by the Office of Technology Assessment, the Congressional Research Service, or their own staffers. Members and their staff often contact universities or companies in their state or district who have technical experts at their disposal. Members of Congress pay particular attention to input from the people who elected them. Most likely to get a member's ear are those who have helped the member politically, represent an influential constituency, or can offer timely insight or information useful to the member's current deliberations.

Engineers can play an important role in helping to shape sound public policy even if it is only by communicating concerns to their representatives in Congress. They possess technical knowledge that is often needed. They are trained as problem solvers to use tools such as systems level thinking, modeling, and quantitative reasoning, which can be applied to the policy development process. They have a responsibility as good citizens to participate in decisions that will affect their future and the future of the country. Scientists and engineers should take special note of William Wells's enjoinder: "All too often we hear scientists and engineers bemoaning the lack of scientific and technical understanding in Congress. If we, as scientists and engineers, expect Congress to understand us, it is essential that we make more of an effort to understand and work with them."[5]

How can engineers effectively communicate with their representatives in Congress? First, they should be aware and knowledgeable about the issues. Newspapers, periodicals, professional publications, and even television can keep them apprised of the important issues of the day. Then they must have a means to communicate their ideas and concerns. Unless they are elected to public office or have a personal relationship with an elected representative, they will need to use the standard tools—the personal letter, the telephone call, and the visit.

Never underestimate the importance of a well-written and informative personal letter. A good letter is written on personal stationary with a return address. It quickly identifies the subject (including the name and/or bill number of any legislation being addressed) and focuses on only one issue. It states the area of concern and what action is desired, using personal examples if possible. It provides supporting reasons based on facts that can be readily substantiated. The letter should be reasonable and not condescending or overly emotional in tone. Finally, it should be concise. Unlike mass-mailed form letters, which arrive and are typically discarded by the bagful, personal letters from constituents are accorded particular attention. They are reviewed individually by staffers who can follow up or make recommendations for consideration by the member of Congress.

Phone calls and visits can also be effective tools. Follow the same guidelines used for written communications—be prepared, informative, and concise. Many individuals, particularly constituents who are seeking help with a problem or concern, hope to communicate directly with their member of Congress. They are discouraged when they are "shunted" aside to a congressional staffer. In many cases, however, a congressional staffer can be the most effective contact, particularly if the staffer has the time to listen and the expertise to understand your issue or concern. Contacts in the senator's or representative's state or district offices are also often good places to start since state or district staffers are usually less harried than their Washington counterparts, often have a better sense of local issues, and will be responsible as case workers for following through on your concern. The best advice is to find out which staffer is responsible for the issue of concern and then communicate with that staffer.

In addition to personal communication, investigate the legislative resources available through an employer, professional or trade association, social groups, and/or local political party organization. Get involved. Don't be dissuaded by the label "special interest." Remember, everyone who communicates with Congress has a special interest.

Finally, engineers and engineering students should take note of programs that provide unique opportunities for participation in the public policy process. For example, a number of organizations, including the Institute of Electrical and Electronics Engineers (IEEE) and the American Society of Mechanical Engineers (ASME) co-sponsor the Congressional Science and Engineering Fellowship program, which places 20 to 30 scientists and engineers each year in one-year fellowships on the staffs of members of Congress or congressional committees. Similarly, the IEEE and the ASME participate in the Washington Internships for Students of Engineering, a highly selective summer internship program for undergraduate engineering students to study the public policy process firsthand while earning academic credit.

4.0 THE EXECUTIVE BRANCH

Popularly elected as our nation's chief executive, the president heads the executive branch of the U.S. government, which includes our huge federal bureaucracy. The president sets the nation's political agenda by using the prestige of the office and the electoral mandate to persuade and cajole Congress to act in certain ways. Without a strong mandate, however, the president's power to influence Congress or direct the bureaucracy is often more symbolic than real. The various executive departments and agencies jealously guard their institutional prerogatives and compete for limited budgetary resources to serve their respective missions.

4.1 Constitutional Powers

Article II, Section 1, of the Constitution provides simply that "the executive Power shall be vested in a president of the United States." The president is elected by electors (i.e., members of the Electoral College), who in turn are popularly elected in each state, with the number of electors from each state being equal to the number of members of Congress representing that state. A vote in a presidential election is, in fact, a vote for the electors who are pledged to vote for the preferred candidate. The president serves a four-year term. The twenty-second Amendment to the Constitution, adopted in 1951 after the four-term presidency of Franklin Delano Roosevelt, provides that no president may serve more than two terms. To be eligible for the office, a presidential candidate must be a natural-born citizen of the United States, at least 35 years of age, and have lived within the United States at least 14 years.

Section 2 of Article II outlines specific powers, noting that the president "shall be Commander in Chief" of the military forces, may grant reprieves and pardons for offenses against the United States, and shall have the power to make treaties and appoint public officials "by and with the Advice and Consent of the Senate." The powers of the presidency are also derived from the customs of nations and by historical precedent.

Throughout U.S. history, the president has played five key roles. First and foremost, the president is the symbolic chief of state, the individual who represents the governmental authority of the United States on formal and ceremonial occasions. Per Article II, the president is also the chief executive, charged with faithfully implementing the laws passed by Congress. As a popularly elected official and a political party leader, the president typically becomes the nation's chief legislator, proposing legislation to Congress to address issues such as health care reform, national service, or science and technology policy to give effect to campaign promises and the planks of the party platform. Consistent with the treaty power outlined in Article II, the president is the nation's chief diplomat, responsible for maintaining our relationships with other countries and promoting the national interest through our foreign policies. Finally, as Article II confirms, the president serves as Commander-in-Chief of the Armed Forces and is responsible for developing and executing national security policy.

4.2 The Organization of the Executive Branch

Although Article II affirms the president's power to appoint heads of executive departments, the Constitution does not specify the organization of the executive branch. The Founding Fathers left it to Congress to create the first executive departments (i.e., the State, Treasury, and War departments) by legislative statute. From the original three executive departments, the executive branch of the United States has grown to encompass 14 departments and 75 independent agencies, as well as dozens of specialized offices, boards, and councils within the Executive Office of the President. Excluding the approximately 1.76 million Americans in military service, the executive branch employs over 2.9 million civilians or approximately 11.8 federal government employees per 1000 Americans.

The Executive Office of the President encompasses the president's senior staff advisors, the various White House staff offices, office of the vice president, the office of the U.S. trade representative, major planning and operational offices such as the Office of Management and Budget and the Central Intelligence Agency, and various policy advisory bodies such as the Domestic Policy Council, the National Economic Council, the National Security Council, and the Office of Science and Technology Policy.

The 14 departments form the next level of government. Dubbed "cabinet departments," each executive department is headed by a presidentially appointed secretary (or attorney general in the case of the Justice Department) who sits on the president's cabinet of policy advisors. Each department was founded by an act of Congress to serve a specific mission, such as the Department of Commerce, which was created to promote business and commerce in the United States. Within the Department of Commerce are a number of subordinate program agencies and offices responsible for a variety of related programs, including the U.S. census, patents and trademarks, development of national measurement standards, national oceanic and atmospheric research, distribution of technical information, trade and export controls, manufacturing extension services, and development of advanced technology.

A large number of independent agencies have been created by Congress to perform a wide variety of executive and regulatory functions. The degree of control exercised by the president over these agencies also varies widely. Some, like the National Science Foundation and the National Aeronautics and Space Administration, operate much like small executive departments and are very responsive to the president's policy agenda. Others, particularly the regulatory agencies like the Interstate Commerce Commission, the Federal Reserve Board, the Federal Communications Commission, and the Securities and Exchange Commission were deliberately structured by Congress to minimize presidential control and encourage their independence from political considerations.

Rounding out the executive branch are a number of government corporations such as the Tennessee Valley Authority, AMTRAK, COM-

SAT, the Student Loan Marketing Association (Sallie Mae), and the largest of them all, the U.S. Postal Service.

4.3 Science, Engineering, and Technology in the Executive Branch

The executive branch is responsible for implementing the science and technology policies and programs outlined in legislation passed by Congress and signed into law. The president also can play a strong role in setting the science, engineering, and technology agenda for the nation. Each new administration typically issues a policy document defining its key science and technology goals and providing a blueprint for federal efforts to promote science and technology. The Clinton administration released such a statement in February 1993 entitled "Technology for America's Economic Growth." It set three broad goals, namely, targeting federal investments in technology development, education, information infrastructure, and transportation to create jobs and promote long-term economic growth; using technology to make government more efficient and responsive; and securing U.S. leadership in basic science, mathematics, and engineering.

The president's science and technology policy is typically developed and coordinated with the assistance of the president's science advisor. Recently retitled the Assistant to the President for Science and Technology, the president's science advisor is equivalent in rank to the president's national security advisor. The science advisor serves as a resource for personal advice to the president as well as an administration spokesperson and diplomat on science and technology issues.

The science advisor has a dual role as the congressionally confirmed director of the Office of Science and Technology Policy (OSTP). Located within the Executive Office of the President, the OSTP was created and charged by Congress to coordinate federal science and technology policy development and research and development programs within the various departments and agencies. OSTP's small staff and limited influence over the federal budgeting process have limited its effectiveness.

Recognizing this fact, President Clinton established a National Science and Technology Council within OSTP in November 1993 to provide a strong mechanism for coordination of federal science and technology policy and budgeting. Chaired by the president, the council's membership is comprised of cabinet-level department heads and science agency directors. Under its charter, the new council will provide advice and make recommendations on research and development programs and funding levels that reflect national goals to the Office of Management and Budget. In addition to his science advisor and the council, the president can call upon the advice of 15 preeminent business leaders and distinguished individuals from the science and engineering community who are appointed to serve on the President's Committee of Advisors in Science and Technology (PCAST). The PCAST is also charged to assist the National Science and Technology Council by securing private sector participation in its activities. PCAST is co-chaired by the science advisor and a nonfederal PCAST member selected by the president.

Through these mechanisms, the president provides direction and policy guidance to the federal departments and agencies with science and technology missions. Each of the departments and agencies has its own specific missions and programs, which are too extensive to describe in detail here.

4.4 Engineers and the Executive Branch

The federal government directly employs approximately 6 percent of the more than 900,000 scientists and engineers in the United States. Their work includes basic and applied research, development, test and evaluation, management, teaching, and related activities.

In addition to the thousands of scientists and engineers who are directly employed by the federal government, there are also hundreds of appointed positions in the executive branch that are responsible for policymaking and management of important scientific and/or technical programs. The Council for Excellence in Government has identified what it deems the 60 toughest government science and technology jobs in Washington. Yet, in its 1991 survey, only three quarters of those positions were filled by individuals with scientific or technical backgrounds.[6]

Why is that so? There are several contributing causes. Washington may seem a foreign place to scientists and engineers. Individuals trained in systems thinking and analytical decision making can find the process of open debate and political compromise irrational. Appointments are typically for a limited term (one to four years) and represent a significant diversion from the typical career path. Government pay and working conditions are seldom comparable to the private sector despite the fact that expectations and job pressure on appointees often outstrip their private sector counterparts. There are, however, many highly qualified engineers who are willing to enter public service for a variety of reasons, not the least of which is the opportunity to be involved in making the decisions that shape our society.

How can scientists or engineers position themselves for government appointment? Knowing what appointments are available and putting themselves forward as candidates are prerequisites to success.[7] Having the right expertise and experience for the job is essential. In that regard, effective communication skills, management experience, and knowledge of governmental processes are every bit as important as technical education. Also important is personal standing and prestige within the profession and in the society at large. Personal characteristics such as age, gender, or ethnic background can also work in your favor if the Administration is looking for diversity. Most important, however, is the political litmus test. How have you helped the individuals who will make or must confirm the appointment? Active involvement in the political process and support of the party in power is an invaluable asset. It is on the latter count that aspiring public servants almost invariably fall short.

5.0 THE FEDERAL BUDGET

With an annual budget in excess of $1.5 trillion, the federal government is by far the largest employer and the largest consumer of goods and services in the United States. Through its budget, the federal government supports the military services and procures weapons for the national defense, pays Social Security and medical entitlements, and invests in discretionary programs such as research and development. Historically, policymakers have looked to the federal budget and to government spending to fuel economic growth in times of economic recession. Today, after decades of deficit spending, the nation is concerned about the accumulated $4 trillion in national debt and its impact on our economy. Clearly, the budget is the chief mechanism by which public policy is implemented and the budgetary process provides an important forum for public policy debate and decision making.

5.1 An Overview of the Federal Budget

Under current law, the federal budget is divided into two basic categories of expenditures—mandatory and discretionary. Mandatory expenditures constitute approximately two-thirds of the budget and include entitlements such as Social Security, Medicare/Medicaid, and income security, as well as payment of interest on the national debt, which accounted for over 14 percent of the fiscal year 1994 budget. These expenditures are termed "mandatory" because laws mandating these expenditures are in place. Congress and the executive branch have little or no control in determining the amount of annual expenditures. The balance of federal expenditures are classified as discretionary. In congressional appropriations for fiscal year 1994, defense spending constitutes just over 50 percent of discretionary spending, domestic programs 46 percent, and international programs (i.e., foreign assistance) 4 percent. Funding for programs within the three discretionary budget categories is allocated annually by Congress in appropriations legislation to specific government departments and agencies, including Congress and the judicial branch.

5.2 How the Budget Is Developed

The federal government operates on a fiscal year, which runs from October 1 to September 30. The process of developing the federal budget for a given fiscal year involves years of analysis and projection that are focused into approximately two years of detailed planning and review by the executive branch and Congress.

The process begins with the president, who provides broad direction to the Office of Management and Budget on budget policy. Based on its preliminary economic assumptions and revenue projections, the OMB provides the departments and agencies with budget planning targets almost two years before the fiscal year being budgeted. After consultation with the agencies, the OMB presents its budget recommendation to the president for approval. By law, the president is required to submit a budget request and budget message to Congress by the first Monday in February.

Based on estimates of budget revenues developed by the Congressional Budget Office and the OMB analysis, the House and Senate Budget Committees then prepare a concurrent budget resolution for congressional approval by April. The budget resolution sets the total amount of federal spending that will be allowed in the forthcoming fiscal year.

Each year, Congress works to complete the appropriations process by October 1, which marks the beginning of the new fiscal year. By custom, appropriations bills originate in the House of Representatives. The House Appropriations Committee submits proposed appropriations bills to the House for action. The Senate Appropriations Committee and its subcommittees review the House proposals and propose amendments. A conference committee is appointed with members from both chambers to consider the

House bill and the Senate amendments. The resulting compromise is reported for approval by both Houses and submitted to the president for signature.

In an effort to control deficit spending, a series of budget laws have been passed in recent years, including the Gramm-Rudman-Hollings Act of 1985, the Balanced Budget and Emergency Deficit Control Act of 1985 (Public Law 99-177), and the 1990 budget agreement (Public Law 101-508). Most recently, the Omnibus Budget Reconciliation Act of 1993 (Public Law 103-66) placed new constraints on the budget process to limit the growth of discretionary spending at 1993 levels through 1998 and to require that funding for new programs be revenue neutral (i.e., offset by decreases in other programs or by tax increases). As a consequence, federal science, engineering, and technology programs must directly compete with other discretionary programs like health, prisons, or veterans for shrinking budget resources.

5.3 Science and Technology in the Federal Budget

In fiscal year 1994, Congress appropriated approximately $71.6 billion to support federal research and development on science and technology programs. This represents just under 5 percent of the entire federal budget or just over 13 percent of total federal discretionary spending. As a source of research and investment funding, the federal government provides over 40 percent of the total national funding, which is second only to industry. Although it is a large source of R&D dollars, the federal government only performs approximately 10 percent of the R&D it funds in federal laboratories. The balance is performed under contract by industry, universities, or nonprofit federally funded research and development centers.

With the end of the Cold War, the emphasis on defense-related federal spending has slowly shifted in recent years toward civilian R&D, which accounted for approximately 45 percent of the fiscal year 1994 R&D budget. There is also an increased emphasis within defense R&D funding on development of "dual-use" technologies, or technologies that have both military and civilian applications.

6.0 THE REGULATORY PROCESS

The Code of Federal Regulations is filled with thousands upon thousands of pages of regulations touching upon almost every aspect of modern economic and social activity. Federal regulations address such diverse subjects as food preparation and labeling, pollution emissions, communications, transportation, and workplace safety standards. Regulation can be described generally as a process by which the government controls private activity to promote the public health, safety, or welfare.

6.1 A Brief History of Federal Regulation

The federal regulatory process can trace its origins to Article I, Section 8, of the U.S. Constitution, which empowers Congress "to regulate Commerce with foreign Nations, and among the several States." Using its authority under the Commerce Clause of Article I, the early Congresses passed laws delegating authority to the president for supervising key governmental activities such as imposing tariffs on trade. Over the next hundred years, additional powers were delegated by Congress to the president under the Commerce Clause, and new agencies were established both within the executive branch and in Congress to promote the growth of fledgling U.S. industries. Agencies and offices created during this period include the Army Corps of Engineers (1824), the Patent and Trademark Office (1836), the Internal Revenue Service (1862), and the Copyright Office of the Library of Congress (1870).

The growth of regulation accelerated near the turn of the twentieth century. In 1887, Congress created the Interstate Commerce Commission to regulate the railroad industry. In the early 1900s, Congress created seven new agencies and commissions to regulate commercial and financial transactions, including the Coast Guard (1915), the Tariff Commission (1916), the Commodities Exchange Authority (1922), the Customs Service (1927), the Federal Radio Commission (1927), the Federal Power Commission (1930), and the Food and Drug Administration (1931).

During the 1930s, President Franklin Delano Roosevelt's New Deal program saw the rapid expansion of economic regulation in an attempt to alleviate both the causes and effects of the Great Depression. In this period, a host of new regulatory agencies were established by Congress, such as the Federal Home Loan Bank Board, the Federal Deposit Insurance Corporation, the Farm Credit Administration, the Securities and Exchange Commission, the National Labor Relations Board, and the Federal Communications Commission. The federal government also undertook important social programs (such as creation of Social Security), which laid the foundation for a new federal role in social regulation that was to follow.

Federal regulation continued its steady expansion after World War II until the 1960s, taking on such new subjects as aviation, atomic energy, and environmental quality. More than 100 regulatory statutes were passed by Congress during the 1970s alone, encompassing a broad array of topics in the fields of consumer protection, environmental quality, workplace safety, and energy regulation. Landmark legislation during this period included the Civil Rights Act of 1964, the National Environmental Policy Act of 1969, the Clean Air Act of 1970, the Clean Water Act of 1972, the Truth in Lending Act of 1968, the Consumer Product Safety Act of 1972, and the Resource Conservation and Recovery Act of 1976.

Despite executive branch efforts during the 1980s and early 1990s to curb federal regulation, important new regulatory statutes, such as the Government Securities Act (1986), the Hazardous and Solid Waste Amendments Act of 1984, the Commercial Space Launch Act of 1984, and the Electric Consumers Protection Act of 1986, continued to fuel its growth. Environmental regulation, in particular, is expanding as public concerns with the environmental impacts of human activity increase. New subjects for federal regulation are emerging with great regularity as the breadth and pace of human activity expands.

Technological change encourages this regulatory growth. New generations of communication technologies have increased the demand for private sector use of the highly regulated electromagnetic spectrum, forcing Congress to consider revamping U.S. communications laws. Congress also responds to expressions of public concern. For example, growing public fears about possible health effects of electric and magnetic fields caused pressure for adoption of federal field exposure regulations.

6.2 The Regulatory Process Described

All regulations begin with passage by Congress of legislation, which defines the purpose of the regulatory scheme, identifies the department or agency responsible for implementing the scheme, provides guidance on implementation, and typically authorizes federal expenditures for this purpose.

Once a law that requires creation of regulations has been passed, the responsible agency proceeds to develop specific rules necessary to implement the law. These rules include prohibitions on certain types of activity, positive mandates, standards, information and reporting requirements, and licensing and permitting schemes. Examples of regulatory mechanisms include occupational health and safety standards for the workplace, environmental impact statements, and construction and operating licenses for nuclear power plants.

The process of creating regulations is governed by the requirements of the Administrative Procedures Act of 1946. Once the process is completed, the regulation is officially published in the Code of Federal Regulations. At this point, the regulation has the same legal status as a law passed by Congress and can be enforced in a court of law.

A final important component of the regulatory process is congressional oversight. By imposing mandatory reporting requirements, commissioning General Accounting Office audits, and holding hearings, congressional committees double-check to make sure that the responsible executive departments and agencies are implementing the legislated intent of Congress consistently and efficiently.

6.3 Engineers and Regulation

Engineers are affected by government regulation in a variety of ways. In addition to the broad social and economic regulations that affect all citizens, engineers are also subject to a wide array of federal, state, and local regulations specific to their fields of technical endeavor. For example, power engineers must be generally familiar with regulations governing the generation, transmission, and distribution of electric power. Engineers compete for contracts to provide services to the federal government under the qualifications-based selection system mandated by the Brooks Architectural and Engineering Act of 1972. All engineers should be aware of the professional licensing requirements imposed by the states in which they practice.

Engineers are not only on the receiving end of regulation. Engineers employed by government or by regulated industries are often called upon to prepare technical analyses used as the basis for developing regulations. In other cases, engineers may participate in the development of voluntary standards, which are subsequently adopted by governments as the basis for regulation or by industry as standard practices.

Engineers can look directly to the Federal Register and other federal publications for advance notice of proposed federal regulations that may affect them and their careers. The Federal Register notices provide information on how to submit comments and recommendations to regulators. Professional associations such as the Institute of Electrical and Electronics Engineers are also a source of information and a channel for input to the policymakers. Large companies often maintain Washington offices to serve similar functions. Companies also frequently band together to form trade associations, such as the Electronic Industries Association or the American Electronics Association, to serve as their collective voice in Washington.

7.0 THE JUDICIARY

The federal judiciary is the third and co-equal branch of the federal government. The constitutional powers and organization of the judicial branch as well as important aspects of the judicial process are briefly outlined in the paragraphs that follow.

7.1 Judicial Powers

The powers of the federal judiciary were originally outlined in Article III of the U.S. Constitution, which provides that "the judicial Power of the United States, shall be vested in one supreme Court, and in such inferior Courts as the Congress may from time to time ordain and establish." Federal judicial authority was further expanded by the Judiciary Act of 1789, which created the first "inferior" courts (i.e., the federal district and circuit courts) and provided that the Supreme Court would have the power to hear appeals from the final judgments of the highest state courts in cases involving "federal" questions. The most important expansion of federal judicial authority, however, occurred in 1803 in the landmark Supreme Court decision in *Marbury* v. *Madison*. In that case, the Supreme Court held certain provisions of the Judiciary Act of 1789 to be unconstitutional, thus ascribing to the federal courts the power of "judicial review." It is this power, as wielded by the Supreme Court, that has made it clearly a co-equal partner in the federal system. As noted by Kelly and Harbison,

> The [Supreme] Court has become the final arbiter of the American constitutional system. Its opinions on the nature and scope of federal and state power, on the functions of the various departments of government, and on the meaning of the written language of the Constitution have built up a great body of living and growing constitutional law. Supreme Court opinions are almost universally accepted as the final word on constitutional questions, so that in a practical, everyday sense it is this body of constitutional law rather than the document of 1787 which comprises the "living constitution" of today.[8]

7.2 The Organization of the Judiciary

The federal judiciary is organized in a hierarchy of three levels, each of which possesses a different jurisdiction. At the lowest level, federal district courts serve as general courts of original jurisdiction or trial courts. One or more federal district courts are established in each state and federal territory, including the District of Columbia, Puerto Rico, Guam, and the Virgin Islands.

Decisions of the district courts can be appealed to the federal circuit courts. Circuit courts do not serve as triers of fact, but focus their review on whether the trial court correctly applied the law to the facts as proven. There are 11 circuits plus the Court of Appeals for the District of Columbia and the U.S. Court of Appeals for the federal circuit. There are also a variety of federal courts with specially delimited trial and/or appellate jurisdictions.

The Supreme Court is the highest judicial authority in the United States. It exercises appellate jurisdiction "both as to Law and Fact" over the district courts, the courts of appeals, and the highest courts of the states. Nine justices sit on the Court and decide all cases. They are appointed by the president with the advice and consent of the U.S. Senate and serve for life. There is no appeal from or final review of Supreme Court decisions, which stand as authoritative statements of U.S. law.

7.3 Science and Technology in the Judicial System

It has been estimated that as many as 20 to 30 percent of the cases tried in the federal courts involve scientific or technological issues. In criminal cases, the issue may be the admissibility of scientific or forensic evidence such as DNA matching. In civil cases, mass tort actions on such subjects as asbestos, breast implants, inadequately tested pharmaceuticals, and dioxin exposures raise numerous scientific questions. Class action cases alleging defective products or breach of warranty often require expert evaluation of design and engineering practices or the use of complex statistical evidence. These examples illustrate just a few of the many areas where judges and juries are asked to consider scientific or technical evidence.

Typically educated as lawyers, few judges are likely to have a detailed understanding of science and technology. Nor is the typical jury likely to fully comprehend the complexity of the technical evidence they are asked to weigh. As a consequence, the ability of the judicial system to handle complex cases involving science and technology has been called increasingly into question.

How, then, can the federal courts more effectively resolve disputes involving science and technology issues and separate the "junk science" from reliable expert advice? There is no easy answer. The prestigious Carnegie Commission on Science, Technology, and Government has brought together experts to examine the question. They urge a sustained effort involving increased education of judges and creation of new mechanisms for interaction between the courts and the scientific and technical community.[9]

7.4 Engineers and the Judicial System

Unless made a party to a federal case or empaneled to serve on a jury, the odds are that the typical engineer might never step foot in a courtroom. One notable exception involves expert testimony in cases involving highly complex technical issues or factual situations. In those cases, attorneys often hire scientists or engineers as expert witnesses.

Another exception is for those engineers who have also studied and are licensed to practice law in federal courts. There are quite a few of these engineer/lawyers who practice in such areas as patent law and intellectual property. Others are found in technologically oriented practice areas such as energy, telecommunications, or space law as well as related legal business areas such as technology licensing and transfer. The American Bar Association maintains a membership section for attorneys interested in science and technology and publishes the journal *Jurimetrics*.

8.0 CONCLUSION: ENGINEERS AND GOVERNMENT

The introduction to this chapter touched briefly on some of the reasons why scientists and engineers should actively participate in their government. The balance of the chapter describes key federal government processes and offers some advice on how engineers can become effectively involved. In conclusion, just a few of the many science and technology policy issues currently faced by the nation on which engineers may be able to make a valuable contribution are presented:

- What roles can and should the federal government play in supporting the competitiveness of U.S. companies in high-technology industries such as electronics or flat-panel displays?
- Should the federal government favor support of big science and

engineering projects such as the superconducting supercollider over small science projects and research done by individual investigators?

- How can government define national needs to set priorities for research and development funding?
- What role can technology play in improving the quality of health care and controlling its escalating costs?
- Now that the Cold War is over, what should be done with the tens of thousands of highly skilled scientists and engineers employed in the defense industry and the national laboratories?
- Is the global climate changing and what steps can we take to stop or adjust to the change?
- Can economical renewable energy technologies or alternative fuels be developed that will reduce or eliminate the nation's dependence on fossil fuels?
- How should the national information infrastructure be structured and what role should the federal government play to assist the private sector?
- How are advances in communications, remote sensing, and computing technologies intruding upon our privacy and what can or should the government do about it?
- Should expensive scientific and technological missions in outer space be undertaken at a time when our society is plagued by poverty, ignorance, and crime?

Decision makers in Congress, the executive branch, and in the federal courts are also wrestling with these and similar questions as they attempt to develop and implement sound public policy. Very few of these decision makers have science, engineering, or technical backgrounds. Yet their decisions will affect engineers, their careers, and the well-being of our nation. Engineers have the knowledge and self-interest to make a contribution to the process. But to make this contribution, they must first get involved.

9.0 RECOMMENDED READING

Carnegie Commission on Science, Engineering, and Government. *Science, Technology, and Congress: Expert Advice and the Decision-Making Process*. Pittsburgh: The Commission, February 1991.

————. *Science, Technology, and Congress: Organizational and Procedural Reforms*. Pittsburgh: The Commission, June 1993.

Cohn, Mary W., ed. *How Congress Works*, 2nd ed. Washington, DC: Congressional Quarterly Press, 1991.

Delphos, William A. *Capitol Capital: Government Resources for High-Technology Companies*. Washington, DC: Venture Publishing, 1993.

Dodd, Lawrence C., and Bruce I. Oppenheimer. *Congress Reconsidered*, 4th ed. Washington, DC: Congressional Quarterly Press, 1989.

Goldinger, Carolyn, ed. *Federal Regulatory Directory*, 6th ed. Washington, DC: Congressional Quarterly Press, 1990.

Lineberry, Robert L. *Government in America: People, Politics and Policy*, 3rd ed. Boston: Little, Brown, 1986.

National Performance Review. *Report of the National Performance Review, From Red Tape to Results: Creating a Government That Works Better and Costs Less*. Washington, DC: U.S. Government Printing Office, 1993.

Oleszek, Walter. *Congressional Procedures and the Policy Process*. Washington, DC: Congressional Quarterly Press, 1989.

Smith, Hedrick. *The Power Game: How Washington Works*. New York: Ballantine Books, 1988.

Trattner, John H. *The Prune Book: The 60 Toughest Science and Technology Jobs in Washington*. Lanham, MD: Madison Books, 1992.

Wells, William G., Jr. *Working with Congress: A Practical Guide for Scientists and Engineers*. Washington, DC: AAAS Press, 1992.

ENDNOTES

1. Corbin McNeill, "Engineers Must Become as Effective in Politics as They Are in Science," *Plant Engineering* (September 3, 1992), p. 92.

2. Richard G. Weingardt, "Engineers Need Broader Perspective and Better Image," *Daily Journal of Commerce* (Seattle, Washington), August 25, 1993, p. 2.

3. William Wells, *Working with Congress: A Practical Guide for Engineers and Scientists* (Washington, DC: American Association for the Advancement of Science, 1993), p. 47 (Table 3-1).

4. James E. Katz, "Science, Technology, and Congress," *Society* (May-June 1993), p. 45. See also Samuel C. Florman, "Engineering and the Concept of the Elite," *The Bridge* (Fall 1991), pp. 11-17.

5. Wells, *Working with Congress,* p. 113.

6. John H. Trattner, *The Prune Book: The 60 Toughest Science and Technology Jobs in Washington* (Lanham, MD: Madison Books, 1992), pp. 5-7.

7. A list of all federal appointive positions, referred to as the "Plum Book" for the color of its cover, is published at the beginning of each new administration by the Government Printing Office. Entitled *Policy and Supporting Positions,* the Plum Book is prepared by the House Committee on Post Office and Civil Service. Several commercial directories, such as the *Executive Yellow Book* published by Monitor Publishing Company, list executive branch positions by department and agency and identify the positions that are appointed by the president both with and without the advice and consent of Congress.

8. Alfred H. Kelley and Winfred A. Harbison, *The American Constitution: Its Origins and Development*, 5th ed. (New York: W. W. Norton, 1976), p. 4.

9. Carnegie Commission on Science, Technology, and Government, *Science and Technology in Judicial Decision Making: Creating Opportunities and Meeting Challenges* (March 1993), p. 24 (notes 2, 3).

12

State Government

Irving J. Gabelman

1.0 BACKGROUND

In 1781 the 13 states ratified the Articles of Confederation that established the first relationship between a central federal government and the state governments. This relationship and the structure of the governments have changed significantly in response to international events, technological advancements, population growth, the admission of new states, and the social and economic needs of its citizens.

The Articles of Confederation created a unicameral Congress whose members were appointed by the state legislatures. The states, protective of their independence, granted the Congress limited powers. It could not tax or regulate commerce, enforce any demands it made upon the states, or directly contact the citizens of the states.

The Congress created by the Articles of Confederation could not deal effectively with the needs of the new democracy. The first of many changes in the relationships of the federal and state government that would occur during U.S. history resulted from the ratification by the states of the Constitution drafted in Philadelphia in 1787. The Constitution created a stronger centralized federal government to which the states surrendered many of their sovereign powers. It established a bicameral Congress composed of delegates from the states, an executive branch headed by the president, and a judicial branch, the Supreme Court.

2.0 FEDERAL CONSTITUTIONAL POWERS

The Congress was given the power to tax, borrow money, regulate interstate and foreign commerce, raise an army and a navy, declare war, establish standards for weights and measures, maintain a militia, establish post offices, issue and control currency, and grant patents and copyrights.

The Supreme Court was given jurisdiction over all cases relating to the Constitution and to those involving suits between states or between their citizens. It was given the power to declare state laws unconstitutional and invalid when they conflicted with a federal law or statute. This power was clearly defined in Article VI, Section 2, which read, "The constitution and the laws of the United States which shall be made in pursuance thereof, and all treaties made, or which shall be made, under the authority of the United States shall be the supreme law of the land; and the judges in every state shall be bound thereby, anything in the constitution or the laws of any state to the contrary notwithstanding."

The Constitution stated specifically those powers that were granted to the federal government. In Article I, Section 8, it also allowed Congress "To make all laws which shall be necessary and proper for carrying into execution the foregoing powers, and all other powers vested by this constitution in the government of the United States or in any department or officer thereof." This "elastic clause" has been invoked by the federal government to augment its powers. For example, under the implied powers granted, it created a national banking system and established various regulatory agencies.

3.0 STATE CONSTITUTIONS

The Constitution recognizes the legal equality of all states. Each state has jurisdiction within its geographic boundaries and is free to govern, restricted only by the powers delegated to the federal government. Every state has a constitution embodying these principles of government. Since 1776, when the first state constitutions were adopted by the colonies, almost all have been rewritten, some more than once.

The 50 states vary widely in geographic features, population size and density, racial and ethnic distributions, and climatic conditions. Some are highly industrialized, while others are largely agricultural. Despite the wide variations in state demographics, their governments do not differ significantly in form or operation. There are differences in the names of the houses of the legislature, length of legislative sessions, numbers and kinds of committees, number and names of elected officials, and so on. Space does not permit a description of the organization and procedures of each state, so that references to state attributes in the following text are those that pertain to most states.

State constitutions are basically alike, providing for the structure, powers, and functions of state and local government; guaranteeing the civil rights of its citizens, and defining the legislative process. The typical state constitution starts with a preamble stating its objectives. The next section is a "bill of rights" that contains provisions affirming the fundamental rights of the citizenry, such as freedom of speech, press, assembly, and religion, exemption from unlawful search and seizure, and many others that duplicate those already found in the federal Constitution. The main body of the constitution presents the structure of the government. All state constitutions establish a government with a judicial branch, an executive branch, and a legislative branch. Every state legislature is bicameral with the sole exception of Nebraska, whose legislature, under a constitution revised and adopted in 1937, is unicameral.

3.1 Judicial Branch

The state judicial system is composed of all courts functioning within the state to protect the rights and privileges of the citizens, try persons accused of perpetration of crimes, determine the constitutionality of a law, oversee the disposition of estates, and rule on contractual and other civil disputes. The state judicial system operates under the laws of the state independently of the federal system except in those cases where federal law has precedence.

The prevailing law of the state is constitutional law. Statute law, the body of law brought into being by acts of the legislature, is next in application. In the absence of these, court decisions are mainly rendered by common law. Common law is law established initially by common usage and is based on precedent. Decisions follow those made in earlier similar cases. The body of laws can further be categorized as civil or criminal.

State courts function at various levels within the judiciary system, with each level characterized by its jurisdictional authority. At the lowest level, the court, in the person of the justice of the peace, functions in rural areas. He is chosen in local elections. The city courts are the next level. The courts hear cases involving traffic offenses, juvenile delinquency, small claims, and so on. City court judges are usually elected, but in some cities they may be appointed by the mayor. Cases dealing with the settlement of estates are heard in county courts. These courts hear appeals from city and justice of the peace judgments and also have limited jurisdiction in criminal and civil actions. Judges are elected officials. Appellate courts, with elected judges, hear appeals from lower court verdicts in criminal cases. The Supreme Court is the highest court in the state. It is usually composed of seven elected judges and hears appeals from any lower court decisions.

3.2 Executive Branch

State constitutions usually provide for popular election of governor, lieutenant governor, secretary of state, comptroller, treasurer, and attorney general. These officials serve in the executive branch. Executive power is divided among these officials who may be members of opposing political parties. This division of authority may hinder administrative actions.

The governors of the 13 colonies were figureheads elected by the legislatures. They had virtually no power and served for only one year. This curbing of authority was a reaction to the tyrannical rule of the royal court-appointed governors prior to the revolution. The governor of today, elected by popular vote to a four-year term, is a powerful figure with not only executive but also legislative and judicial powers. His executive powers are generally not clearly defined in the constitution and accrue to him through legislative statutes. Other undocumented powers stem from the prestige of the chief executive office and his influential position as nominal head of his political party.

The governor heads the executive branch and is the chief executive officer of the state. A state's governmental activities are vested in departments, usually about 20. The governor appoints or approves the heads of most of these departments and those of the numerous boards and commissions that help in the administration of the business of the state. He or she is responsible for the preparation of the annual state budget. In the state of the state address, he or she presents his or her objectives and desired program, which provides guidance for legislation. Legislation is further influenced by the governor's veto power. The potential threat of a veto discourages submission of bills that oppose gubernatorial objectives. The power to call special sessions of the legislature allows the governor to concentrate attention on selected issues. Judicial powers are limited to exercise of executive clemency, commutation of sentences, and granting of pardons.

The lieutenant governor succeeds the governor should he or she die, become disabled, be removed, or unable to serve for any other cause. The lieutenant governor presides over the senate. He or she does not have a vote on senate matters except in the case of a tie, in which case he or she may cast a deciding vote.

The secretary of state is chief executive of the State Department. He or she uses the state seal to make state documents official. The department publishes and distributes the minutes of the legislative sessions and other legislatively mandated state publications, issues corporation charters, signs proclamations, aids municipalities in organizing local government, supervises elections, corresponds with the federal and other state governments, and performs various other functions.

The comptroller is the chief fiscal officer of the state and executive head of the Department of Audit and Control. This office approves the need for expenditures requested by the various state agencies and authorizes the state treasurer to pay billings. It performs postaudits of agency expenditures, certifying that the funds were spent as intended and in accordance with the law. It acts as custodian and investor of state and other funds entrusted to it. The office prepares and submits to the legislature plans for improving the financial status of the state. Arrangements for bond issues and other borrowings to meet the revenue needs of the state are its responsibility.

The treasurer has no real executive power. He or she is the keeper of the state finances, and when authorized by the comptroller, pays bills submitted to the state. In some states the treasurer is a governor appointee.

The attorney general is the chief legal officer of the state. The activities of the office are directed toward protecting the citizens of the state. These include prosecution of organized crime figures, advocating civil rights, acting to protect the environment, and ensuring safe disposal of toxic and radioactive waste. The office prepares legal opinions on state litigation, represents the state in the courts, and advises the legislative and executive departments on legal matters.

The commissioner of education supervises the administration of the state educational system and enforcement of school laws.

This function may include the design of instructional programs, the establishment of qualifications for obtaining teacher certificates, the allocation of funds to school districts, and the operation of a state university system.

3.2.1 *Departments, Boards, and Commissions*   The administration of state affairs is a very complex task, complicated by the division of executive authority among the elected executives. Administrative functions are carried out by departments, agencies, boards, and commissions.

The number of departments vary from state to state and is limited by some state constitutions. Typically among them will be Agriculture and Markets, Banking, Commerce, Health, Motor Vehicles, and Taxation and Finance. Most of these department heads are appointed by the governor. The comptroller heads an Audit and Control Department. The Department of Education is under the commissioner of education and the attorney general directs the Department of Law.

The executive branch has the responsibility for implementing state policies and enforcing laws and regulations in many areas that are of engineering interest, such as science and technology, licensing and registration for the professions, cable television, waste management, power authority, oil and gas, and many others. Each of these areas is usually assigned to a board or commission. Boards and commissions may be established by the state constitution, by an act of the legislature, and by the governor. The method of appointment of members to these bodies and their executive power varies widely from state to state. Board and commission positions may be civil service, appointees, or elected officials. The council, recognizing the public service obligation of the engineering community, should encourage its members to apply for positions in these units. Engineers should be available to serve as agency members, advisors, or in any capacity where their specialized knowledge could be used for the public benefit.

3.3 Legislative Branch

There is an ever-increasing load placed on the state legislature to initiate and pass laws that are needed for the effective government of our complex society. Further complications are introduced by rapidly advancing technologies and the changing relationship between federal and state government. The state legislatures vary from state to state, not only in name but also in number of members, their compensation and qualifications, length and dates of sessions, and number of bills introduced in a session. With the exception of Nebraska, all state legislatures are bicameral. In most states, the lower house is called the "House of Representatives" and the upper house, the "Senate." The lower house is also called the "Assembly," the "General Assembly," and the "General Court." The term of the members of the lower house is usually two years and of the upper house, four years. All members of both houses are elected by popular vote. The presiding officer of the senate is the lieutenant governor in most states. In some states the presiding officer is a member of the senate chosen by his peers. A speaker is chosen from among the members to preside over the house of representatives.

The legislature has executive powers such as the confirmation of gubernatorial appointments and impeachment. It exercises indirect control over various state functions through its appropriation, investigative, and budget approval powers. Its chief and most time-consuming task is the consideration of bills and resolutions. If a bill survives several legislative hurdles, it becomes a law. A resolution is a proposal for some course of action such as the establishment of a special group. The volume of bills and resolutions introduced during a legislative session ranges from about 1,000 in Wyoming to more than 20,000 in New York.

3.3.1 Committees   The difficulties arising in trying to debate and discuss large numbers of bills and resolutions, encompassing as they do a broad spectrum of topics, led early on to having them first considered by committees. Members of these committees are appointed by the Speaker in the lower house and in the upper house by the house as a whole, the lieutenant governor, a committee on committees, or a committee on rules. The review of bills is one of the many tasks delegated to these committees. They analyze budgets, pass on appropriations, perform research, mediate differences between the houses, and undertake various other time-consuming tasks. Committees are indispensable, and they are employed by every state legislature. The number of committees, their influence, and their importance vary from state to state.

There are several kinds of committees, and each house has its own complement. The membership is appointed by the speaker in the lower house and in the upper house by the senate as a whole, the lieutenant governor, or a committee on committees. This power of appointment indirectly affects legislation since the political attitudes of the membership influence strongly the enactment or defeat of a bill.

Standing committees are the most important. A standing committee is permanent and is established for each area of legislative concern such as appropriations, finance, budget, revenue, agriculture, labor, utilities, commerce, health, labor, education, public safety, and so on. These committees may appoint specialized subcommittees on a permanent or temporary basis to expedite further the consideration of bills. The full committee, recognizing the competence of the subcommittee, usually accepts its recommendations.

Special committees are formed for researching aspects of current or proposed bills. Interim committees perform similar functions between legislative sessions. Committees may be created to investigate irregularities or other unusual occurrences and to obtain information for the enactment of pertinent legislation. Joint committees, composed of members from both houses, coordinate action on bills and resolve differences between the two houses. They may introduce a bill directly and thus avoid the need for companion bills and dual consideration.

Gathering information on which to base a legislative decision is a difficult and time-consuming task because of the breadth of topics addressed in the bills that are introduced in a session. All states provide the committees with professional staffs to assist them. Expert advice is also offered by lobbyists and interest groups. Since they are trying to foster favor, the data supplied, though biased, is almost always accurate and reliable. Committee hearings are held to solicit views and comments from the public. This avenue, extensively used by the federal government, is not generally employed by the states. These hearings tend to attract highly biased groups who dominate the proceedings, allowing only their views to be expressed.

3.3.2 Legislative Process   A bill becomes a law after successful passage through several legislative actions which parallel those of the U.S. Congress. Bills have multiple sources. Many are introduced by a legislator or a group of legislators. Others originate outside of the legislature from constituents, interest groups, legislative committees, state executive branch agencies, municipalities, and other concerned entities.

Since enactment of a bill results in a law, the phraseology must precisely convey the intent of the originator in language that allows for exact implementation or enforcement of its provisions. Drafting a bill is a complex and laborious task accomplished by legislative professionals on the staff of the sponsor or by a commercial legislative agency. After it is drafted, the bill is submitted to the clerk of the house and assigned a number giving it official status. A bill may be introduced in either house. After approval, it will be sent to the other house. Alternately, it or a similar companion bill may be introduced into both houses at the same time. Introduction is merely the "first reading" when the bill is announced. It is then referred by the presiding house officer to a standing or other committee for consideration and appraisal. Almost all bills are sent to committee; however, where consideration of a bill is especially urgent, it may go directly to the floor for debate.

Committee jurisdiction is loosely defined, and complex bills may fall under the purview of more than one committee. The presiding officer at times has a choice of two or more standing committees. For example, a bill related to the training of dental technicians might be assigned to an education standing committee or to one dealing with health issues. This ability allows political bias to enter, for the presiding officer can assign the bill to that committee most sympathetic to his or her views. Additional political advantage is obtained by his or her power to appoint committee chairmen. State committee chairmen are not as powerful as those in the federal government, but they do influence the choice of calendar and other committee actions.

There are political advantages accruing to a bill sponsor. The bill may reflect special interests of the sponsor's constituency and thus ensure their continued support and their votes at election time. Sponsors of key bills achieve recognition from their peers and thus further their political aspirations. Sponsoring legislators will submit a memorandum of support to the committee to indicate an active interest as opposed to bills sponsored for political motives. Without this memorandum, a bill may not be seriously considered by the committee. The committee chairman may place its review at the bottom of the agenda so that it is not reached and will be killed in committee. Because the introduction of a bill is a relatively simple task, a large number of bills, greater than can be considered in a legislative session, are sponsored.

If favorably reported out of committee, the bill is given a "second reading" and presented to the house floor for discussion, possible revision or amendment, and in some states a final vote. Most states require a "third reading" before a vote is taken.

If passed, the bill is sent to the other house where these actions are duplicated. Failure to pass in either house will kill the bill. When the versions of the bill passed by the upper and lower houses differ, a conference committee is established to reconcile the differences. In some states the house leaders make the adjustments. The final version is then sent to the governor who may sign it into law or veto it. If vetoed, it is sent back to the legislature. If the governors' veto is overridden by a legally designated vote of each house, the bill becomes a law.

3.3.3 Lobbying Executive officials and legislators are subject to pressure by groups who attempt to influence the conduct of government in order to benefit the special interests of their members. The number of such groups is extremely large. They differ in size, power, financial resources, and objectives. In 1993, there were 1791 lobbyists, representing 1111 clients, in New York State. Chambers of Commerce, National Association of Manufacturers, National Association of Realtors, and American Bankers Association are representative of business groups. The American Medical Association represents doctors and the American Bar Association, lawyers. There are unions working to benefit plumbers, carpenters, auto workers, and so on. Some groups such as the League of Women Voters and Common Cause pursue altruistic goals for the public good. Still others have the advancement of ethnic or racial interests as their goal.

The affluent groups maintain offices in the capital of those states where the legislature has lengthy sessions. A full-time staff including professional lobbyists and public relations personnel plan and implement their lobbying strategies. They research, extensively, complex issues and supply results to legislators to help them in the drafting of a bill. Bills beneficial to their members are drafted for a supportive legislator to sponsor. They are available for informational briefings on any one of the large number of bills under consideration in a session and also on similar bills being considered or already acted upon by other states. In the past, this information gathering capability was valuable; however, with modern computer communications equipment, legislative staffs have easy access to this data.

The group office staff may include a lobbyist or an independent professional hired as a consultant. There are many such independents in the state capitals who have one or more groups as clients. They often are former legislators well versed in the strategies employed to enact a bill into law or to block its passage. Adversarial positions may be taken on some provisions of a bill by lobbyists representing different interest groups. If passage of the bill is desired by both groups, the lobbyists try for a compromise solution, acceptable to both factions and to the responsible committee so as not to impede the bill's transit through the legislative stages.

The lobbyist understands the crucial role that committees play in the legislative process and tries to influence the selection of committee members and chairmen. The lobbyist interfaces with the legislators, acting as a conduit for supplying the services just described. He or she works closely with political action groups (PACs) that contribute funds to incumbents who tend to support his or her interest group or to the opposition when they do not.

The lobbyist has had a poor public image, often being seen as using his or her ability to deiver services and financial support in order to unduly influence legislators. Responding to this perception, the states have required registration and reports of their activities. Every state has enacted statutes that define a lobbyist. The criteria for determining lobbyist status varies. In most states, an individual receiving compensation for supplying engineering information or advocating a position on a bill is required to register.

4.0 EMERGENCE OF THE STATES

For most of our nation's history, the states have subordinated their powers to those of the federal government. The country's involvement in foreign wars and its visible and direct participation in international organizations and in domestic events of sweeping national impact, elevated the stature of the federal government so that our citizenry looked to Washington for leadership.

This attitude was reinforced by the weakness of most state governments, some of which were visibly corrupt and dominated by political machines. Staffs were small or in many cases nonexistent, so that legislators depended on lobbyists and executive agencies for information. Legislative districts were drawn so that party choices were elected. Racial and ethnic group discrimination was the rule.

In 1962, a Supreme Court decision (Baker v. Carr) resulted in reapportionment of the legislative districts so that the principle of "one man, one vote" was observed. The Civil Rights Act of 1964 and other companion legislation ensured that the state legislatures more accurately represented the voters and were more responsive to their interests. These reforms were followed by others initiated within the states, gradually transforming the state governments into more responsive entities. Forty states have rewritten or amended their constitutions since 1960. Legislatures have streamlined their procedures, improving the scheduling and consideration of bills. Computers have automated the storage and retrieval of bills and pertinent data. Laws controlling lobbying and campaign financing have been enacted. Staffs have been greatly increased and augmented with specialists. In 1993, over 40,000 staff members served the legislators of the 50 states. The increasing number and complexity of the bills introduced caused most states to meet annually in longer sessions and in special sessions called by the governor. Legislator salaries have been raised to compensate for the additional demands on their time. The higher pay and the possibility of political advancement has made government service an attractive career opportunity.

The governors in this period were also modernizing, strengthening, and consolidating their leadership position. Seventeen states increased their two-year term to four years, bringing the total states with four-year terms to 47. New Hampshire, Rhode Island, and Vermont retain the two-year tenure. Many state administrative elected officials were changed to governor appointees. The governors' personal staff has been increased with the addition of budget and policy planning specialists. Communication among the governors was facilitated with the formation of a National Governors Association in 1977.

The revitalization of state governments continued in the 1970s and 1980s. Welfare systems were revised. New approaches in precollege education emphasizing mathematics and science were instituted. Enacting environmental control laws received a high priority in legislative calendars. Offices for economic development were created to encourage entrepreneurial enterprises and to invite the establishment of national and international corporate plants and offices. Meanwhile, the federal government was coping with a mounting national debt and defense budget. Under President Reagan, federal grants to the states were decreased. Additional responsibilities were imposed on the states by federal mandates directing activity in school desegregation, abortion, waste disposal, busing, prison population restraints, environmental pollution control, and occupational health care standards. These mandates forced the states to undertake new programs at their own expense. While imposing these added burdens, the federal government not only did not supply additional funds but actually lessened its financial aid.

The states, adopting a more aggressive stance, responded to the expanded areas of responsibility imposed by various mandates of the federal government with new and innovative programs. They established offices to promote economic development, provided grants for and encouraged research and development in high technologies, improved educational methods and facilities, rebuilt infrastructure, revamped welfare and health care systems, protected the environment, and generally assumed a leadership role in many other governmental areas. The 1990s has seen a continuance of this independence; however, decreasing revenues has caused budgetary problems with an accompanying slowdown in entrepreneurial undertakings.

5.0 STATE POWERS

The U.S. Constitution did not list specifically the powers delegated to the states, nor did it preclude exercise of those same powers by the states unless they were withheld by federal law. The Tenth Amendment states that "all powers not delegated to the United States by the Constitution, nor prohibited by it to the states, are reserved to the states respectively or to the people." James Madison, commenting on the Tenth Amendment, wrote that "The powers reserved to the several States will extend to all the objects which, in the ordinary course of affairs, concern the lives, liberties, and properties of the people and the internal order, improvement, and prosperity of the State."

The states traditionally have been concerned with those social and economic issues that affect their citizens. They enjoy wide latitude in dealing with these issues, constrained only by the powers given to the federal government by the Constitution.

The powers assumed and exercised by the states fall broadly into three categories: police power, public services, and the determination of the structure and function of local government. Police power allows the states to place restrictions on individual rights and liberties and regulations on business enterprises when they are necessary to protect the public health, interests, morals, and welfare and safety. This power is best exercised by the states, rather than the federal government, since their proximity to local conditions allows for more effective handling of problems. Police power is exercised in the chartering of corporations and partnerships, enforcement of antitrust laws, regulation of banks, insurance companies, and public utilities. The state police enforce all laws and regulations, including those issued by local governments. They share this responsibility with municipal police, sheriffs, and other local law enforcement personnel.

Educational facilities, highway construction, public transportation, health care, and welfare assistance are provided under the public services power.

A partial listing of subject areas of direct technical concern to the engineering community that is controlled within these broad categories would include environmental pollution, licensing, building codes and standards, vehicle operation and safety, radioactive waste disposal, solid waste management, water facilities, zoning, public transportation, road construction, electric power production and transmission, computer usage and security, nuclear energy and other alternative fuel and energy sources, architecture, and surveying. There are other socioeconomic areas where the state may exercise control in which the engineering community will have interest, such as tort reform, foreign competitiveness, and health care.

6.0 ROLE OF SOCIETIES

Engineers tend to immerse themselves in their disciplines, solving the ever-emerging problems created by advancing technology. They are generally politically naive and indeed apathetic about participation in government activities that could affect them socially and economically. In 1993, less than 1 percent of the approximately 7500 state legislators were engineers. Lawyers are very aware of the importance of legislative process involvement. Their numbers are an impressive 16 percent of the total. Seville Chapman, director of the New York State Assembly Staff from 1971 to 1976, recognized this attitude, stating "Scientists and engineers are accustomed to isolating their problems, in which case the solutions are often straightforward. But it is pointless to solve a problem technically by an economically or politically infeasible method. In matters of public policy, problems cannot be isolated, so I urge people to work with the system we have and where possible contribute to making it more effective. When scientists, engineers and academic experts begin to mix equal numbers with public officials and administrators, they may develop the opportunities to use their expertise in the development of technically sound public policy."

In the past two decades there has been a growing realization in the engineering community that their interests should be made visible, and their expertise available, to the lawmakers and executives of our state and federal governments. Engineering societies have actively advocated these interests at all levels of government. As early as 1974, a group of 30 scientific, engineering, and technical (SET) societies sponsored conferences and workshops wherein methods for interaction between the legislatures and the SET community were discussed. Three such conferences were held. The first conference on "Energy and the Environment" was held in Albany, New York, in 1974, the second on "Lawmaking, Technology and Quality Growth" in Boston, Massachusetts, in 1976, and the third on the "Energy Dilemma" in Annapolis, Maryland, in 1977.

The engineering societies most active in promoting the socioeconomic interests of their members are the Institute of Electrical and Electronics Engineers (IEEE), the American Society of Mechanical Engineers (ASME), and the National Society of Professional Engineers (NSPE).

The IEEE United States Activities Board (USAB), since 1972, has carried out many programs promoting the economic and social well-being of its members. Activities at the state level are the responsibility of the State Government Activities Committee (SGAC). SGAC guides the establishment of State IEEE Legislative Activities (SILA). SILAs try to influence the legislature's disposition of legislation of interest to the IEEE membership. They provide information to legislators on the technical content of such legislation. SGAC prepares position papers, maintains a data base on state activities, and disseminates information on noteworthy state legislation nationwide.

The American Society of Mechanical Engineers (ASME) has also recognized the importance of interacting with state and local governments. Their two principal programs aimed at realizing these objectives are the Legislative Fellow Program and the State Government Coordinator Program, initiated, respectively, in 1980 and 1983 by A. Bruce Conlin, the ASME director of State and Local Government Affairs. ASME state government coordinators are active in 17 states. They provide engineering information to legislators, advise members, and comment on pending legislation. They provide an interface between the legislature and the society. ASME fellows have been appointed in 9 states. They serve for one or two years, working with state scientific and technical offices as staff members.

Influencing legislation that affects their members is a high-priority objective of the National Society of Professional Engineers (NSPE) and the American Consulting Engineers Council (ACEC). Both maintain offices in most of the state capitols, staffed with salaried personnel who monitor legislation, prepare position papers, and keep state society members informed of relevant legislation. At least one staff member is a registered lobbyist who conveys the society position to legislators.

6.1 State Councils

While the independent efforts of the engineering societies are laudable and have been effective, it was recognized at national levels that they could have greater impact if they coordinated their efforts through an umbrella organization, the American Association of Engineering Societies (AAES). The AAES comprises 26 member societies with a combined membership of over 700,000. Quoting from its public policies and priorities pamphlet, "The American Association of Engineering Societies is a multidisciplinary organization of engineering societies dedicated to advancing the knowledge, understanding and practice of engineering."

The advantage of SET organizations acting in concert on socioeconomic and technical issues has been recognized in several states. Umbrella engineering councils, with representation from the various engineering, scientific, and technical entities within the state, have as a broad objective the promoting of the stature of the engineering profession.

They initiate activities, such as "Engineer's Week," that increase public awareness of the engineering community and that enhance the image of the engineer. They are a source of unbiased engineering and scientific information for the executive and legislative branches on the wide range of technical disciplines found in the regulatory and legislative issues that impact upon the health, welfare, and safety of the general public and upon those issues of socioeconomic interest to the engineering community. They serve as a forum for discussion and development of policy positions on these issues. They sponsor and participate in educational programs that have as their subject matter environmental, technical, and scientific issues that affect the citizens of their state.

In the states where state councils are operative, the engineering community has enjoyed its greatest success in influencing public policy and attitudes. Some of the more active engineering councils are the following:

Washington Architects and Engineers Legislative Council

Michigan Council of Professional, Scientific and Technical Associations (MCPSTA)

California Legislative Council of Professional Engineers

Indiana Engineers Society Legislative Forum

Colorado American Consulting Engineer's Council of Colorado

Illinois Engineers Council

Virginia Legislative Advisory Council

Idaho Technical Advisory Council

Oregon Engineers Coordinating Council of Oregon

Tennessee Joint Engineering Action Group

Washington, DC, District of Columbia Council of Engineering and Architectural Societies

Appendices 12.1 and 12.2 are suggested models of the bylaws and charter for a state council.

Except in those states with active state councils, the engineering community has been noticeably absent from those interest groups that promote the objectives of their constituents. National engineering societies have almost without exception focused their efforts and attention on Congress, with secondary consideration being given to the states. Now that more legislation of socioeconomic interest to the engineering community is state initiated, they should endorse the concept of state councils and should encourage participation by their regions and sections in state council activities. A state leader should be appointed or elected to coordinate activities within the state. Funds should be made available for organizational efforts.

Generally state councils are low-budget operations financed by moderate dues paid by the member societies. They cannot compete directly with wealthy lobbies that contribute substantial campaign funds to legislators via political action committees and buy expensive media time to further their interests.

However, the combined constituency of the council member societies can wield considerable political clout by using a grass roots approach. Society members can provide testimony at state committee hearings on proposed legislation. Positions and opinions can be aired on local radio and television and published in newspapers. Part-time lobbyists, often individuals whose livelihood comes from other sources, can be employed to interact with state legislative committees and their staffs. Any lobbying by the council of state legislators during the busy legislative sessions should be supplemented by direct contact of the legislators in their home districts. In almost every state a constituent who expresses his position on legislation to a legislator is not considered to be a lobbyist unless he is paid.

The council could establish a network of minute men within the state, one in each legislative district, to disseminate position papers and organize legislator contacts by telephone, letter, or visit. Legislators will usually receive few, if any, communications pertaining to a bill so that receipt of a relatively small number of letters or telephone calls can influence a legislator's vote. They are sensitive to opinions voiced by voters upon whom they depend for reelection. The Institute for Government Public Information Research, American University, Washington, DC, queried legislators on the relative effectiveness of 30 types of communications. "Spontaneous letters from constituents" and "telephone calls from constituents" ranked first and second. "Visits from constituents" ranked sixth, while "visits from lobbyists" was nineteenth.

Section newsletters could alert council members to their societies' position on relevant pending legislation. The council can provide legislators with expert advice on the wide spectrum of engineering disciplines that may be the subject of a bill. It can make available to legislators a listing of volunteers who could give briefings and who could testify in committee hearings. It could sponsor workshops, prepare video and audio tapes, and give seminars on subjects of public interest.

By supplying unbiased reliable information clearly, concisely, free from technical jargon, well in advance of a vote, engineers and scientists can establish a rapport with legislators that will insure that their opinions receive proper consideration. This source of technical information is essential to intelligent consideration of many proposed bills; however, realization of technical benefits is only one of many factors that influence the legislator's final vote. It is not always the deciding factor. Political considerations, such as party position and the opposition of other interest groups, may override them.

RECOMMENDED READING

Colman, William G. *State and Local Government and Public-Private Partnership.* Westport, CT: Greenwood Press, 1989.

Henry, Nicholas. *Governing at the Grass Roots.* Englewood Cliffs, NJ: Prentice Hall, 1984.

Keefe, W. J., and M. S. Ogul. *The American Legislative Process.* Englewood Cliffs, NJ: Prentice Hall, 1985.

Rosenthal, Alan. *The Third House.* Congressional Quarterly Press; Washington DC: 1993.

———. *Governors and Legislatures Contending Powers.* Congressional Quarterly Press; Washington DC: 1990.

———. *Legislative Life.* Congressional Quarterly Press; Washington DC: 1981.

Van Horn, Carl E. *The State of the States.* Congressional Quarterly Press; Washington DC: 1989.

APPENDIX 12.1

CHARTER OF THE STATE OF _____ ENGINEERING COUNCIL

Article I — Name and Objective

1.1 The name of the organization shall be "The State of _____ Engineering Council," hereinafter referred to as the "Council."

1.2 The objective of the Council shall be to enhance and promote the stature of the Engineering profession in the State of _____.

1.3 The Council shall be governed by these Articles of Association and by the appended Bylaws.

Article II — Membership

2.1 The full membership of the Council shall comprise designated and authorized delegates from engineering, scientific, and technical societies and councils. Affiliate membership shall be open to any organization which has an interest in and endorses the Council objective.

Article III — Funding

3.1 The member organizations shall provide financial support.

Article IV — Officers

4.1 The officers of the Council shall be the Chairperson, the Vice-Chairperson, the Secretary, and the Treasurer.

Article V — Committees

5.1 Standing committees deemed necessary for the conduct of the Councils affairs shall be established.

5.2 The Chairperson of each committee shall be a member of the Council.

Article VI — Publications

6.1 The Council may have an official publication and may sponsor other publications which in the Council's opinion will contribute to the attainment of its objective.

Article VII — Responsibilities and Limitations

7.1 An action taken by any officer, member, or committee shall not be binding on the Council unless such action has the prior approval and sanction of the Council.

7.2 Nothing in these Articles shall prohibit or inhibit any of the member organizations from pursuing or refraining from pursuing any specific legislative or governmental endeavor on its own, provided that full cognizance of the position and efforts are made known to the Council. All collective representations shall be made only when there is unanimous approval by the members of the Council.

Article VIII — Amendments

8.1 Any voting member of the Council may submit a written petition requesting an amendment or amendments to these Articles of Association.

Article IX — Code of Ethics

9.1 The Council shall adopt and act in accordance with a code of ethics. Failure to comply with this code by any member shall be dealt with by appropriate disciplinary by the Council.

Article X — Dissolution

10.1 In the event of the dissolution of the Council, all assets not required for payment of liabilities shall be distributed by the Executive Committee, subject to the approval of a majority of the Council members, to nonprofit educational or scientific organizations.

APPENDIX 12.2

BYLAWS OF THE STATE OF _____ ENGINEERING COUNCIL

Section I — Objective

The Objective of the Council as stated in the Articles of Association shall be achieved by:

A. Generating public awareness and providing public education on engineering, scientific, technical, and environmental issues that affect the citizens of the State of _____.

B. Serving as a forum for discussion and developing and establishing positions on those engineering, scientific, technical and environmental issues which are the subject of legislative or regulatory action by governing bodies in the State of _____.

C. Coordinating with other technical, professional, engineering and scientific societies in areas of common interest, in order to obtain strength in numbers and more effectively utilize existing resources. Encouraging and developing contacts between constituent organizations and government entities.

D. Developing technical positions and plans for a promotion of such positions which utilize the resources and capabilities of member constituent organizations.

E. Providing engineering and scientific information to state administrative officials and to the legislature to clarify the technical aspects of regulatory or other legislation.

Section II — General

A. The activities conducted by the Council will be for and on behalf of the citizens of the State of _____ regardless of age, creed, color, national origin, or sex.

B. All activities of the Council shall be in accordance with Section 501(c)(3) of the Internal Revenue code and in accordance with the laws governing nonprofit organizations.

C. The entire income of the Council shall be used in furtherance of its objectives, and no part of such income shall inure to the benefit of any individual or individuals except for necessary expenses incurred by a delegate or delegates for purposes furthering the Objective of the Council.

D. A constituent organization may veto a Council position on a given issue following which the Council may not take a position on that issue until or unless the veto is renewed.

Section III — Financial Support

A. The member organizations shall provide financial support to the Council as set forth in Section XII.

Section IV — Membership

A. Qualifications: Membership in the Council shall be open to any engineering, scientific, or technical society.

B. Application: Any engineering, scientific, or technical society desiring membership on the Council shall file written application executed by its chief elected officer and its secretary. Such application shall be accompanied by a copy of the constitution and bylaws of the applicant organization.

C. Admissions: Each application for admission shall be passed on by the Committee on Membership which committee shall report its findings and recommendations to the Council. Admission to membership on the Council shall be by a two-thirds affirmative vote by the Council.

D. Termination: Any member of the Council in good standing and having its dues fully paid may terminate its membership by written notice of resignation, executed by its chief elected officer. Any member of the Council whose dues for the current fiscal year are unpaid by the end of the year shall be subject to suspension of voting privileges and, if such dues are unpaid three (3) months thereafter, shall be dropped from membership. Due notice of this contemplated action shall be given to the chief elected officer of the constituent organization thirty (30) days prior to termination. The fiscal year shall be concurrent with the calendar year.

Section V — Representation

A. Number of Council Members: Each constituent organization shall designate two delegates to the Council.

B. Appointment: A designated delegate to the Council shall take office when the delegate is certified to the secretary of the Council by written notice signed by the chief elected officer or the secretary of the organization the delegate represents.

C. Terms of Office: It shall be recommended to each constituent organization that Council delegates from their organization serve for staggered two-year terms with one of the initial delegates appointed to a one-year term.

D. Votes: Each constituent organization shall have only one vote which may be voted by either delegate as designated by their respective constituent organization.

Section VI — Meetings

A. Frequency: The Council shall meet at least four times per year. The fourth of these meetings will be the Annual Meeting. It will be held on the first Saturday in December. Additional meetings may be called by the Chairperson. Special interim meetings may be called by any five Council delegates.

B. Conduct: "Roberts Rules of Order" shall govern the procedure followed for the conduct of meetings. At any meeting, a quorum shall be reached when a majority of all constituent organizations on the Council are represented by their respective duly authorized delegates.

Section VII — Officers

A. Terms of Office: The Chairperson and Vice Chairperson shall serve a one year term and may not be reelected to a second consecutive term. The secretary and treasurer shall be elected to two-year terms and may not be reelected to a second consecutive term.

Section VIII — Nominations

A. Not less than ninety (90) days before the annual meeting, the chairperson shall, with the approval of the Council, appoint a Nominating Committee of three Council delegates. No constituent organization shall have more than one member on the nominating committee.

B. Not less than sixty (60) days before the annual meeting the Nominating Committee shall secure acceptance of the nominations from their nominees.

C. The Chairperson shall be nominated from among the delegates serving on the Council during the previous year.

D. The secretary shall send a list of these nominations to each Council delegate at least thirty (30) days before the annual meeting.

E. Other nominations may be presented from the floor at the annual meeting.

Section IX — Elections

A. Election of Council officers shall be by the majority of votes cast by secret ballot at the annual meeting, provided that a quorum is present. If no candidate receives a majority of the votes cast, then the candidate receiving the least number of votes shall be eliminated and voting continued until an election is obtained.

Section X — Duties of Officers

A. The Chairperson shall preside at all meetings and shall have general charge and care of the business of the Council. The Chairperson may appoint the members of the standing committees and may appoint such other committees as may be deemed necessary for the proper conduct of the Council's affairs. The Chairperson shall be an ex-officio member of all appointed committees.

B. The Vice Chairperson shall have such powers and duties as may be assigned by the delegates and in the absence of the Chairperson or the inability of the Chairperson to act, the Vice Chairperson shall exercise the functions and perform the duties of the Chairperson.

C. The Secretary shall prepare with the Chairperson an agenda for each meeting. Agenda items may be suggested by any of the constituent organizations. The secretary shall make arrangements for all meetings and distribute meetings notices to constituent organizations and their delegates not less than forty-five (45) days prior to the scheduled meeting. The Secretary shall take notes of all minutes and distribute copies to all constituent organizations and their delegates. The Secretary shall maintain a list of all member organizations. This list shall be available for review by the constituent organizations of the Council. The Secretary shall distribute to all constituent organizations any opinion or position sent the legislature on behalf of the Council.

D. The Treasurer shall maintain full and accurate records of receipts and disbursements of monies of the Council and shall deposit and disburse funds of the Council in accordance with directions from the Council. The Treasurer shall submit an annual financial statement at the close of the fiscal year. A preliminary financial statement shall be presented by the treasurer at the Annual Meeting.

Section XI — Standing Committees

    A. Executive Committee

       1. The four officers and the immediate past Chairperson shall comprise the Executive Committee.

       2. The Executive Committee shall act on behalf of the Council when the Council is not in session. All actions taken shall be reported to the Council at its next meeting. These actions shall be subject to review and must be approved by the Council before becoming an official act.

       3. The Executive Committee may conduct a business meeting provided a quorum of its members are present. A quorum is represented by three or more members. A business meeting may be conducted by telephone conferencing or by letter ballot.

       4. Meetings of the Executive Committee may be suggested by any member of the Committee and shall be called by the Chairperson.

    B. Membership Committee

       1. The Membership Committee shall review applications for membership and shall report its findings to the Council. (See Section IV.C.)

    C. Nominating Committee (See Section VIII)

    D. Finance Committee (to be described)

    E. Legislative Committee (to be described)

    F. Charter and Bylaws Committee (to be described)

    G. Education Committee (to be described)

H. Public Affairs Committee (to be described)

I. Ad Hoc Committees

1. Committees may be appointed by the Chairperson with duties and terms of office determined and authorized by the Chairperson.

Section XII — Dues, Expenditures, and Contributions

A. Dues : Annual dues shall be assessed each constituent organization in accordance with the following schedule:

1000 or more members $300
Fewer than 1000 members $200
Regional councils $100

Constituent organizations shall be billed by the Treasurer on or before January 1 of each year. Organizations joining the Council after January 1 shall be billed on a pro rata basis.

B. Expenditures: The Council shall have control of all disbursements.

C. Contributions: Contributions to the Council treasury shall be subject to Council approval.

13

Local Government

Ruth Barwick

1.0 BACKGROUND

The study of local government typically receives less attention than it deserves in surveys of American politics. National issues, and the national government itself, capture the largest share of media attention and attention by scholars as well. Yet local politics are closer to the day-to-day lives of most people.

Local governments touch our lives every day in many very personal ways. From grade school to university, education is dominated by public schools, roads are maintained by local and state governments, water is generally provided through a publicly owned water company, and waste water is carried away by a public sewer system. Opportunities for employment are much greater with local governments than with other governmental units; in fact, local governments employ more people than the states and federal government combined. Protecting you from diseases when you eat at a restaurant, protecting you and your children against fire and crime, and requiring drivers to "buckle up" for their safety are a few in a long list of ways in which local government enters our lives every day.

Local governments continually experiment to provide services efficiently, effectively, and equitably and are increasingly able to respond to change, make effective decisions, and manage conflict. Local governments have shown tremendous increases in their ability to respond to needs over the past two decades. Their development has been tempered, however, by the reality of federalism—a system in which power is distributed between levels of government and characterized by both cooperation and conflict.

2.0 FEDERALISM

The framers of the Constitution of the United States had to struggle with the proper allocation of power and responsibility—between allowing citizens a strong voice in their government and restraining them. Three mechanisms were used in the Constitution to control factions and yet allow for democratic government. One was the system of representative government, another the division of the federal government into three branches, and finally, the organization of the government as a whole as a federal system.

Federalism was seen by the Founders as protection against tyranny. If the newly formed national government threatened people's liberties, the states would protect them, and vice versa. Federalism, which the Constitution put in place in 1789 and under which the nation functions, is a union of people. The national government and state governments receive power from the people and exercise authority directly over them.

2.1 Power of Local Government

A critical feature of federalism is that the central government and the states derive their powers from a common source—the Constitution. Neither level of government gives powers to the other. However, local governments are never mentioned in the Constitution and, therefore, do not derive their powers from that document. They are instead created and endowed powers by the states. Every local government—whether school district, city, village, or town—is a creature of the state. All their powers are derived from the state; each state's constitution details what local governments can and cannot do. Courts have consistently upheld the dependency of local government upon the state. In a precedent- setting decision in 1868,[*] Judge John F. Dillon ruled that local governments may exercise only those powers

[*]Dillon's rule, as it became known, was first written in the case of the *City of Clinton* v. *Cedar Rapids and Missouri Railroad Co.* (1868).

explicitly granted to them by the state or those clearly implied by the explicit powers. Where there is any doubt, the courts have ruled in favor of the state.

Therefore, local governments have little discretionary power. When a local government wants to assume a new responsibility or provide a new service, it must first receive permission from the state legislature. All power is vested in state governments; local governments exist only as agents of the states and may exercise only those powers given to them. Their powers may, therefore, be viewed as borrowed. It is important to note that powers forbidden to the states by the Constitution are also forbidden to every arm of the state.

Since the early days of the country, state legislatures have been able to organize local government as they wished. They have granted, amended, and repealed city charters, established counties, determined city and county structures, set debt limits, and passed laws for the local units. To allow more local discretion, since 1900 most states through their constitutions have provided for "home rule." This is a legal arrangement by which the state allows chartered local governments discretion and flexibility in their operations. These constitutional amendments authorize cities, and in some cases counties, to run their own affairs and limit the power of state officials to interfere in local matters.

Once created, local governments have always had to care for themselves and historically have been dependent upon the property tax. Since World War II, the costs of "governing" have been very high, and it has been necessary for local governments to receive assistance from the state to provide for such things as education, welfare, highways, criminal justice, finance, and health. As states have become more involved in local government operation, so too has the federal government, which now provides grants for a variety of needs.

3.0 TYPES OF LOCAL GOVERNMENTS

Myriad services may be offered by the various kinds of local governments. Some governments provide many of these services; others, however, have a specific purpose and perform only one function. This is the distinction between *general-purpose* and *single-purpose* governments. The former perform a wide range of functions and services and include counties, cities, and towns; examples of single-purpose governments are school districts and fire districts, which are created specifically to perform a particular function.

3.1 County Government

Counties are general-purpose units of government and are the principal divisions of all states except Louisiana and Alaska. In Louisiana they are called parishes, in Alaska, boroughs. There are over 3000 counties in the United States.

Unlike a city, a county is not created at the request of its citizens. Originally, counties were set up by the state at the state's initiative to manage the administration of certain state functions at a local level. However, through the years, counties have become much more of a vehicle for local self-government.

Functions of counties vary from state to state and even from county to county within a state. Many counties still, at the request of the state, perform selected state functions such as voting registration, vehicle registration, issuance of automobile licenses and/or hunting permits, and so on. Typical county functions commonly include:

AirportsPublic safety
Coroner/medical examiner
Health
Highways planning
Hospitals
Justice
Law enforcement/sheriff
Libraries
Nursing homes
Parks, recreation
Property assessment
Public safety
Services to senior citizens
Vital statistics
Welfare

The importance of a county to the average citizen generally depends upon whether the person lives in a city or in a rural area. Cities normally supply their residents with most of the services for which rural residents look to the county. When a city is established within a county, the county may withdraw most of its services from the city. To avoid the layering of jurisdictions, some highly urban counties are also cities or city/counties, for example, Denver, San Francisco, Honolulu, and Philadelphia. Although most counties receive little public recognition, some, such as Westchester County, New York; Dade County, Florida; Cook County, Illinois; Bucks County, Pennsylvania, are as well known.

There is no such thing as a typical county; there are great variations in population (ranging from less than 1000 to over 8 million) and area (ranging from less than 24 square miles to 20,00 square miles).[1] Counties are rich, poor, urban, rural, agricultural, industrial, flat, mountainous, fertile, arid, and so on. The number of counties within each state also varies; western states tend to have fewer and larger counties than eastern states.

There is generally a county board, known by various names in different places. The county board may be called a board of supervisors, legislators, representatives, or commissioners. The chief administrator may be an elected county executive or an appointed county administrator, or the chairman of the board may serve as chief administrator. The commission form is the most common form of county governmental organization with an elected board of three to five members, with no one person on the commission with administrative responsibility for the county. Commissioners may be elected from single-member districts or at-large.

Although counties have no clear-cut or "standard" governmental organization, a few generalizations can be made. The "typical" county has numerous, separately elected officials who run their own departments with little or no coordination between departments and without any supervision by a higher authority.

In general, the same civic and political interests that influence state legislatures and city halls are also found at the county level. Politics may be less publicized at the county level, but if a major controversy arises, those with positions of power and influence in the county will be at the forefront. County government may be the least visible layer of government, but those in positions of power make decisions about who gets what, when, and how much it will cost.

Some counties have a very small population, which makes for inefficiencies in providing services. Studies have shown repeatedly that consolidation of counties would save money. However, rural residents do not want to lose their identity; office holders and their friends and families do not want county jobs to disappear; those involved in commerce and business know that people are drawn to the county seat for services, which is good for local business. There are many reasons why consolidation seldom takes place, and the status quo does not change in regard to either consolidation of services or county lines.

3.2 Cities

Cities and municipalities are one and the same—the terms refer to a specific, populated area, operating under a charter from the state. Residents of an area must petition the state for a charter of incorporation to establish a city. Certain criteria, which vary from state to state, must be met. A referendum is generally required, enabling the citizens to vote on whether they wish to incorporate.

Most states have enacted home rule provisions for cities that allow extensive decision-making authority and discretion. City governments are usually one of three forms: mayor-council, city commission, or city manager. Within these types there are variations such as strong mayor-council or weak mayor-council, and opinions vary on which form is best. The voters in a city must decide what works best for them, and having decided upon one form, can always vote to change. Cities have both a chief executive and a legislative body. Cities generally offer more services than villages or counties.

Both governmental structure and power are delineated in the city's charter, which is granted by the state. The charter sets forth what the state prohibits and allows; it lists major officers, how they are selected, and their powers; it includes a geographic description of the city and describes how the charter may be amended.

3.3 Towns

Towns (called *townships* in some states) are general-purpose units of local government. Only 20 states, mainly in the Northeast and Midwest, have designated towns or townships. Towns in New England, New York, New Jersey, Pennsylvania, Michigan, and Wisconsin have fairly broad powers. In the other township states (Illinois, Indiana, Iowa, Kansas, Minnesota, Missouri, Nebraska, North Dakota, South Dakota, and Ohio), government is generally limited to roads and law enforcement.

Towns in New England are different from towns or townships elsewhere. A New England town is intended to provide government for both rural and urban areas within its boundaries and is the principal unit of local government practicing direct democracy.

Towns outside of New England do not have these characteristics and

have been described as "the least glorious of all government."[2] The demise
of the town has been predicted by some observers, who believe that as rural
areas become more populated, towns will eventually meet the population
requirements and become municipalities.

Elsewhere, counties have taken over the functions of towns,[3] while in
other places, towns have endured and taken over functions of villages which
have then disappeared!

3.4 Villages

In states where villages exist, they are general-purpose municipal corporations formed voluntarily by the residents of an area of one or more towns.
Their function is to provide more urban-type services than towns do. When
a village is created, its area remains part of the town where it is located, and
residents continue to be residents and taxpayers of that town. To incorporate, a village must meet certain statutory requirements set by the state, such
as size of land area and population. Patterns of village government are
similar to those of cities although the scale of operation is smaller.

3.5 Suburbs

Since World War II, suburbs have been among the fastest-growing areas in
the United States. Defined as the area around cities, suburban populations
have increased (at the expense of cities) for many reasons—less expensive
land, lower taxes, more open space, better services, less crime, and the
changing character of inner cities. Industries moved from the city in search
of cheaper land, lower taxes, and more lenient building codes. Businesses
then followed the people and industries. While the suburbs were growing,
the poor and the dispossessed migrated from rural areas to central cities,
especially in the northeast and north central regions.

To speak of suburban "government" is a misnomer and can be very
confusing. In fact, there is no suburban government as such, and in most
cases there are *many* governments in suburban areas dealing with a multi-
tude of issues, problems, and services. Problems of crime, traffic, and health
do not stop at city lines. Many urban problems defy city and county
boundaries. There are also many special districts (discussed shortly) that
provide special services for local or regional areas. Lines of special districts
do not necessarily follow lines of general-purpose governments, further
complicating the picture. Special districts for transit, recreation, water, and

so on organized on a regional basis may make good sense economically, but they can also pose challenges for existing governmental units.

3.6 Single-Purpose Governments

Single-purpose units of government, often called special-purpose districts or simply special districts, provide a single service or type of service rather than the array of services provided by the traditional general-purpose government. The most numerous form of local government, single-purpose governments account for half of all units of local government in the United States.[4] Some single-purpose units of government are called *authorities*, some are called *boards*, some are known as *corporations*—the most frequently used name is *district*. These single-purpose units include school districts, fire districts, drainage and flood control districts, water supply districts, soil conservation districts, sewerage districts, park districts, transit districts, and many others.

Generally, special-purpose districts are created because other local governments cannot or will not meet service needs in a particular area. Cost is very often a factor in the creation of a special district—an area wants water service, trash collection, or a library, and the county or town does not want to tax all its residents for this service. A special district allows the costs for the service to be borne by those who receive the service.

3.6.1 School Districts   School districts are a particular kind of single purpose or special district and have unique characteristics. The responsibility for establishing, supporting, and overseeing public schools is reserved to the states under the Tenth Amendment and is specifically provided for in state constitutions. Day-to-day operating authority is delegated to local governments by all states except Hawaii. Ninety percent of primary and secondary school systems are operated by independent school districts, but cities, counties, towns, or townships operate the school systems in some states.

"Local control" is a popular rallying cry, but in reality, states have always been the dominant policymaker concerning elementary and secondary education. The state decides such things as the duration of the school year, curriculum requirements, textbook selections, teacher certification, compensation, minimum graduation requirements, and pupil-teacher ratios. Hiring and firing of teachers, certain budget decisions, management, and operating details are carried out locally.

Public schools in the United States are financed by local government

(48 percent of the cost), state government (44 percent), and the remainder by the federal government. This last component has been steadily decreasing in terms of percentage of overall expenditures, while state involvement is growing.

4.0 FINANCING LOCAL GOVERNMENT

Government's purpose is to provide services; services cost money. Money is raised through taxes and fees. Through decisions made in the voting booth, citizens decide what range and quality of services they want.

In the eighteenth and nineteenth centuries, people expected few services from state and local governments. Property taxes were the major source of revenue for those limited services. As the number and level of services increased, governments developed more revenue raising methods: income tax, sales tax, taxes on particular items, as well as fees and permits.

State and local fiscal systems are linked to and influenced by those of the federal government. Revenues are shared to a great extent. Local governments rely heavily on the state, and to a lesser degree upon the national government for both financial authority and assistance. Again, it should be noted that the states authorize localities to levy taxes and fees, incur debt, and spend money, and in turn, state regulations place many conditions on local taxing and spending practices; for example, cities have debt limits placed on borrowing, sales tax rates are regulated by the state, and so forth.

4.1 Taxes

Although each level of government has a different tax base, and each tax hits some groups harder than others, all taxes ultimately depend on the productivity of the American people. There are many ways of evaluating different taxes, but the overriding test has always been that it should be fair—usually meaning that the burden of the tax is distributed in accordance with ability to pay.

The property tax is the chief revenue source for local governments. Although its importance in both municipal and county budgets has decreased, it still provides about a third of the revenue cities collect and about 44 percent of counties' revenues.[5] It is the only major tax common to all 50 states and is the oldest tax levied in the United States.

Although valued for its reliability, many now consider the property tax regressive, difficult to administer, and lacking in accountability. These difficulties with the property tax helped precipitate Proposition 13 in California. Property values rose dramatically and property taxes doubled and tripled. People whose liquid assets did not keep up with the appreciation of their property, such as seniors living on fixed incomes, were especially hard hit.

The sales tax is less stable than the property tax but is favored by many voters as being more equitable. It has become the most important tax source next to the property tax. Both cities and counties collect sales taxes. Its relative popularity among taxpayers results from its low visibility and from the fact that it is collected in small increments over a large number of transactions. However, when applied to all merchandise, it too is regressive—the poor spend a larger portion of their income on food and clothing. There is also some evidence that although the sales tax generally does reduce the property tax burden, it also may increase local government spending.[6]

A few very large cities, such as Philadelphia, New York City, and Baltimore, and counties in Indiana and Maryland[7] also rely on the income tax to raise revenues. However, the local income tax has never achieved the same political acceptance as the sales tax. There are other taxes that can assist localities in raising revenues, each of which has its proponents and detractors, its virtues, and its deficiencies. Most students of local government believe that a medley of different taxes represents the fairest and most stable way to finance local services.

4.2 Indebtedness

States require local governments to balance their operating budgets. Most states limit borrowing by local governments. In addition to limiting the size of the debt, some states limit the purposes for which local government can borrow. In a few states, there must be a vote before a locality can borrow.

These legal limits usually restrict only that borrowing accomplished through sale of general obligation bonds, which are a charge against general revenues. Revenue bonds, another form of borrowing, are frequently exempt from borrowing limits because they are charged against the revenue of a particular revenue-producing government enterprise such as a transit authority or water authority. Buyers of revenue bonds gamble on the ability of the enterprise to repay them, whereas buyers of general obligation bonds have a claim on the general credit and taxing power of the locality.

Almost all states place constitutional or statutory restrictions on local government borrowing. Some have maximum levels of indebtedness, others require votes by citizens to either approve borrowing or to exceed the debt limit. The bond market places its own restrictions; it rates a jurisdiction's capacity to repay its debt by looking at a locality's existing debt level, contingency funds, market value of real estate, population growth, per capita income, employment levels, and so on, which together measure a community's financial health and solvency. The market then rates the community—AAA, AA, A, B, C. Any B variation is considered medium to high risk. C is used if there is danger of default. The average interest rate on low-rated bonds exceeds top-rated ones by one and a half to two percentage points. This difference has a major effect on the size of interest payments the locality must then make and ultimately, on project feasibility.

4.3 Mandates

A state mandate is a requirement that a local unit of government undertake a specific activity or provide a particular service. Local government officials believe that states, through the use of mandates, prefer to dictate to local governments how to solve their problems rather than letting the local governments develop their own solutions. Unfunded mandates have evolved as a way of setting standards and ensuring certain governmental "behavior" without cost to the state and are the most common source of friction between levels of government. From the perspective of state government, mandates are necessary to ensure that policies are uniform from one jurisdiction to another within the state, for example, the operation of polling places, hours in a public school year, and so on.

Because of the fiscal and political problems state mandates have created, states have started to adopt mandate reimbursement requirements. These requirements stipulate that states must reimburse local governments for the costs of state mandates or give local governments enough revenue-raising ability to deal with them. About one-third of the states have passed mandate reimbursement legislation.

5.0 REGIONAL GOVERNMENT

Areas formed from suburban communities and small towns have become the places where most Americans live, learn, work, shop, and play. These areas now show signs of age and are developing some of the problems of the inner city. However, in terms of governmental structure, these "fringe" areas do not follow jurisdictional lines and require new solutions and mechanisms for dealing with continued growth and more recently, with deterioration.

Regional government offers some solutions. Under a regional government, the myriad local governments give up some power and authority in exchange for areawide responsibilities and solutions to local problems. State legislatures are important players in the creation of regional governments because they generally help orchestrate the reorganization and develop the rules for regionalization to follow.

The closest thing to regional government in the United States is city-county consolidation in which the functions of local government are provided by a single jurisdiction. There are 23 such consolidated governments[8] in the country. Although regional government may seem very reasonable, it has not proven to be the ideal solution, either at the polls or in practice. Costs do not necessarily decrease while government becomes larger and further removed from the people.

Regional coordination has emerged as a more acceptable alternative. Councils of government or regional planning commissions are examples of regional coordination. No formal merger of jurisdictions takes place. Certain federal legislation has furthered the formation of these bodies, such as the U.S. Housing Act of 1954, which provided funds for metropolitan planning, and the Model Cities Act of 1966, which required metropolitan planning agencies to review grant applications from all agencies within a region.

Areawide planning is one activity councils of governments do well; others are technical assistance (grant writing), professional services (budgeting, engineering), and collection and analysis of information (socioeconomic data for the region). To date, councils of government have not been very popular, but they have made two major contributions—areawide planning has become a reality in many functional areas such as criminal justice, water quality, housing, and transportation planning. In addition, councils have substantially improved the operational capacity of rural local governments by providing technical expertise.

6.0 CITIZEN PARTICIPATION

Elected and appointed officeholders rarely act alone. They are affected by the wants and desires of other persons; they are affected by influences,

pressures, inducements, persuasions, motivations, biases, urgings, and seduc-
tions of every sort. . . . One cannot begin to list all the influences to which
officeholders are susceptible, but it is a fact that public officials are influenced. . . . Being influenced is not always evil. After all, the whole idea of
democracy is that officeholders will respond to the public . . .[9]

Democracy assumes citizen participation in public decision making.
If the American system of government is to function properly, citizens must
actively participate in its operations at all levels, but it is especially important at the local level. Citizens should keep themselves informed and should,
if possible, play meaningful roles in determining local public policy.

6.1 The Engineer as Government Employee

There are many opportunities for engineers to work in local government.
Their skills are called upon each day in a wide array of situations in both
appointed and civil service positions. Without distinguishing here between
the many kinds of engineers, it should be noted that the engineer is
employed by local government in a variety of capacities. A partial list of
the kinds of jobs include the following:

- *Streets and highways:* planning new ones, altering the routes of
  existing ones, repairing existing streets and bridges, routing and
  rerouting traffic, installing and maintaining traffic signals
- *Urban development and redevelopment:* adopting building standards, issuing building permits, redesigning neighborhoods, demol-
  ishing abandoned or unsafe buildings
- *Public health:* water distribution systems and water quality, sewer
  systems, solid waste treatment, environmental health concerns, hazardous waste removal, infectious disease control
- *Airports:* location, approaches, and design

6.2 The Engineer as Citizen

The individual has numerous ways to influence government: serving on
boards or committees, writing letters, joining interest groups, attending
public hearings and open meetings of legislative bodies, and, of course,
voting for public officials or holding elective office. Additionally, participation in party politics presents opportunities for influencing public actions
through selection of candidates, petitions, getting out the vote, and so on.

There are also ways, which vary from state to state, in which citizens can vote directly on issues instead of delegating that right to the legislators. These are called initiatives (proposed laws that are placed on the ballot by citizen petition to be approved or rejected by popular vote), referenda (in which people vote directly on actions taken by legislature), or recalls (which allow voters to remove an officeholder by popular vote).

As citizens, engineers can and should bring their expertise and insights into the arena of citizen participation. In public hearings, development of legislation, promulgation of building codes and standards, environmental issues hearings, during political campaigns, and in local party politics, engineers should bring their professional knowledge and opinions before the local leaders.

The valuable and relevant experience of the engineer can serve the community in many ways. In a democratic society such as ours, there are many opportunities for the engineer to make his voice heard.

ENDNOTES

1. Robert S. Lorch, *State and Local Politics—The Great Entanglement,* 4th ed. (Englewood Cliffs, NJ: Prentice Hall, 1992), p. 232.
2. Ann O'M. Bowman and Richard C. Kearney, *State and Local Government,* 2nd ed. (Boston: Houghton Mifflin, 1993), p. 329.
3. Lorch, *State and Local Politics,* p. 253.
4. Ibid. p. 254.
5. Robert L. Bland, *A Revenue Guide for Local Government.* (Washington, D.C.: International City Managers Association, 1989), p. 27.
6. Ibid., p. 61.
7. Ibid., p. 90.
8. Bowman and Kearney, *State and Local Government,* p. 376.
9. Lorch, *State and Local Politics,* p. 95.

Index